BLUES AND EVIL

BLUES AND EVIL

JON MICHAEL SPENCER

The University of Tennessee Press / Knoxville

Frontispiece: Photograph courtesy of Hampton University Archives.

The paper in this book meets the minimum requirements of the
American National Standard for Permanence of Paper for Printed
Library Materials.   ∞   The binding materials have been chosen
for strength and durability.

LIBRARY OF CONGRESS CATALOGING IN PUBLICATION DATA

Spencer, Jon Michael.
     Blues and evil / Jon Michael Spencer.
          p.   cm.
     Includes bibliographical references and index.
     ISBN 0-87049-782-0 (cloth: alk. paper)
     ISBN 0-87049-783-9 (pbk.: alk. paper)
     1. Blues (Music) — Religious aspects. I. Title.
ML3521.S63   1993
781.643—dc20   92-33008
                                          CIP
                                          MN

To black "blues people" worldwide

who have been marginalized

for being centered in the truth

CONTENTS

Acknowledgments	ix
Introduction	xi
1. The Mythologies of the Blues	1
2. The Theologies of the Blues	35
3. The Theodicies of the Blues	68
Conclusion	99
Notes	139
Select Bibliography	159
Index	167

ACKNOWLEDGMENTS

The initial impetus to write this book came during my last year of teaching at Duke University Divinity School, when and where it became clear to me that I was destined to be a "bluesman"—one who is, as my dedication implies, marginalized for telling the truth about life and liberty, but who is well "centered" in that peripheral situation. My divinity students that last year at Duke, especially that final semester, were absolutely divine, and they gave me a heartfelt send-off to my new faculty appointment at Bowling Green State University. That send-off included their "blues" testimonies and a recording of John Lee Hooker's new blues album, *The Healer*. Knowing the wounds I suffered as a black bluesman, one of the students (who used to bake homemade bread for my wife and me) encouraged me by saying, "There is a balm in Bowling Green to make the wounded whole." Another of my students, at that final send-off where they put me on the "train" to ride, sang those words to the tune of the spiritual, "There is a Balm in Gilead."

The "train" (I thought of it as the "underground railroad") arrived safely in Ohio, the old abolition state. But Bowling Green seemed hardly to have any balm at all for me, and it seems I became a bluesman all the more. It was the right time to teach a course on the blues and to write this book; and as I wrote it, my soul often bathed deeply in my memory of the "blues" discoveries my students and I at Duke Divinity (all thirty of us) made together about life's religious realities. I also submerged my mind and spirit in the black sounds of the thousands upon thousands of blues recordings in the famed Popular Culture Library at Bowling Green State University. My body moved. I listened and sang and hummed and moaned and sometimes cried; my blues students at Bowling Green saw the tears in my eyes, as had my students at Duke. Perhaps here, after all, was the "balm"—those uncountable blues.

A good portion of my thought about the blues was worked out during the 1990–91 academic year, the first of my two years of teaching in Bowling Green's Department of Popular Culture. During the fall semester I taught an undergraduate course titled "American Blues Music" and a graduate course titled "Evil in Popular Culture." For the spring semester I taught a graduate course on the blues and an undergraduate course entitled "Rap and Race" (rap being the new blues of the twenty-first century). The students in my graduate course on the blues, who were doctoral students in American culture studies and English and masters students in popular culture and art, provided creative and well-informed responses to the material I shared with them. I learned much from them.

I was especially fortunate to have had Angela Nelson, an African-American doctoral candidate in American culture studies who has now completed her degree, as my teaching assistant for the undergraduate classes I taught. She is an excellent teacher, and her research assistance during the academic year and summer was enormously beneficial to me as this project progressed. My work that summer was also helped by a small grant from the Faculty Research Committee of Bowling Green State University. And I am grateful to Kenneth Surin of Duke University's Department of Religion and Lawrence Mamiya of Vassar College's Department of Religion for reading and helpfully commenting on the finished manuscript of this book. As well, I am grateful to Stan Ivester, Managing Editor at the University of Tennessee Press, for seeing this project through publication. Above all, I am indebted to Kay Sergent, who patiently prepared this manuscript throughout the year it was being written, while also functioning as the secretary to the academic journal I edit, *Black Sacred Music: A Journal of Theomusicology*. Without her work of high quality and her devotion (I believe she has glimpsed my vision), *Blues and Evil* would not have been completed as smoothly and promptly as it was. To Kay Sergent, Angela Nelson, Kenneth Surin, Lawrence Mamiya, and Stan Ivester, I am beholden.

INTRODUCTION

I n a 1988 article in the esteemed higher-education periodical *The Chronicle of Higher Education,* ethnomusicology professor and blues scholar David Evans detailed American blacks' and whites' renewed interest in the blues in recent decades. He spoke of the publication of dozens of books on the blues and of nearly a dozen blues magazines in more than ten countries, the release of thousands of recorded and reissued albums, and increased performances of the blues on television, radio, and at music festivals in America and abroad. Yet, in spite of these developments, Evans expressed discontent with the majority of this renewed interest having come from nonacademic blues enthusiasts, with fewer than ten American academicians publishing books on the blues during the last three decades.[1]

My reason for writing this book is somewhat related to Evans's dismay that few academicians have published books on the blues, but my purpose is even more related to Langston Hughes's complaint almost a half-century ago. Hughes wrote in 1944, "I do not know why Negro writers have been so backward in writing about popular music and musicians. There are several excellent books by white writers largely devoted to analyzing, describing, and praising Negro music and its interpreters. But I know of no book by a Negro writer. There are several white magazines, a large portion of whose pages are devoted to extolling the ecstasies of Negro jazz, blues, and swing as expressed through our performers and composers. But I know of no such Negro magazines."[2] My concern, then, is that the dozens of monographs on the blues during the last thirty years include a mere handful by black scholars—LeRoi Jones (Amiri Baraka), James H. Cone, Julio Finn, Albert Murray, and Daphne Duval Harrison—and that this neglect in black scholarship has had some bearing on the reading public's misunderstanding of the blues and the people whose culture created the music. In response to blues scholar Jeff Titon's remark that perhaps black scholars will one day discover "their music" if they have any interest in it,[3] my principal interest is not that scholars such as Evans and Titon have discovered "our music"; my concern is that they, as outsiders to the culture that produced the blues, have failed to capture the music's pervading ethos—its religious nature!

One of the first scholars to write on the blues in the tradition in which Evans and Titon are firmly rooted was Paul Oliver. Oliver had sufficient insight from the beginning to understand that whites used the blues to support their stereotypes of blacks as immoral and sexually promiscuous,[4] but he repeatedly negated this insight by accepting the more egregious stereotype that essentially encompassed the foregoing ones: using a Victorian model of morality, he validated the notion that the blues was "devil's music." Oliver was not simply "playing the devil's advocate" when he called the blues "devil's music," for he neglected to explain that this designation was accusational on the part of the church faithful of the old South's black society. Blues scholar Giles Oakley at least made it fairly clear that the designation "devil's music" was applied from the perspective of the church.[5] But both Englishmen failed to clarify that this accusation resulted from the imposition of Christianity's bifurcating worldview (the sacred versus the profane) on the holistic cosmology of this people of African origin. That Oliver, especially, intended "devil's music" to signify "evil music" was evidenced by his claim that the blues was "somewhat bereft of spiritual values."[6] With the Egyptians being the acknowledged originators of religion, philosophy, and ethics, this is identical to Hegel saying in his *Philosophy of History* that among the Negroes of Egyptian culture "moral sentiments are weak, or more strictly speaking, nonexistent."[7]

Ingeniously, the "dirty work" of flushing out the meaning of Oliver's carefully stated proposition about blues being "somewhat bereft of spiritual values" was handed over to the writer of the foreword, African-American novelist Richard Wright. Compromising his claim of two decades earlier, that blues were the "spirituals of the city pavements,"[8] Wright said that the theme of spirituality was banned in the blues because blues singers had an "atheistic vision of life."[9] Possibly giving Oakley the idea for the title of his book, *The Devil's Music: A History of the Blues* (1977), Wright praised Oliver's work as "the first history of those devil's songs."[10]

Just as Wright's foreword set the tone for Oliver's position, which permeated his book, so did Oliver's scholarship set the tone for most of the academic and amateur blues historiography that has followed it. Rather than blues scholars critiquing Oliver's work for the misinformed Victorian perspective that it was, a tradition of interpretation has been built upon it, interpretation that includes a preoccupation with the theme of sex. The insurrection of subjugated sexualities in the blues—the blues singers' flaunting of metaphors implying immense sexual capacity—has teased their Victorian sensibilities. Finding it impossible to reconcile the seeming disparity between sex and ethics, scholars who are not natives of the culture that produced the blues have been unable to see beyond its eros to its deeper spiritual ethos.

Another by-product of Oliver's extensive blues scholarship is the fascination his "followers" have had with the devil-lore surrounding the so-called "devil's music." Their failure to correct his contention that blues is in effect evil has resulted in their making light of the serious relationship between blues and evil. Take for instance one writer's narration of the life of blues singer Robert Johnson in a magazine piece titled "Satan, Now On CD," written upon the 1990 reissuing of Johnson's music on compact disc. The narration began with the writer saying that various blues musicians have long been vying to be declared Johnson's official heir, which was an impossibility because the devil, the one to whom Johnson sold his soul at a crossroads, was his "heir." The writer went on to identify Johnson as the "original singer of American evil," a black man who "played like the devil" and "died like a dog." He "died like a dog," the writer said, because one day in August of 1938 the devil came to collect his due— Johnson's soul—which was taken away by means of whiskey poisoned by a jealous husband: "Bob died, down on all fours, barking." The writer's tale ended with reference to one of Johnson's famous recordings: "He had to die that way, of course, the 'hellhound on my trail' having caught up with him, possessing him at last."[11] Julio Finn's negative critique of this sort of storytelling was that it merely adds to the charm of "blues life," and, he said (mocking the attitude of these tale-bearers), "it sells records: so better leave it in."[12]

This kind of tale-telling by persons who are not natives of the culture that produced the blues has resulted in the moral ambiguity of their calling the blues "evil" and then celebrating it ("Satan, Now On CD!"). When the meaning of the blues is explained in a way in which evil is celebrated, it is because the *mythology* surrounding the lives of blues singers is more interesting than their reality and what the authentic *mythologies* inherent to the blues can reveal about that reality. This enthusiasm that has resulted in blues musicians being mythologized as tragic heroes—musicians who played like the devil and died like dogs—is a kind of escapism in that it distracts scholars from the task of establishing a society in which black people are no longer the subject and objects of evil. This failure to demystify the devil-lore surrounding the blues also means that the use of the language of evil ("blues is devil's music") is pseudo-religious and qualifies neither as a recognition of the synchronous duplicity of the blues (that is, blues being both sacred *and* profane) nor as discourse about its religious nature.

To call the blues "devil's music" and then to celebrate it seemingly would be to use the designation in a metaphorical sense, as Paul Garon tried to do in his surrealist approach in *Blues and the Poetic Spirit* (1975). Garon claimed that the ethos of revolt in the blues could not be assimilated into Christian culture except by dilution or falsification because the "moral attitude" of the blues was one that embraced evil.[13] He said, "The 'Devil's music'—that is, the music of the damned, the music of the excluded—embraces the revolutionary principle of *evil* which Hegel long ago recognized as the form in which the motive force of historical development presents itself."[14] According to the German philosopher of science Paul Carus, in his book *The History of the Devil and the Idea of Evil* (1899), the devil was generally portrayed in this light in the popular literature of verse and fable:

> In popular literature the Devil plays a most important role. While he is still regarded as the incarnation of all physical and moral evil, his main office has become that of a general mischief-worker in the universe; without him there would be no plot, and the story of the world would lose its interest. He appears as the critic of the good Lord, as the representative of discontent with existing conditions, he inspires men with the desire for an increase of wealth, power, and knowledge; he is

the mouth-piece of all who are anxious for a change in matters political, social, and ecclesiastical. He is identified with the spirit of progress so inconvenient to those who are satisfied with the existing state of things, and thus he is credited with innovations of all kinds, the aspiration for improvement as well as the desire for the overthrow of law and order. In a word, he is characterised as the patron of both reform and evolution.[15]

The blues, however, was not really a "popular literature," except when it actually thematized popular tales about such folk heroes as Railroad Bill, Stackolee, and Devil Winston; otherwise it was the embodiment of an actual religious cosmology. Thus, despite Garon's surrealist reading of the blues, his attempt to use the designation "devil's music" ("the music of the damned") in a metaphorical sense was fuddled. He failed to recognize the so-called "atheism" of the blues as nothing more than a polemical moment for blues singers to stand in opposition to a history of oppression by white "theists" (Christians), a polemical moment that by no means precluded blues being fundamentally religious. But to have done this would have undercut Garon's subversive, surrealist politics. Because he took the surrealist view that there is no such thing as a poetry of religion in that all true poetry is pure revolt,[16] he had to de-religionize the blues in order to claim it as poetry. In Oliver's case, any possible attempt to use the designation "devil's music" metaphorically was precluded simply by his claim that the blues was "somewhat bereft of spiritual values."

The scholarship of Oliver and his academic and amateur descendants is no less guilty of perpetuating the stereotype of the blues being evil than the article "Satan, Now On CD." In turn, the latter, obviously written by a blues enthusiast and avid capitalist, is no less guilty than the advertising of the white-owned record companies that exploited the blues beginning in the 1920s. In 1924, for instance, Okeh Race Records advertised Sippie Wallace as a blues singer whose contralto voice was perfectly suited for the "low-downs."[17] A year later, Okeh promoted her "Devil Dance Blues" as though the "low-downs" were in fact "devil's music," calling the piece "the darkest, blackest sort of blues that ever skipped around an Okeh Record."[18] A year after that, in 1926, Paramount Records advertised Ma Rainey's "Slave to the Blues" with a picture of a woman about to be clutched by the long, thin, pointy fingers of a dark, shrouded figure identified as "Blues."[19] Jeff Titon said these advertisements reveal "the nature of white uncertainties,"[20] but so does the Oliverian tradition of scholarship of which Titon is a part. Any scholarship that neglects to demystify the blues for its authentic mythologies reveals "white uncertainties." The "uncertain" white scholars of this ilk do not explicitly describe the blues as "lowdowns," Robert Johnson as one of the "original singers of American evil," or personify blues as the devil; but those blues scholars essentially engage in the same stereotyping when not qualifying their semantics—"(d)evil"—or when not contesting the widespread and entrenched belief that blues was irreligious, anti-religion, and atheistic. The essence of these "white uncertainties" is, based on the foregoing evidence, the perpetuation of the psychological intentions that motivated the minstrel tradition. What literary and cultural critic Houston Baker said about the ritual of theatrical minstrelsy is also true of literary, scholarly, and academic minstrelsy: "The device is designed to remind white consciousness that black men and women are *mis-speakers* bereft of humanity— carefree devils strumming and humming all day—unless, in a gaslight misidentification, they are violent devils fit for lynching, a final exorcism that will leave whites alone."[21] Thus, the blues is not devoid of spiritual values; it was Oliver and those of his ilk who devalued the spirituality of the blues.

Finn made the latter point when he said that this tradition of stereotyping—specifically calling the blues "devil's music"—is just another form of moral scapegoating that has resulted from an inherent "anti-black" stance in American culture.[22] In other words, identifying "blues" as evil is like identifying "black" as evil; it is a practice rooted in the custom of the most powerful (and guilty), who always deal with evil through various means of scapegoating at the expense of their victims. This observation coincides with Charles Keil's recognition that some white blues scholars, such as Oliver, practice a variant of the "white man's burden" tradition,[23] which obviously has little to do with being pro-black and a lot to do with being burdened with guilt. This "burden" of guilt, to explicate, is what was evidenced in the confession of ethnomusicologist Alan Lomax: "The black and evil blues will roll on and on, troubling the minds of many American citizens until we all join in expunging this guilty stain from the hearts of our countrymen."[24]

Another reason white scholars have been unable to get at the truth about the black blues is that the blues has an elusive cultural element that defies their attempts at *representation* (description, transcription, and analysis). By matching the music creator's achievement with the achievement of scholarly representation, it is natural for scholars—in their own eyes or in the eyes of colleagues—to feel that they have attained a kind of peer status (or even superiority) to the music creator, particularly if the representation involves judgment, either positive or negative.[25] For similar reasons, white musicians who perform the blues may feel as though they have attained a peer status with black blues singers. This is what rock-blues musician Eric Clapton was implying when he said, "I think the blues is actually more of an emotional experience than one exclusive to black or white, or related to poverty."[26] It may be that the wide availability of blues representations—books, magazines, recordings—gives white musicians the inclination that, if they can understand the representations and objectify them in performance (the twelve-bar form, the "blue note," the technique), then they too can be authentic blues singers, real "blues people." But if one reads Clapton's views carefully, he also said that all he was doing was "presenting a case" for the music he loved. "I was just its *representative*," he said.[27]

The practice of white musicians always producing representations of black music is what black music critic Nelson George was implying when he said blacks create and move on while whites document and recycle.[28] Langston Hughes said the same thing four decades earlier. "[W]hite folks are always imitating us, especially in the entertainment field, taking our material, our song styles, our dances and making a million dollars from them," he said. "Look at the dozens of imitators of Sarah Vaughn, Billie Holiday and Louis Armstrong."[29] Hughes continued with a point also made by W. C. Handy.[30] He said, "there are some Negro entertainers who, instead of continuing to originate, seem to think the ideal thing to do is imitate the imitations of ourselves. . . . But they come out such pale carbon copies that no wonder audiences are subconsciously bored."[31]

This is the reason W. C. Handy, the so-called "Father of the Blues," commented that, "I have a feeling that real blues can be written only by a Negro, who keeps his roots in the life of the race."[32] Although there are many who have questioned the notion of whether Handy's blues were "real blues," the answer to the question of what he meant and why his "St. Louis Blues" was "the blues" was demonstrated when he was Jim Crowed at the Park Plaza hotel in the city he helped make famous.[33] These kinds of experiences are what gave impetus and character to the blues. Having an understanding of this is why Zora Neale Hurston commented that whites wrongly think blacks are easily imitated, when in fact she personally had never seen a white performance of black music that was entirely realistic. "And God only knows what the world has suffered from the white damsels who try to sing Blues," she said.[34] Amiri Baraka went so far as to say that the idea of a white blues singer seemed to be a contradiction, even more of a contradiction than the idea of a black middle-class blues singer. "The materials of the blues were not available to the white American," explained Baraka, "even though some strange circumstance might prompt him to look for them."[35]

This distinction between black and white musicians playing the blues parallels the prevailing scholarship on the blues. I believe Alan Dundes surmised correctly when he said, "If being a Negro is a prerequisite to playing the blues, it may also be one for understanding all the nuances of the blues."[36] Del Jones, an African-American journalist and cultural critic, pushed this point further than anyone else in his small but extremely provocative book, *Culture Bandits* (1990). He said that, while white musicians during the sixties co-opted the blues into their cultural reality in part to profit from it, white intellects set themselves up as expert critics of the music they could never really understand.[37] This was easy to accomplish, he said, because the mass media—the record and radio broadcast industries as well as the print media—were almost solely under white control.[38] Jones is not alone in making these kinds of accusations. Ngugi wa Thiong'o, the Kenyan novelist, called culture banditry a "cultural bomb," a bomb Molefi Asante said destroys all but that which is stolen. "Many scholars have behaved toward African culture and history as pirates aboard a ship, they have taken as much as they could put under their belts and discarded the rest."[39] These comments are by no means the ranting of irrational black radicals. Jacques Attali, the French economist and scholar, said of jazz created by black Americans (with later reference to blues), "Whites would steal from them this creativity born of labor and the elementary forms of industrialization, and then turn around and sell it back. . . . White capital, which owned all of the record companies, controlled this commercialization process from the start, economically and culturally."[40]

But it was not just the blues that was incomprehensible, according to Langston Hughes. Hughes had his comical cultural critic, the fictitious Jesse B. Simple, say these words about the origin and meaning of bebop: "Be-bop music is certainly colored folk's music—which is why white folks find it so hard to imitate. . . . The ones that sing try to make up new Be-bop words, but them white folks don't know what they are singing about."[41] In response to the question of exactly where be-bop came from, Simple answered, "the police":

> From their beating Negroes' heads. . . . Every time a white cop hits a Negro with his billy club, that old club says, "Bop! Bop! . . . Be-Bop! Mop . . . Bop!" That Negro hollers, "Ou-o-o! Oooo-ya-koo! Ou-o-o!" But old cop just keeps on. . . . That's where Be-bop comes from, beaten right out of somebody's head into them horns and saxophones and piano keys that plays it now. Do you call that nonsense? . . .
>
> That's why so many white folks don't dig Bop. . . . White folks do not get their heads beat just for being white. But you, me, a cop is liable to grab me anytime and beat my head—just for being colored. . . .
>
> And that is where Bop comes from—out of them dark days we have seen. That is why Be-bop is so mad, wild, frantic, crazy. And not to be dug unless you have seen dark days, too. That's why folks who ain't suffered much cannot play Bop, and do not understand it. They think it's nonsense.[42]

To apply the metaphor, white blues scholars do not fully understand the blues because they do not understand the threat and experience of getting their heads beaten.

Oliver, for instance, did a decent job of discerning "meaning *in* the blues"—that is, in reading history through the blues and providing the historical background for topics in blues lyrics—but he missed the true "meaning *of* the blues," and he even admitted it. He said, "For those who had the blues, for those who lived the blues, for those who lived *with* the blues, the blues had meaning. But for those who lived outside the blues the meaning of the blues was elusive. For the blues was more than a form of folk song, and though its meaning became clearer with an understanding of the content of the verses, the reason why Blacks sang the blues and listened to the blues is still not wholly explained."[43] The meaning *of* the blues was elusive to Oliver and his followers because they lived "outside" the blues. In this regard, Wright rhetorically asked and wrongly answered the crucial question in the foreword to Oliver's book: "Can an alien, who has never visited the *milieu* from which a family of songs has sprung, write about them? . . . I answer a categoric and emphatic Yes."[44] The answer, I will demonstrate in this book, is a categorical and emphatic No, unless the writer becomes immersed in "the milieu." The fact is, white blues scholars' representations of the blues—despite what Langston Hughes described as their excellent books largely devoted to analyzing, describing, and praising the music—generally leave those who are natives of the culture that produced the blues with the impression that all these scholars have accomplished is to reduce the *subject* of blues to an *object*.

The blues is not simply a good man or woman feeling bad; it is, as Robert Johnson sang in "Preaching the Blues," "a lowdown aching old heart disease, like consumption, killing me by degrees." The blues was more than the "bad luck" it was portrayed as in a front-page news piece of 1950, captioned, "Billie Holiday Ill Has Right to Sing Blues." "Billie Holiday had the right to sing the blues last week," the newsbrief began. "Police grabbed her new Lincoln Cosmopolitan sedan and her chauffer, too . . . because he had dope in his possession. And Billie? She was reported ill in a Los Angeles hospital."[45] The blues was more than that, more than simply personal; it was social, political, and economic. Political cartoonist Jay Jackson captured this in a political drawing composed for *The Chicago Defender* in 1948. Titled "Blues in the Blackbelts," it referenced some of the political and economic losses blacks faced during the forties, principal among them being Mississippi Senator Theodore Bilbo's 1946 filibuster of the bill to establish a permanent Fair Employment Practice Commission (FEPC), the racialist employment policies of the Tennessee Valley Authority, which was supported by the anti-FEPC Mississippi Senator John Rankin, and the postwar demise of the Office of Price Administration (OPA), one of the few wartime agencies that practiced fair employment policies. Jackson's political drawing pictured an aged blues musician with his shoulders rounded over an old piano, a cigarette dangling from his lips, and a piece of sheet music on the piano titled "Columbia-Tennessee Blues." The woman leaning heavily on the piano was the blues singer, and she was holding pieces of sheet music titled "The FEPC Breakdown" and "We Took a Spankin from Bilbo and Rankin." On the floor was a piece of music titled "The OPA Has Gone Away." The verses she sang were:

The FEP was snatched from me.

The OPA has scampered.

In Tennessee we're up a tree

'Cause justice has been hampered!

The KKK is on the climb.

Bilbo and Rankin winners!

A dollar bill is worth a dime

When seeking rooms or dinners!

So, jack, I'm solid in the blues

As blue as blues can be.

They've taken all that we can lose.

Oh, who can help poor me?

As the blues saying goes, "You can't play the blues until you have paid your dues."[46] Correlatively, the best writer on the blues is not simply one who does good theoretical scholarship, but one who knows the "lowdown shaking chill" of living at the political, economic, and social underside of history.

One reason the representations of white blues scholars seem counterfeit is that they often take the form of reduction to the language of ethnomusicology, which is not an a theoretical methodology indigenous to African-American culture. I found, as this book attests, that I could glean an even deeper understanding of the people who created the blues through a theological (theomusicological) study of blues, particularly as it relates to evil. As Jeffrey Burton Russell said in his history of the devil, the question of what evil is and how it came to be is one of the most ancient and intricate of human queries, and the "problem of evil" seems even more pressing today than ever.[47] As Burton understood, there is a wide semantic field covered by the words "evil" and "devil," so that the study of a people's popular beliefs regarding the sources and nature of evil reveals submerged realities about their nature as religious human beings. This is because the study of evil is essentially the study of morality, for evil cannot be examined without some comprehension of the parameters of what is perceived by a people to be good, sacred, and holy.[48] In turn, the study of morality involves the study of human cosmology (worldview), namely, a people's mythologies, theologies, and theodicies. Not only can we learn much about the cosmology of blues singers, but also much about that of black churchgoers and white writers who, in accusationally defining blues as evil, revealed much about their own view of humanity.

In studying blues and evil, we find much that actually is good, sacred, and holy in and about this music, in part because the teachings and the spirituality of the church overflowed into the secular world and its cultural products. It is by means of what sociologist Bruce Reed termed "representative oscillation" that this religious connection between the sacred and the secular can be partly understood. Viewing religious participation as movement from daily, self-autonomous life to the spiritual world of religious ritual and heightened forms of community, Reed derived three categories that describe the extents to which people participate religiously. There are those that attend church weekly (which is normative for the church faithful), those who attend infrequently and therefore depend on the weekly attendance of a relative or friend ("representative oscillation"), and those who never attend but are dependent on the existence or symbolic presence of the church.[49] Another sociologist, Andrew Greeley, created a similar model of measurement, but listed three times as many categories. His categories included church attendance: never, less than once a year, about once a year, several times a year, about once a month, two or three times a month, nearly every week, every week, and several times a week.[50] These nine categories Greeley then reduced to what was essentially Reed's three categories of religious participation. Greeley spoke of those who are "quite religious," "somewhat religious," and "rather unreligious."[51]

Blues singers, despite the strictness with which church folk criticized them, were customarily among those who were "somewhat religious." Virginia Piedmont blues singer John Cephas, for instance, considered himself to be a Christian—one who believes in God, Jesus Christ, and reads the Bible—even though he was not a regular churchgoer.[52] If "blues people" did not attend church themselves because of the church's mandate that "you cannot play the devil's music and serve God," then a relative was their religious representative. This was not only a common practice among blues singers; it was, as Tommy Johnson's "Lonesome Home Blues" illustrated, a common belief. Johnson sang that one morning he woke up to say his morning prayers because he no longer had a woman to speak in his behalf. Joe McCoy seemingly borrowed and slightly paraphrased this verse in his "My Wash Woman's Gone." Lightnin' Hopkins finally repented to his "representative" after becoming wild from running around with women against his mother's good advice. In the last verse of his "Mama's Baby Child" he said he was going home to fall down on his mother's knee to ask her, "Please, ma'am, pray for me." Jimmy Oden, in "Going Down Slow," asked someone among his listeners to write his mother and tell her the shape he was in, "Tell her to pray for me, forgive me for my sin." Robert Wilkins sang in "I'll Go With Her Blues" that every time he heard the lonesome church bell ring he thought about the song that his baby used to sing.

The secular domain, then, was that sphere of behavior among the "somewhat religious" that involved mythologies, theologies, and theodicies principally derived from the church. Thus, the blues was not *of* the church, but "blues belief" (and therefore "blues people") existed on the periphery of the doctrinal enclave of Christianity. While the "quite religious" had the opportunity to express their mythologies, theologies, and theodicies in their church music, the "somewhat religious" expressed their cosmology and religious ponderings in the blues.

Ethnomusicologists who have written on the blues have totally disregarded these kinds of considerations, considerations that could fall within the domain of their discipline if only they would learn to ask the pertinent questions. Part of the reason for this neglect is that ethnomusicologists, white scholars in general, have paid no regard to the first important work by a black scholar to begin to uncover the theology of the blues, James H. Cone's *The Spirituals and the Blues* (1972). By ignoring or glossing over Cone's interpretation of the blues, ethnomusicologists have been just as misled as historical musicologists, who, in a rather "high-hat" way, have fully turned a deaf ear to the blues. In both instances, the problem lies in the general devaluation of black culture and scholarship by those writers who do not share the black experience of subsistence at the underside of history. As explained by Houston Baker, the problem white scholars have in understanding black culture is that they have neglected to immerse themselves in the whole of discourse about it, including conversing with the natives of that culture.[53] "Furthermore," said Molefi Asante, "without culture immersion the researcher loses all sense of ethical value and becomes a researcher 'for the sake of research,' the worse kind of value in the Afrocentric approach which sees research as assisting in the humanizing of the world. In a European world one can have intercultural communicationists doing intercultural research who do not believe in intercultural communication, except as a way to sell market products, attitudes, or beliefs."[54] To summarize my point, reversing Charles Keil's claim that scholars find in the blues what they expect to,[55] I have discerned that white blues scholars tend not find in this black music what they tend to be incapable of finding.

Does the fact that I am an African-American scholar who has been immersed in the whole of discourse about black culture (including dialogue with Cone's interpretation of the blues) make my treatment of the music any less a reductive representation than that of scholars who evidently have not so immersed themselves? We might as well ask if Cone is any more justified than scholars of the latter sort in saying "I am the blues."[56] What Cone means by saying "I am the blues" is that he understands what it means to be black in America, in part because he has fully immersed himself in conversation with the natives of black culture who also know this racial experience. The way Cone phrased it, "To be black is to be blue,"[57] is identical to bluesman Memphis Slim's statement that, "I think all black people can sing the blues more or less."[58] Houston Baker would agree; and that he can sing the blues more or less is why he was able to take the blues as the basis of a theory for Afro-American literary criticism.[59] Langston Hughes and Sterling Brown could also sing the blues more or less, which is why they were able to attain noncounterfeit representations of the blues in their poetry. The culture-bearing of these literati was much akin to the noncounterfeit representations of black southern lore that Paul Laurence Dunbar, Jean Toomer, James Weldon Johnson, and Margaret Walker were able to attain in their literature. Then, am I, as a black scholar, more capable of a noncounterfeit representation of the blues than nonblack scholars who neither live at the underside of history nor immerse themselves in discourse with the natives of black culture? Baker answers that black cultural critics who are participants in black history and discourse are not automatically cultural authorities but do have a greater chance of fashioning "thick descriptions."[60]

I certainly do not feel that I am an automatic authority on the blues. I do not even feel that I can say "I am the blues," as could Memphis-born bluesman Booker T. Laury. "I am the blues—I'm the truth about the blues," said Laury.[61] For me to declare that "I am the blues" is essentially for me to say, using Laury's language, "I am the truth," which is to claim automatic cultural authority. First of all, to say "I am the blues," when I am a fairly comfortable academic, is to sidestep the truthfulness and the tragedy of the real blues life. In fact, to declare "I am"—whether it is "*I am* an African American" or "*I am* the blues"—is to claim selfhood among a community of affirmed *beings,* whereas those who created and sang the blues were constantly trying to affirm their personhood in the face of abject racialist bombardment and "head-bashing" by the overculture. This constant attempt to affirm black personhood is the "attitude" of the blues, the distinguishing factor between the technique of "playing the blues" and the mystique of "singing in the blues." As Baraka said, white musicians understand the blues principally as a form of music and seldom as a kind of attitude.[62] Similarly, blues scholars who are nonnatives of black culture understand their scholarship as an acquirable skill rather than as a particular racial disposition.

Though I do not feel I can say "I am the blues," I can say comfortably (as can the other black scholars who have written on the blues) that I "belong to" the blues, part and parcel, because I know what it means to be black and currently living at the underside of history. I know the feeling out of personal experience and from having immersed myself in the multi-leveled discourse of my people, who also know the feeling. Thus, I am claiming that this book, *Blues and Evil,* like all other books on the blues, is naturally a representation of the blues; but because I belong to the blues, it is a representation comprised of "thick descriptions," descriptions thicker than the work of scholars who have neglected to immerse themselves deeply and continuously in the whole of discourse about black culture.

Because of the neglect on the part of white blues scholars to demystify the blues for its authentic mythologies, this book intends to contest the stereotypic notions that blues *is* evil and that blues singers are anti-religion, irreligious, and atheistic. I will argue that blues is replete with mythologies that reveal blues singers' religious thought on the origin and description of evil (chapter 1), that it is a music that is theological and that talks about evil in folk theological language (chapter 2), and that it is a music that posits "theodicies" reconciling the seeming incongruence of evil existing in a world believed to be created and ruled by a good God (chapter 3). In other words, jazz musician Noble Sissle's comment about all of the elements that went into making jazz was also true of the blues. "[The] music . . . did not just happen. . . . There is a history to the birth form of our music. There is every element of life in it—religion, romance, tragedy, faith, hope and primitive abandon—brought together and paid for at a tremendous price."[63]

Out of the first and third chapters on the mythologies and theodicies of the blues evolves my theory of African-American cultural understanding. This is centered around the African trickster-god, a personage that is both superhuman and subhuman, female and male, sacred and profane, benevolent and malevolent, and who walks with a limp because one foot moves in the realm of the mundane and the other in the realm of the divine. This trickster figure is not only symbolic of what blues is when personified, but prototypal of a paradigm of personality and morality in African-American cultural history. Given the synchronous duplicity or holistic tenacity of African-American culture, the blues singer is one of many African-American personages that fits within the personality scheme of the trickster and that shows the blues to be a symbol of black cultural and ontological reality. This synchronous duplicity in the blues, this unification of apparent opposites, was captured in what a group of "experts" (scholars, critics, and performers), gathered for a ten-day discussion to define jazz, concluded about the music of bluesman John Lee Hooker. Hooker sang "both the blues and religious songs" in a style the "experts" agreed was "amazingly complex yet authentically primitive."[64]

Given the synchronous duplicity of the blues, it is no coincidence that the two indigenous literary theories of criticism developed by African-American scholars are based on the blues and the Signifying Monkey.[65] The blues was created by people who saw in the trickster personality an emulative model of behavior to cope with oppression, and the Signifying Monkey is itself an African-American trickster figure. With respect to Baker's *Blues, Ideology, and Afro-American Literature: A Vernacular Theory* (1984), Earl Conrad, back in 1945, spoke of a "blues school of literature," a phrase he borrowed from Ralph Ellison's essay, "Richard Wright's Blues."[66] Regarding such novels as Chester Himes's *If He Hollers*

Let Him Go and Richard Wright's *Native Son,* Conrad said this school of literature brought to the consciousness of the American public characters whose behaviors and personalities revealed the problems of racism, thus turning a negative into a positive.[67] In other words, what Molefi Asante said of Ellison's novel is essentially true of the other literature that comprised the "blues school of literature"—"above all else this is a blues poem, an expression of a condition, a will to escape, even if that means making yourself invisible by living underground."[68]

Given that theomusicology is an indigenous theory that evolved out of my study of the blues, it is also no surprise that my trickster theory of Afro-American cultural understanding is a by-product of my theomusicological (theological) approach to culture-study. What all of this means is that, contrary to Oliver's claim that blues is "somewhat bereft of spiritual values," the trickster personality illustrates that the blues can be a source of theory for the fashioning of an African-American ethics. I strongly believe a blues-based ethics is a positive possibility, despite Alan Dundes's suggestion that any positive sense of black identity in the blues is but a reaction to whites considering it evil music. "If white folks regarded blues as evil music (in contrast to the spirituals)," said Dundes, "then to the extent that Negroes wished to form their own aesthetic judgments independent of white values, it is reasonable for them to find a positive sense of identity in the blues."[69] I am positing the possibility of a blues-based African-American ethics in spite of, not because of, my initial reaction to "white folks'" claims that blues is evil. These ideas, though someday I hope to develop them in a project on the philosophy of African-American music in its entirety, will be implicit throughout this book.

After I discuss the mythologies, theologies, and theodicies of the blues in the three chapters that comprise the body of *Blues and Evil,* my conclusion (which is a substantive chapter in itself) describes, in painstaking detail, the process by which these religious elements of the blues diminished as the music moved out of its "country" context into the "city" where it developed into a sophisticated "urban" art form. The blues continuum that I will use to delineate the changes that occurred in the blues is: country blues → city blues → urban blues. Baraka and Keil first employed this essentially historical, geographical, and stylistic continuum in their books; but I have added a decidedly theological interpretation to the continuum derived from my indigenous theomusicological approach to the blues.

Because my continuum is largely theological (while still being geographical and stylistic), I have not included the field or forest hollers in the continuum. These "made-up songs," which bluesman Muddy Waters remembered singing back in the days he worked on a Mississippi plantation ploughing and chopping cotton,[70] seem to be mainly the musical and emotional predecessors of country blues rather than its religious precursors. The soloistic expression of the guitar-accompanied country blues, as well as its unstandardized forms, inconsistent pulse, spoken introductions and endings, emotional interpolations, and occasional falsetto articulations, all reveal the musical and emotional influences of the hollers. While it is difficult to say, given the relatively few recordings of hollers, whether these "made-up songs" were the thematic predecessors of the country blues (in terms of the latter's mythologies, theologies, and theodicies), what I will illustrate in this book is that "country blues"—the blues of Robert Johnson, Son House, Charlie Patton, Bukka White, Blind Willie McTell, and others—was a music that was religious in the foregoing three respects.

"City blues" of the 1920s and beyond was essentially an urbanized or "citified" country blues, as was evidenced in the music of Lonnie Johnson, Tommy McClennan, J. B. Lenoir, Peetie Wheatstraw, Blind Lemon Jefferson, and Memphis Minnie. With electric guitar replacing the "box" (the folk guitar), city blues became an intensified country sound. It was also "country" in that it was fundamentally a verbal genre (revealing its kinship with the hollers). In city blues, as in country blues, even the guitar had to be a "talking guitar," one that not only responded with interpolations to the blues singer's articulations, but would, as a blues singer might have said, "sing it by itself." Although the sound of city blues was not as stylized as the sophisticated "urban blues" that developed from it beginning around the 1940s, the music was characterized by standardized forms. Usually (but not always), city blues involved two or more instruments—often piano rather than (or in addition to) electric guitar. The important point is that the impact of the city was quickly felt in the musical aspect of the blues but not in its mythologies, theologies, and theodicies, since these things involved an entrenched religious cosmology. City blues, in short, was religiously "country," an ethos Langston Hughes captured in his review of Memphis Minnie's performance on the eve of the 1943 new year. Hughes said, "through the smoke and racket of the noisy Chicago bar float Louisiana bayous, muddy old swamps, Mississippi dust and sun, cotton fields, lonesome roads, train whistles in the night, mosquitoes at dawn. . . . All these things cry through the strings on Memphis Minnie's electric guitar, amplified to machine proportions." The music had so much in it, concluded Hughes, that sometimes it made the folks holler out loud.[71]

"Classic blues" fits into the category of "city blues" because it was essentially a wedding of southern folk cosmology and the jazz-like accompaniment of a piano or small ensemble. Among the "queens of the blues," who insinuated their country upbringing into the stiff musical phrasing taught them by band leaders, were Alberta Hunter, Ethel Waters, Bessie Smith, Ma Rainey, Victoria Spivey, and Ida Cox. This countrified "insinuation," in a word, is represented by the title of Ethel Waters's blues of 1921, "The Down Home Blues." To illustrate the point, Ida Cox's "How Long Daddy, How Long" (1925), a banjo-accompanied blues with a very prominent "downhome" sound, captured a strong remembrance of "home" (the context) and the hollers (the texture). In fact, when Cox recorded "Lawdy Lawdy Blues" thirty-six years later (in 1961), well into the urban blues phase, her "singing the blues" remained textually, texturally, and contextually identical to her above-mentioned piece of 1925, despite the sophisticated jazz accompaniment. Thus, while the musical style was modified in "classic" (city) blues, the linguistic *texture* (stress, inflection, tone, timbre, pitch), the *text* (mythologies, theologies, theodicies), and the *context* (the ritual blues gathering) remained largely unaffected.[72]

Although city blues was still situated in the worldview of the rural South, over the decades the city setting took its toll. Country blues became city blues, Jim Crow became "James Crow," and the devil became Kluxism, Nordism, and Bilboism rather than a "big black man" with an ambrosial curl, a top hat, and a frock coat that hid his forked tail. The result of the city taking its toll was the evolution of "city blues" into "urban blues," the music of T-Bone Walker, Bobby Bland, Jimmy Reed, Jimmy Rushing, Otis Rush, and B. B. King. This urbane blues was less folkloric and more assimilative in its sound than city blues. It was a blues more subdued than its precursor, in part because its rhythms were more refined, more danceable. The African-rooted spirituality basically continued untouched; but the nonarticulations (moans and hums) were less dissonant and menacing, and the "oh Lord" interpolation and its myriad permutations were, if not actually more absent, less convincing ritualistically.

Part of the reason for these changes that comprise urban blues is that many of the musicians of the post–World War II era learned to play the blues by listening to records and the radio rather than from the downhome musicians who sang the blues in a context unfettered by the wishes of white record executives and the limitations of the three-minute recording. The original context was an environment replete with a certain religious cosmology and a certain memory that Skip James alluded to in "Cypress Grove" when he sang, "Well the old people told me baby but I never did know." What makes blues singing authentic was not the ability to imitate the text and texture, both of which were relatively concrete, but learning these in the context where the reason the text and texture were as they were could be witnessed firsthand and explained by the "old people" who knew. To the extent that the original context was foreign to the younger urban musicians when they were learning the blues, urban blues became an artistic representation of the folk blues of the old-time bluesmen who remembered and witnessed what the "old people" knew and had told them. As a result, folk elements, when used, were often "borrowed." As Alain Locke explained, the use of folk elements did not necessarily result in the creation of folk music. "When folk elements are stereotyped and artificially imitated," Locke said, "we have popular music with a folk flavor."[73] In summary, urban blues developed from city blues, which developed from country blues; and as the continuum proceeded, each genre increasingly became a representation or reduction of what blues was religiously when it first began to evolve following Reconstruction.

This is what this book is about—what the blues once was in its reflection of a people's religious cosmology, including a constant reminder of how white scholars have misinformed us about what the blues once was. The blues is still the blues; but it is not the blues that it used to be because, as I will show in my conclusion, it was eventually denatured of its traditional mythologies, theologies, and theodicies. Before detailing the process of this denaturement, the body of this book will give close attention to the trinary religious cosmology of the blues: "The Mythologies of the Blues" (chapter 1), "The Theologies of the Blues" (chapter 2), and "The Theodicies of the Blues" (chapter 3). We will begin with the mythologies because this comprises the overarching rubric in which theologies and theodicies are subsequently fashioned.

CHAPTER ONE

THE MYTHOLOGIES
OF THE BLUES

I n the old American South, from the era of slavery to the early twentieth century, the Bible was the principal source of religious authority referred to by the people of African origin for explanations regarding the mythical and the mysterious. Among blacks who mixed African religious retentions into the new religion of Christianity, it was a great conjure book that documented such heroic acts of conjuration as Moses dividing the Red Sea.[1] The sacredness of the holy book was such that, according to superstitious belief, it was supposed to be kept in a central location—such as the center of a table—and no other books or objects could lay atop it.[2] Even as blacks moved out of the rural South to the urban North during the great migration and as the rural residue of religion began to diminish in the new city milieu, biblical lore remained deeply embedded in the heritage and narratives of Afro-America. The scripturality continued into the modern era of urban blues, even though biblical meanings may have been forgotten increasingly, even modified beyond recognition.

Given the Bible's cultural interiority and influence, it should not be surprising that the two myths on the origin and description of evil prevalent in the old South and its blues were biblical—the Adamic and the tragic-hero myths. In the Adamic myth, the "problem of evil," traced back to a human ancestor, supervenes on God's perfect creation. In the tragic-hero myth, fault is traced back to a deity rather than to human ancestors. Although the Adamic myth includes recessive elements of the tragic,[3] the Adamic is, in African-American religious thought, the myth par excellence that prevents evil, no matter how radical, from being symmetrical with good and that characterizes evil as a mere "staining" of that which is primordially unblemished.

Because blues singers of the old South were customarily brought up as churchgoers, and the blues, as I will detail in the next chapter, was a music deeply rooted in the theological world outlook of Afro-Christianity, the Adamic myth constituted the mythology of evil that predominated in blues lyrics and "blues life." I find this to be true not simply because the narratives of blues singers (interviews, biographies, and autobiographies) document their traditional literalist reading of the Bible, but also because the Adamic myth was occasionally thematized and frequently implied in the lyrics of the blues—blues such as Talking Billy Anderson's recording of 1927, "Adam and Eve."[4] Folklorists Howard Odum and Guy Johnson in their book of 1926, *Negro Workaday Songs,* recorded two blues that thematized the Adamic myth. One blamed "the woman" for causing "po' Adam's fall," and the other blamed "Mudder Eve" for "Daddy Adam's fall."[5] Jimmy Oden's "Patience Like Job," co-written by Sunnyland Slim, similarly thematized the Adamic myth. He sang, "Adam and Eve made sin, what more can we do?" Kokomo Arnold thematized the myth in "The Twelves," a vaudeville-like treatment of the creation and the subsequent disobedience of Adam. Arnold sang, with seeming reckless humor, that God made Adam stout and gave him a snout, then gave him a tail to fan flies and then some eyes. Next, God made Adam's "yas, yas, yas" so he was unable to turn a "trick" (sex), which made him sick; but then he got his "trick." Consequently, as the final verse summarized, God made Adam sick but then made him well; "you know by that," sang Arnold, "the big boy's coughing in hell." Tommie Bradley, in his "Adam and Eve," also parodied the perceived sexual theme in the so-called "temptation" narrative. He sang, "Adam said to Eve, 'you been so cute, you wouldn't give me of that forbidden fruit.'" But Bradley figured, as had Arnold, that Adam got some "fruit": Since they had one child named "Cabel" and another named "Ain," Bradley sang, "you know by that they must have shook that thing."

Hociel Thomas's classic blues, "Adam and Eve Had the Blues," also involved the traditional (Augustinian) sexual overtones. The piece was co-written by Thomas's aunt, blues singer Sippie Wallace, who said her inspiration to write it came from a soured marriage that resulted from her husband's infidelity—a sin she believed all men committed because of the primordial fault of Eve. "Eve is the cause of all of us having the blues," Wallace said.[6] Rendered in the "classic" blues style, Thomas retold the Adamic myth in a more familiar and serious fashion than Arnold and Bradley. She said that, when Adam and Eve were in the Garden of Eden, Eve called her husband to her side to show him the fruit tree that could make them wise. Eve convinced Adam they could eat of the fruit now that the good Lord was gone, and Adam agreed that it would not take them long. But when they ate, they committed a "sin" and their troubles began, and they are still, sang Thomas, having troubles yet. When the good Lord came down, Adam and Eve found out what their troubles were all about. The Lord said to Adam and then to Eve that they had been seen eating from the forbidden tree. Then (with a bit of vaudeville humor via a double entendre), Eve said to the good Lord, "don't blame poor me, because every woman's wild about a good old tree." Despite her pleading, because they ate of the tree that they were "refused," Adam and Eve "had the blues."

When this explicit thematization of the Adamic myth is considered alongside the uncountable allusions to "the fall" (which I will detail in chapter 2), it is obvious that the Adamic myth had either significantly influenced or actually dominated blues singers' thought regarding the origin and description of evil, not to mention that it also accounted for the cosmological perspective blues singers held regarding life and death. Kokomo Arnold sang in his "Rocky Road Blues" that his mother always told him when he was but a child, "Son you must always remember, Lord, that you was born to die."

Within the Adamic mythological rubric are recessive themes from the tragic myth, the myth in which the divine and the diabolical (let us say, God and the serpent) are indistinguishable. According to the tragic myth, when a person is tempted and led astray by a deity working through human weaknesses, the fault lays in the initiative of the deity.[7] The counterpart of Adam, here, is the "tragic hero," who, though he commits no fault on his own accord, is nonetheless guilty—a "guilty innocent."[8]

But this mythology of the guilty-innocent tragic hero is unspeakable as a thought-out theology because it blames God for the "problem of evil." Since blaming evil on God cannot be rationalized by the worldview dominated by the Adamic myth (the myth that professes God to be innocent of evil), then the recessive tragic theme in the Adamic myth cannot be articulated, only unknowingly exhibited. This exhibition, which comprises part of what I have termed "the mythologies of the blues," included both the lyricizing of lore about traditional black tragic heroes and the embodiment of the tragic personality by living blues singers. As I will explain later, the character of the tragic hero became a paradigm of personality for blues singers who saw in him a behavioral means of coping with oppression. Thus, in the mythologies of the blues, a theology for the tragic myth was never worked out reflectively. Rather, it was thematized by means of "characters" that were storied in African-American lore and lyric and by means of drama that was lived in the lives of black "blues people."

If, in this thematizing and realizing, the recessive "tragic" trait of the predominant Adamic myth did not eventually give way to its host myth, as was usually the case (as I will show in chapter 2), then the end of evil and the beginning of salvation could only occur through the medium of human pity. This pity was described by Christian existentialist Paul Ricoeur as "an impotent emotion of participation in the misfortunes of the hero, a sort of weeping with him and purifying the tears by the beauty of song."[9] This is the very thing Zora Neale Hurston was saying about pity as it was manifested in African-American storytelling: "It is singular that God never finds fault, never censures the Negro. He sees faults but expects nothing different. He is lacking in bitterness as is the Negro story-teller himself in circumstances that ordinarily would call for pity."[10] This pardoning pity, capable of activation through the beauty of song, typified balladry about such tragic "badman" heroes of African-American legendry as Stackolee, Railroad Bill, and George "Devil" Winston.

For those whose understanding of evil was informed by the Adamic myth, a tragic theology could not be articulated, let alone fathomed, to pardon these badmen of their crimes, these black victims of their guilty-innocence; but in the dramatization of their lives in African-American lore and lyric, pity could keep them alive, even resurrect them. Because death could not contain them, these immortal heroes either took control of the underworld and gave the devil himself "hell," or they wandered about the earth, as bluesman and tragic hero Robert Johnson said he would in "Me and the Devil Blues." Johnson instructed his survivors to bury his body "down by the highway side" so his evil spirit could easily "get a Greyhound bus and ride." Picking up and protracting the tendency of secular African

Americans to "save" their tragic heroes—those whose lives lived out that peculiar personality—Peter Guralnick, in *Searching for Robert Johnson* (1989), carefully portrayed Johnson as, in his words, "a modern-day Orpheus."[11]

That blues singers actually could triumph as "tragic heroes" when, according to the Adamic myth, they died as "prodigal sons" also has been sensationalized and dramatized in storytelling about the life and death of Blind Lemon Jefferson. According to lore and lyric, bluesman Jefferson (a *real* blind man!) died in a Chicago snowstorm following a successful recording career (a career tainted "only" by the exploitation of Paramount Records). One night, Jefferson left the Paramount studio to sing at a house-rent party, but he never arrived at his destination. The following day he was found in the street covered with snow, frozen to death, his guitar laying beside him in the white tomb. While Paramount claimed Jefferson died innocently of a heart attack, others believed (implying the fault of the exploiters) that the blind man froze waiting for his driver or the streetcar. Samuel Charters, who narrated the story in his classic *Country Blues* (1959), left the mystery intact, thus dramatizing the tragic motif and evoking the pity of his readers. "There is probably no way of ever knowing," lamented Charters, "what happened to Lemon in the darkness of that winter night."[12]

The mystery of Jefferson's death somewhat paralleled those of the deaths of Robert Johnson and Peetie Wheatstraw. One of the pieces Wheatstraw recorded at his last studio session was "Bring Me Flowers While I'm Living,"[13] recorded a mere twenty-six days before a fatal car accident in 1941; the final recording Jefferson did for Paramount on the day he died was "Empty House Blues." The seeming premonitions of these bluesmen were *tragic:* men driven into exile, driven to sing the blues, and then having to make a living of it (like having to sport blackface), knowing that the hard life of exile often led to premature demise. The entire drama, often replayed, was tragic: exploitation, death, and pardon—pardon through our "weeping with him and purifying the tears by the beauty of song." So pardoned, Jefferson was memorialized in a Paramount record entitled "Wasn't It Sad about Lemon."

The same sentiments were purifying and edifying of Walter Barnes, a jazz-band leader who died with nine members of his group and a total of two hundred black people in the tragic fire of 1940 that burned down the Rhythm Night Club in Natchez, Mississippi. Although the morality of jazz was hotly debated beginning in the 1920s and on up through the 1940s, *The Chicago Defender* advertised "a pair of sad but tuneful numbers" by the Bronzeville Five that eulogized Barnes, one of the city's own citizens. The advertisement said about the disk's two sides, "Mississippi Fire Blues" and "Natchez Mississippi Blues," that "The numbers are written in a way to laud the efforts of Walter Barnes toward saving the patrons in the hall and also carries a saddening note for the many who lost their lives in the fire."[14] Thus, akin to the sinner who traditionally could be "preached into heaven" by a eulogy that portrayed the sinner as a "saint," Jefferson, Johnson, Wheatstraw, and uncountable others were pardoned for being "blues people," just as Barnes was pardoned for being associated with jazz. This pardoning was a kind of tragic salvation attained not through religious purification or justification but through the emotion of piteous mercy.[15]

While the tragic myth loomed large in the secular lore and lyric of old-South Afro-America and typified aspects of mythologized "blues life" protracted by the pens of infatuated blues enthusiasts, it was the Adamic myth that prevailed when the narratives of "blues people" gave explanations for the origin (and description) of evil and when the drama of the "prodigal son," to be discussed in the next chapter, was fully played out.

FROM TRICKSTER TO BADMAN TO BLUESMAN

In African-American folk-heroic literature, such personages as the trickster, the conjurer, and the badman were partial answers to the "problem of evil." Having long helped African Americans of the old South to adapt to the recurring evil of racial oppression, these heroes were fashioned and refashioned out of conscious and unconscious needs that resulted from the oppressive conditions.[16] From the perspective of the dominant Adamic myth of the Afro-Christian old South, these figures were essentially tragic heroes.

One of the characters of African-American life and lore that stood outside this tragic hero tradition, and therefore helped define what the black community perceived to be the boundaries of heroism, was the "bad nigger." The "bad nigger" was the kind of person or pariah bluesman Will Shade was probably singing about in "I Packed My Suitcase, Started to the Train." Shade sang, "Hey black folks [that] is evil do anything that you want to do." During slavery and afterwards, the "bad nigger" did anything he wanted to do; he defied everyone—oppressor and oppressed alike—in order to improve his personal lot in life.[17] While some folklorists have argued that the "bad nigger" is the prototype of the heroic "badman,"[18] African-American folklorist John Roberts, in his book *Trickster to Badman*, has argued that blacks did not perceive the "bad nigger" to be a hero because his behavior threatened the solidarity that was their community's only defense against the destructive ways of white dominance.[19]

The black blues singer was traditionally viewed by the constituency of the "overculture" (the culture of white dominance) as a "bad nigger." The coverage *Life* magazine gave the two gubernatorial pardons of bluesman Leadbelly for murders committed in Texas and Louisiana is perhaps an adequate metaphor for the point. The caption to the article of 1937, no doubt representing the view most whites had of blues singers, read, "Bad Nigger Makes Good Minstrel."[20] From within the "underculture," however, blues singers (Leadbelly included) characteristically were not perceived as "bad niggers." The good minstrels were "badmen" whose personalities were rooted in the traditions of the African trickster and conjurer.

The "badman" was the heroic figure that especially captured the folk imagination of African Americans during the 1890s, because of his uncanny ability to trick the sheriff and the judge through acts of defiance.[21] This ability to defy "the law" resulted from the badman character evolving as a synthesis of traits from the trickster and conjurer traditions, which were African religious retentions among the enslaved communities.[22] For instance, the Mexican boll weevil, which ravaged the South's cotton crop during the decades leading to the great migration, was often lyricized by the freedmen and descendants of the enslaved communities as an animal trickster, a carry-over from Yoruban trickster lore; but as depicted by Ma Rainey in her "Bo-Weavil Blues," the notorious worm was somewhat of a conjurer. "That bug is so evil," the blues mother sang, "I'm afraid it might poison me."

Antebellum and postbellum African Americans saw in the tradition of this figure of wit and guile, capable of manipulatively procuring sustenance in the face of abject oppression, an emulative model of behavior that they transmitted in their trickster tales.[23] When African-American singers and storytellers merged the traits of the trickster with those of the conjurer—a hero with supernatural powers believed to be purchased from the devil—the resulting "badman" character was, in effect, a "supernatural trickster."[24] The tradition of the black conjurer, particularly the notion that his power was derived from the devil, played a principal part in the development of the badman character as having gleaned his powers from the devil or the devil's evil influence in the world.[25] Stackolee, probably the most notorious of the black badmen (because of his womanizing, gambling, and homicide), was said to have been born with supernatural powers that were enhanced when he later sold his soul.[26] Because of the badman's relationship to evil and his worldly behavior, his natural habitat, according to African-American depictions, was the secular world of jukes, barrelhouses, and nightclubs, a characterization that had much to do with his portrayal as "bad."[27] According to the doctrinal teachings of the black church, as articulated in its ongoing attack against the morality of "blues people," the badman was basically a sinner who either paid for his sins in hell or atoned for them through conversion.[28]

On occasion, badman heroes appeared as protagonists in the lyrics of country and city blues. However, even when they were lyricized, it was generally the blues singer himself or herself who was portrayed as the "baddest." In an article on boasting in the blues, Mimi Melnick said the blues singer, in no uncertain terms, established himself as a hero.[29] She went on to say that, "A particular status is gained from dealings in sin and from defiance of law and order. Complete indifference to the consequences of liquor, reefers, drugs, gambling, women and assorted crimes lends the badman boaster a kind of wildman glamour as well as a high position in his competitive society."[30]

For example, one badman character frequently sung about in ballads and occasionally in the blues was Railroad Bill. Will Bennett, in his blues titled "Railroad Bill," said Bill ought to be killed for seducing his wife. But Bennett did not stop at pursuing the badman with a forty-one derringer; he also decided he was going to kill everyone that ever betrayed him. Lonnie Johnson, in "Sam, You're Just a Rat," similarly proved himself to be the "baddest" of men by confronting a badman named Sam, telling him that if he wanted a woman he had better get his own and leave his wife alone. He sang, "because if I ever catch you with my wife, you hell bound sure as I'm born." Melnick is correct: When the blues singer thematized the heroic badman, it was the singer himself, as the protagonist of his own songs, who triumphed as hero. Blues scholar William Barlow seemed to sense this point in his suggestion that blues singers, who saw in the badman a model of heroic action worth emulating, created a pantheon of tragic heroes. "Blues personas achieved mythical stature in the black community," said Barlow, "constituting a black pantheon separate from—and in many ways antithetical to—the white heroes and heroines of middle-class America."[31]

The foregoing portrayal of the badman, whose personality served as a model of heroic action for oppressed African Americans, strikingly resembles biographical and autobiographical profiles of country and city blues singers. In terms of what is meant by "the mythologies of the blues," the mythology (in this case) was not necessarily reflected in the blues *text*, as was the Adamic myth; this aspect of the mythologies of the blues was reflected in the persona of the blues singer, a persona that was a product of the traditional black southern cosmological *context*. The blues lyrics of Peetie Wheatstraw were hardly replete with the religious folklorisms, African retentions (voodoo-hoodoo), and European superstitions characteristic of the blues of Victoria Spivey and others; but Wheatstraw's life itself embodied the mythology of the badman. This was first signaled by his transmutation from William Bunch of Ripley, Tennessee, into the infamous Peetie Wheatstraw of East St. Louis, known among his fans and friends as "the Devil's Son-in-Law." That the character of Wheatstraw in turn became a paradigm for subsequent badman characterizations was evidenced by Wheatstraw's numerous imitators. Floyd "Dipper Boy" Council recorded at least one blues on which he was identified as "the Devil's Daddy-in-Law"; Harmon Ray was referred to as "Peetie Wheatstraw's Buddy" on Bluebird labels and as Herman "Peetie Wheatstraw" Ray on Decca; Jimmie Gordon was designated "Peetie Wheatstraw's Brother" on a Decca label; and Robert Lee McCoy on Decca as "Peetie's Boy."[32] To illustrate how this paradigm of personality was picked up and perpetuated in African-American literature, Ralph Ellison included a character in his classic "blues" novel, *Invisible Man,* who identified himself as "Peetie Wheatstraw . . . the Devil's son-in-law . . . a piano player and a rounder, a whiskey drinker and a pavement pounder."[33]

Robert Johnson has been especially remembered in blues lore as a badman with notoriety somewhat akin to that of the legendary Stackolee of badman balladry. Johnson was believed by some to have made a pact with the devil that enabled him to play the guitar incredibly well. His alleged payoff—death—was, according to true believers and blues enthusiasts, foreshadowed by his "Hell Hound on My Trail." In a kind of protracted moan, Johnson sang that he had to keep on moving amid the blues "falling down like hail" since there was a hellhound on his trail. His

"Me and the Devil Blues" also seemed to suggest to true believers (within the culture) and blues enthusiasts (without it) that Johnson was in fact possessed by the devil. In this blues, Satan knocked at Johnson's door and together they walked "side by side" to the home of his woman so he could beat her until he was "satisfied." His woman's response to his behavior was that the way he dogged her around was "evil" and must have been the work of that "old evil spirit so deep down in the ground"; to which Johnson replied that when he died she should bury him down by the "highway side" so his "old evil spirit" could catch a Greyhound bus and "ride."

What led to the initial suspicion regarding Johnson's possible supernatural connections was neither his "evil" behavior toward his woman nor his suggestive lyrics, but both of these in connection with his rapid acquisition of musical skill and his mysterious death at the young age of thirty-six. In the old South, it was generally believed among African Americans that any sudden acquisition of luck or talent was the consequence of conjuration and that sudden death, particularly when preceded by delirium, was the work of witchcraft.[34] Evidently poisoned by a jealous husband or girlfriend, Johnson, in the hours leading up to his expiration, was said to have deliriously crawled on all fours and barked (maybe "barfed") like a dog. Similarly, native South Carolinian Blind Gary Davis had such a notorious reputation as a gifted bluesman around the "Bull City" (Durham, North Carolina) that many of the local folks told stories about his having sold his soul to the devil and about his guitar having been buried beside him because the evil one possessed it.[35]

The foregoing characterizations of Johnson, Wheatstraw, and Davis seem to suggest that, of the two character elements said to comprise the persona of the badman, it was the conjurer rather than the trickster trait that was dominant. However, it was the trickster element that seemed to be prototypal of a paradigm of personality in the African-American community and archetypal of what the blues was when personified. This means of understanding an aspect of African-American cultural personality can bring a corrective to David Evans's claim that the personified representation of the blues was a malevolent being or trickster whose character was similar to the devil's.[36] This was a stereotype similar to that in the Paramount Records advertisement of Ma Rainey's "Slave to the Blues," which peculiarly pictured a fair-skinned woman about to be clutched by the pointy fingers of a dark evil figure identified as "Blues."[37]

As I will explain even more as we proceed, the character that personified the blues hardly resembled Paramount's demonic figure or the devil as portrayed in European lore. Rather, he resembled, to emphasize the point, Peetie Wheatstraw, Robert Johnson, and Lemon Jefferson. He was not an appearance, per se; he was a personality principally. Personified blues was the personality of the African trickster-god and his African-American derivatives, which functioned as models of heroic action for those who fought for sustenance at the underside of history. Of all the African trickster-gods, it is Legba, of the Dahomean Fon, who probably best personified the blues. After all, the Yoruba and the Fon provided a considerable portion of the "slave market" in the Americas, so that their traditions were particularly prominent in African-American religious traditions. Thus, it was specifically the personality of Legba, an emulative model of heroic action, that the blues person embodied, the trickster's character that the "tragic hero" dramatized. Legba, whom the Fon never depicted as an animal in their myths and icons, is a being of synchronous duplicity, a duplicity like that in the blues. He is both malevolent and benevolent, disruptive and reconciliatory, profane and sacred, and yet the predominant attitude toward him is affection rather than fear.[38]

This synchronous duplicity in the blues and in the blues personified was illustrated in Son House's explanation of how he came to title his famous blues "Preachin' the Blues" at a time in his life he was both preaching and playing the blues. "I'm preaching on this side and the blues is on that side," he said. "I says, well, I'll just put them together and name it 'Preachin' the Blues?'"[39] In Columbia Records's attempt to understand the blues in order to better market and profit on their line of race recordings, they unknowingly stumbled onto this aspect of the blues when they advertised Bessie Smith as both "lowdown" *and* "sweet." The advertisement read, "Bessie is Sweet and Low Down in the Mouth."[40]

"Thus a 'mythology' of human life is not only possible but necessary in order to express the human situation according to the truth of our being."[41] That was trickster scholar Robert Pelton's conclusion in his interpretation of the trickster persona as a universal or cosmocultural (transcultural) personality that *is* the human being as most honestly and ontologically realized. The cosmocultural aside, it is the people of African origin who have consistently illustrated monoculturally Pelton's contention that the trickster reveals the human being to be a symbol.[42] Thus, the trickster's mythological importance is that he/she, as the revealer of the human situation through her/his behavior, symbolizes the reality of what it means to be people of African cosmology. Given this, what Pelton further stated about the character of the trickster perfectly explains how blues singers revealed the sacred element of secular life, thereby sanctioning the ordinary in all its contradiction and anomaly. Read "blues singer" in lieu of "trickster" and the elusive sacred element of the blues's secular ethos is partly disclosed: "The trickster's doubleness becomes both the source of his transforming power and the reason for his banishment from the community; as profaner of the sacred he becomes a sacred being, yet remains an outsider, the victim of his own violations. Radically impure by reason of his unbounded sexuality, gluttony, and mendacity, the trickster nonetheless helps to give the individual access to the sacred power by which his society is built."[43]

This characterization of the trickster (and the blues singer) helps explain the parallel between early white missionaries in Dahomey identifying Legba as Satan and scholars of European orientation perpetuating the notion that blues, when personified, is the devil. Legba's and the blues singer's "badman" qualities—trickiness, capriciousness, lawlessness, and rampant sexuality—have been, from the Victorian or Eurocentric perspective, interpreted as demonic rather than as holistic. These qualities have been perceived as causing anarchy rather than as functioning to open up social and psychological boundaries, to enlarge the scope of the human, and to turn repressive dead-ends into liberative crossroads.

More important than gleaning some comprehension of white attitudes toward the black blues is that we have discovered a valuable paradigm of personality by which to understand certain character traits that arise in African-American cultural reality. We can understand bluesman Sam Collins's statement in "Devil in the Lion's Den"—that he has "ways like the devil"—as a recognition of that suppressed side of the human personality that is part of "the truth of our being." The same thing can be said of Sylvester Weaver's insatiable sexual appetite sung about in his "Can't Be Trusted Blues." Weaver warned everyone to pull down their windows and lock their doors because he had "ways like the devil" and was sneaking around "on all fours." The trickster paradigm of personality also helps us contextualize and comprehend Peetie Wheatstraw's phallic boasting in "Peetie Wheatstraw Stomp," in which he vaunted that throughout "this land" people were raving about his talent and how he had women "going from hand to hand." He identified himself as "Peetie Wheatstraw the high sheriff from hell" and swaggered about the way he could strut his "stuff."

Both Weaver's cautioning that he could be neither trusted around any woman nor sexually satisfied and Wheatstraw's warning that his sexual prowess not be broadcast lest all the women become inflamed with curiosity, were not unbounded, inexplicable evil. That interpretation has resulted from a Victorian model of morality being projected upon another culture, a culture that Pelton, like Jung, would agree is more in tune with "the truth of our being." To those of African origin who saw in the trickster persona a model of emulative behavior, Wheatstraw, Weaver, and Collins were "bad" individuals who came to understand a truthful aspect of "our being."

It is the capricious element of the trickster's synchronous duplicity—an element that the Dahomean Fon were quite willing to accept in Legba—that was decontextualized and emphasized by those scholars and blues enthusiasts who have reduced the broad mythologies of the blues to mere mythic fiction, namely the fictitious belief that the blues personified is the devil or that the blues is "devil's music." To restate this with reference to the Paramount advertisement of Bessie Smith, it was the "lowdown" element that has been decontextualized and emphasized in the scholarship of those who are not natives of the culture that produced the blues. Because the misinterpreters of the mythologies of the blues have failed to grasp the synchronous duplicity of the blues and of black "blues people," they have also failed to comprehend the doubleness of African-American ontology and the elasticity of black reality, which together account for the depth and strength of black spirituality found in the blues.

THE CONFLATION OF MYTHOLOGIES IN THE BLUES

As I will explain in chapter 2, blues singers were prodigal sons and daughters whose belief system took them to the periphery of the strict doctrinal enclave of Protestant Christianity—a location of human openness and mythological potentiality. At this periphery, as the foregoing pages have begun to show, there existed a conflation of mythologies that, along with the Adamic myth, comprised the mythologies of the blues. This conflation of mythologies was a mixture of Christian (the Adamic and its recessive tragic) mythology and African (the trickster and subsequent badman) mythology, plus a plethora of European belief and superstition. As one Mississippi ex-slave admitted, folks back then were religious and superstitious; they believed in divinities and ghosts as well as in signs and hoodooing. "Our religion and superstition was all mixed up," he said.[44]

This "mixing" was such that being a conjure-doctor or herbalist often did not preclude individual claims to Christian faith, some conjurers (like some blues singers) also being preachers.[45]

The African retentions in America that derived from the voodoo-hoodoo religion of Africa were less repressed among the free-thinkers who sang the blues at the open spaces of "the periphery" than among the church faithful, who tended to lean toward Euro-American puritanism in pursuit of social respectability. No doubt, Afro-Christians would frequently (but unadmittedly) lay aside that repressive and unnatural puritanism to attain ends by means of traditional Africanisms, but this was even more true of the "blues people" who, either by force or by choice, kept some distance from the church. For "blues people" at the periphery of Afro-Christianity, this religion given them by their European captors was only an outer form in which they could encase their African religious worldview while paying only lip service to orthodox Christianity. Thus, at that peripheral location of radical openness and mythological potentiality, the blues made visible the invisible—the often unarticulated religious retentions of the native homeland, Africa.

The occasional laying aside of Protestant puritanism to embrace certain Africanisms that were suppressed in the church led to the practice of "tipping out." Folks who were regular or fairly regular churchgoers occasionally "tipped out" to the juke joints or clubs to receive the kind of therapy-of-remembering that only the blues singer could offer. This practice was akin to that of Afro-Catholics in Haiti or New Orleans "tipping out" to the voodoo rituals for the kind of therapy-of-remembering that only the voodoo priest could offer. From the perspective of the Christian "center" (in the strict doctrinal sense), such persons were religionists of the Christian periphery, at which location of human openness and mythological potentiality traditional Africanisms (voodoo-hoodooisms) were remembered and embraced. From the broader cosmological perspective, the most significant of these Africanisms was the blues singer's holistic worldview—an African-centered synchronous duplicity that is the "truth of our being," as opposed to the dichotomous ethics and ontology of European religion and reality.

The most significant Africanism to blemish the periphery of the doctrinal Christianity that blacks received at the hands of their captors was voodoo-hoodoo. As in Haiti, African-American voodoo, which was able to survive in New Orleans, embraced divination, manipulation, and herbalism.

The threatening, manipulatory aspect of the religion was hoodoo, which deemphasized the voodoo ritual—the dances and the worship of the African deities. Hoodoo practices, such as the placing and removing of curses, the giving of luck and sexual powers, and the causing of death by means of the ominous "death dance,"[46] were among the hoodooisms that found their way into the lyrics of country and city blues. As one Mississippi ex-slave said around the late thirties, "There is folks today what thinks everytime they gets sick that some one has put the jinks upon them, and when a woman's husband leaves her she thinks another woman has conjured him into leaving."[47] The manipulatory character of hoodoo is probably the reason blues scholar Jeff Titon said blues lyrics tease the boundary between religion and magic.[48] (In voodoo-hoodoo, of course, there is no boundary; religion and magic are one and the same.) Eventually, voodoo-hoodoo, along with the blues, was carried to the northern cities by southern black emigrants, especially during the great migration that commenced during the second decade of the twentieth century. Just as the services of hoodooists were made available in the northern cities, so did hoodoo belief find its way into the lyrics of city blues. In fact, some of the advertisements of hoodoo in black-owned newspapers of the urban North could have been words right out of an Ida Cox classic blues of the twenties or thirties. One early thirties advertisement promoting New Orleans Luck Powder began, "Why be blue and low?" and proceeded to assure potential customers that thousands of people believed in the New Orleans powder to bring luck, love, success, and happiness, just as well as other known powders, like the Adam and Eve root.[49]

The blues repertoire, up through at least the early forties, was replete with references to hoodoo, as evidenced in such popular songs as Muddy Waters's "Louisiana Blues" and John Lee Williamson's "Hoodoo, Hoodoo." Both of these bluesmen spoke of their need to sojourn to Louisiana—particularly New Orleans, the voodoo capital of North America—to procure a "mojo hand" from a hoodoo practitioner for the purpose of conjuration. Hoodoo practitioners (known as "hoodoo doctors," "medicine men," "root doctors," and "conjurers") were generally men paid by clients such as Waters and Williamson to "hoodoo" someone. Their victims were persons who were made to act against their will, generally by means of having drunk or eaten a potion or having worn a charm. According to "Louisiana Blues," Waters wanted to get the good-looking women of Chicago to treat him "good." Williamson, in "Hoodoo,

Hoodoo," wanted to get his woman to stop loving another man.

One of the popular hoodooisms Waters and Williamson could have used to bring about their desired ends was Good Luck Dust. It was probably this dust, rather than Goofer Dust, that Ida Cox and Little Willie Littlefield sang about in their respective songs, "New Orleans Goofer Dust Blues" and "Goofey Dust Blues." The dust Ida Cox sang about was for the purpose of attaining romantic security. The "goofy, loofy, groovy" stuff Littlefield sang about in his recording of 1953 was a "dust" he was eager to spread on himself as he moved to the city to learn its "crazy ways." Goofer Dust, on the other hand, was dirt, taken about arm-length deep from a cemetery grave, that was used to harm or destroy an enemy.[50] It was the dust Charlie Spand sang about in his "Big Fat Mama Blues," when he warned his "good lookin' mama" that he was going to spread some around her head (on her pillow) so that she would one morning wake up and find herself dead.

While the tenets of Christianity (especially as interpreted by the white church) led the masses of black Christians to believe that voodoo-hoodoo was mere "black magic," blues singers, at the periphery of Christianity's doctrinal enclave, were open to embrace the retentions of African religion that their historical memory and cultural intuition affirmed. Black blues scholar Julio Finn clarified this point as regards such "hoodoo bluesmen" as Robert Johnson and Muddy Waters: "Churchless, he praised God in his songs, and his listeners were reminded of the powers of the *loas*, of the forces the enemy could not understand, of their past glory and the history of their native land. These powers were their birthright; they symbolized and brought into focus those half-felt thoughts, those forms which unexpectedly dropped in during the night." [51] As Zora Neale Hurston stated the same point, voodoo kept the powers of Africa alive.[52]

Not only were the forces of the *loas* (spirits) incomprehensible to the enemy, but blues singers who embraced this belief system might have thought of these spiritual forces as ultimately unconquerable by the enemy. Certainly they sensed and could partly articulate the disruptive effect of the Christian church in their lives and their traditional cosmology. Like voodooists in Haiti during the era of slavery, they might have believed that the *loas* were certain to triumph over the oppressive Christianity they referred to as the "magic of the whites."[53] As Finn alluded above, voodoo was a collective memorization of African religious traditions, a language expressing African resistance to oppression, and a testimony of the will of the oppressed to maintain African values in the face of forced Christianization to the deity of white magic.[54] Zora Neale Hurston made this same point about the "signifying" of early African-American storytellers, for whom "the devil" (in name) was but Legba, the powerful god of voodoo who competed successfully with what Haitians called the deity of white magic. Hurston strongly suspected that the devil was an extension of the storytellers, and that God, an extension of the white master, was, in spite of his seeming omnipotence, nevertheless defeated by the blacks.[55]

Despite the general Africanizing of Christianity by black spirituality, there was, in "blues belief," an underlying tension between Christianity and the African traditional religious cosmology. Additionally, within the Adamic-tragic/trickster-badman mythological rubric, which also involved some tensions, was a mixture of other folkloric beliefs and superstitions. There was, for instance, a prevailing belief in myriad kinds of spirits. At one extreme were the malevolent (but harmless) "haunts" that were detectable by sight and sound; at the other, the murderous witches whose master was the devil.[56] Also reflected in an occasional blues lyric was the fear of the falling star. This occurrence meant that someone residing in the direction of the star's descent would soon die, possibly, if one accidentally pointed to the star, a relative or friend.[57] A shooting star also meant bad luck—that there would be a death in three days (possibly of a family member) or that another soul had passed into heaven or was about to be bought by the devil.[58] This was the reason "classic" blues singer Lizzie Miles, according to her "Shootin' Star Blues," engaged in several countermeasures when she spotted a shooting star. She sang in her blues that she was not superstitious, as evidenced by the fact that she would allow a black cat to cross her trail or would walk through a funeral line. She probably would not have paid any attention to the "superstition" that if you drop a comb you will sing the hard-time blues.[59] However, when the stars started shooting, Miles was certain that it was a sign of bad luck and had nothing to do with superstition. Because "a shooting star means evil," she sang, and she had never seen that sign to fail, she turned to hoodoo—she boiled a black cat bone, tied it in a sack, and walked off talking to herself.

Also thematized in the blues, as in Victoria Spivey's "Red Lantern Blues," was the frightful apparition of European lore known as the "Jack-o-lantern" or "Jack-o-my-lantern." This flickering light from a lantern being carried by a ghostly goblin "hot from hell" or a restless spirit of a deceased person was utterly bewitching. If precautions were not taken—

shutting the eyes, plugging the ears, holding the breath, throwing oneself to the ground, or simply turning and running—the seduced person would be led into quicksand in a swamp or thickets in the woods never again to be seen alive.[60] All of these beliefs—the superstitions and voodooisms— merged with the Adamic-tragic and trickster-badman myths to constitute the mythologies of the blues. A principal player in these mythologies was the character commonly referred to as the devil.

THE DEVIL IN THE BLUES MYTHOLOGIES

Joe Evans, in his blues, "New Huntsville Jail," was "almost dead" as a result of his imprisonment that had something to do with his woman. He sang, "Ashes to ashes and dust to dust . . . , if God don't have me you know the devil must." Joe McCoy, in "Someday I'll Be in the Clay," also said to his woman that when he died, "if I ain't gone to heaven, you know I gone to hell." Bill Wilber, boasting of his love for his woman in "My Babe My Babe"—how she "tore up" his troubles and "broke up" his misery—said, "fare you well" and "if I don't meet you in heaven you know I'll meet you in hell." The devil and his place of residency, hell, were principal parts of the mythologies of the blues.

Mississippi blues singer James Son Thomas, upon recounting the mythology of how the devil came to inhabit hell, said the evil one was once in heaven and the saints were feeling the threat of imminent danger. "The devil took his tail and drug down three thirds of heaven while he was up there," said Thomas. "That's why the Lord put him in a sealed-up place where he can't get out."[61] Skip James told a similar story. According to what he had heard, the onetime angel got so unruly and desirous of power that God evicted him from heaven. But before he actually departed, God allowed the devil to take along some angels, thus bringing sin to earth. After residing on earth for a while at God's granting, the devil and his rebel angels settled in hell, from which locale they continued to persuade people to do evil.[62] Perhaps this is the mythology Joe Williams was curious about in "Mr. Devil Blues," when he said he was going to write a letter and "mail it in the air" in order to ask "Dr. Jesus" if the devil had ever been there.

This devil-lore began to be dismissed as southern superstition by blacks who, starting around the time of the great migration, moved to the northern cities and got caught up in the thrust toward cultural assimilation and middle-class status. I will explain the reasons this occurred in my conclusion; but for the purpose of our understanding the mythologies of the blues, this lore should not be taken lightly as mere tale-telling. At the folk level, it was easier for people to talk in terms of evil divinities than to theologize formally about evil.[63]

What we can gather from stories such as the foregoing is that evil, according to the old-South African-American cosmology, was perceived to be a material entity that was morally and physically threatening, the kind of threat Son Thomas said made the hosts of heaven feel they were in danger. In other words, the evil of which bluesmen Thomas and James were speaking was not merely of the descriptive sort, simply a synonym for the criminal, sinful, bad, worthless, ugly, or sad. "Evil" or "the devil," in the descriptive or "weak sense" of the word, was implied in such common blues phrases as "I'm gonna give you the devil," "raising hell" and "devilment." It is in this sense that we are to take Peetie Wheatstraw's statement in "Sweet Home Blues," that an unhappy home "will be the devil." Similarly, Blind Percy sang in "Coal River Blues," "Woman's so doggone evil wants every woman's man." Bluesmen customarily referred to their women as "evil" in the descriptive sense when they felt they were being mistreated, as illustrated in Leroy Carr's "Evil-Hearted Woman" or James Wiggins's "Evil Woman Blues." Women were also called "evil" if they broke up other women's homes, as Six Cylinder Smith said women customarily do in "Pennsylvania Woman Blues." It is in this descriptive sense, not the "strong sense," that Lonnie Johnson equated blues and evil in "Devil's Got the Blues." Johnson said the blues was "like" the devil because it would leave a heart full of "trouble" and a mind full of "hell."

As the foregoing accounts of Son Thomas and Skip James suggest, evil in the "strong sense" was personified as that rogue angel known as the devil and as his compatriot evil spirits and demonic apparitions, all of which were thought to be mortally harmful. Based on all that has been said thus far, it should not be surprising that this depiction of evil was the same as that portrayed by the church, for both James and Thomas (like most blues singers) were brought up in the church and indoctrinated with its mythologies. For instance, the religious conversion narratives of ex-slaves, documented around the early 1920s, confirm that the devil and his submerged domain were viewed as a moral and mortal menace. Hell was portrayed in these narratives as a dark, deep chasm beneath the earth's crust, a roaring pit fraught with blue and green flames, ravenous beasts that grotesquely protruded their tongues, and hellhounds that violently growled and barked, within which "jaws of hell" were "weeping and gnashing of teeth" among the damned souls spinning around on hell's "big wheel."[64] Summarily put by a former slave and preacher, under whose teaching a few future blues singers were probably raised: "There is a real heaven and hell. The hell is the devil and his angels. They are evil spirits and are ever present with us to tempt and try us. They are at war with the heavenly host and seek to dissuade those who would serve God."[65]

Because the likes of Son Thomas and Skip James were raised under this sort of preaching, the blues was replete with the foregoing kinds of beliefs regarding the nature and depiction of the "strong sense" of evil. Bessie Smith's "Blue Spirit Blues," to emphasize the point, was mythologically indistinct from the "fire and brimstone" gospel song she recorded in 1930, "Moan, Mourners." In her gospel song, akin to other gospels of that day, Smith warned sinners that "down below" there was burning "hot brimstone" and that Satan was laying in wait for anyone who neglected to fall down on bended knees and send up to the Lord repentant pleas. That "Blue Spirit Blues" came from the same mythological cosmology as "Moan, Mourners" was probably evident to her record-buying audience, despite the vaudeville-like sound of the accompaniment. In "Blue Spirit Blues" Smith recounted a dream in which she was dead and led down to that "red-hot land" by the devil. Not unlike depictions of hell given in Afro-Christian conversion narratives, she saw all sorts of frightful creatures—fairies and dragons that spit blue flames and demons whose eyelids "dripped blood" as they dragged sinners to their "brimstone flood." The printed advertisement of this blues was also a bit vaudeville-like, with its illustration of a horned, tailed, hoof-footed, pitchfork-carrying, dark man leaping into hell's fires, pulling behind him a fair-skinned woman.[66] Despite the minstrel mood of the piece, that fair-skinned woman could have been Smith herself, for according to a traditional folk belief, dreams were real experiences in which the "dream soul" visited another world.[67] Smith's black audiences thus might have interpreted "Blue Spirit Blues" as her making light of a somewhat frightening dream experience.

Newbell Niles Puckett's assessment of this devil-lore was that southern blacks gave more attention to the devil than their white counterparts did,[68] a point he made in *Folk Beliefs of the Southern Negro* (1926). Despite the cultural biases that permeate Puckett's work, anthropologist Melville Herskovits later agreed with his assessment in *The Myth of the Negro Past* (1941), the first seminal anthropological work on African

Americans by an American anthropologist.[69] During the late nineteenth and early twentieth centuries, Puckett's and Herskovits's claims might have been accurate, but the opposite was probably true from the time the British colonized North America up to about the late nineteenth century. John Ashton said in his book of 1896, *The Devil in Britain and America,* that "North America had been colonized by the British long enough to have enjoyed visitations from the devil. And the present Americans, judging by the amount of literature written thereon, seem rather proud of his having dwelt among them; it gives an air of antiquity, and an old-world tone, to the favoured States, which is sadly lacking, and not otherwise procurable, in those unvisited by his Satanic Majesty."[70] There is little question that the devil was a principal player in African-American religious belief and lore and therefore in the mythologies of the blues, and it is most probable that the emphasis on devil-lore among southern blacks was an early modern Europeanism dating back to the thirteenth century. Paul Carus, the turn-of-century German philosopher of religion and science, said the devil reached his acme of influence at this time: "With the belief in witchcraft a new period begins in the evolution of mankind. The Devil becomes greater and more respected than ever; indeed, this is the classical period of his history and the prime of his life. Contracts were made with the Devil in which men surrendered their souls for all kinds of services on his part."[71] This European demonology was brought to bear on American Protestantism by its Calvinistic adherents who, out of a deep fear of the horrible death of sinners, excessively sensationalized scriptural teachings.[72]

Other early modern Europeanisms absorbed into African-American lore were the depictions of the devil as a blackfaced, clubfooted man with cloven feet, claw-like hands, and fiery red eyes, who had a ball and chain attached to his leg and a pronged fork in his hand. These depictions were first witnessed in the testimonies of witches in Europe as far back as the sixteenth century.[73] It was not unusual for the devil to appear to the early British as a bear, lion, rat, toad, hare, white dove, or yellow cat,[74] but when in human form, the devil almost always appeared as a "big" or "great" "black man,"[75] a description also found throughout African-American lore. For enslaved blacks to have alone conceived of depicting the evil god as black is as unlikely as the ancient Egyptians, had they really been a Europoid race, always painting and depicting their gods Isis and Osiris as (as they in fact always appeared) black.

Clearly, the depiction of the devil as a "black man" when he assumed human form was an early Europeanism. In an essay written in England in 1600, "A True Narration of the Strange and Grevious Vexation by the Devil of 7 Persons in Lancashire," the author, Rev. John Darrell, documented testimonies of the possession and later "dispossession" of the female victims. One of the women said that the devil, in attempting to repossess her, "came to her like an ugly black man with shoulders higher than his head."[76] Another testified, "It went out like a great breath, ugly like a toad, round like a ball, and within an hour after, it returned like a foul big black man"; but she resisted and it departed.[77] In another case, documented in 1664, a woman testified that the devil appeared as a "black man" with cloven feet riding upon a black horse.[78]

Even when described as "a man in black" or "a man in black clothes,"[79] the implication among the early modern British was that this "gentleman"[80] was a "black man," a view obviously passed along to the enslaved Africans in America who perpetuated it in their lore. For instance, the claim by a British informant, around 1591, that the devil was a "black" preacher who, from his pulpit, forced his servants to testify as to the evil they had committed in his behalf,[81] was strikingly similar to some of the southern lore surrounding even the era of city blues. In an advertisement of a recorded sermon by the well-known African-American evangelist Rev. A. W. Nix, titled "The Prayer Meeting in Hell," a dark devil was pictured preaching from a lectern to a miserable congregation of the damned.[82] The notion that the devil was "black" thus evolved from the same religious symbology and ideology that taught blues singers such as Lil' Son Jackson to sing, as he did in his "Evil Blues," "I'm black, I swear I'm evil," and Alice Moore, as she did in "Black and Evil Blues," "I'm evil, need watching 'cause I might make a midnight creep."

The idea of making a "midnight creep" was also connected with the symbolism of blackness in early modern British belief. One of Britain's leading authorities on the devil's manifestation in witchcraft and sorcery during the sixteenth century argued that the devil was a spirit which, when appearing in bodily form, was but an apparition, unless an actual body had been lent him to wear.[83] Puckett also claimed that the devil of early African-American lore customarily borrowed human skin in order to masquerade as a person while he or she was sleeping.[84] Given the foregoing examples of early modern British belief and the similarities found among the former slaves of the British colonizers of North America and their American descendants, the devil seemingly preferred borrowing the body of a "black man." Let us make no mistake, Paul Carus in his book of 1899, *The History of the Devil and the Idea of Evil,* interpreted this "black man" to be a "negro."[85] If this were not the case, then what better explanation would account for the fear and prejudice whites in Britain and America had toward blacks or for their interpretation of the blues as "devil's music?"

Slaveholders steeped in this British devil-lore were evidently responsible for passing it on to their African slaves, a theory folklorist Richard Dorson would have agreed with due to his general belief that African-American folklore, though containing African retentions, was largely a part of the European tradition. Ex-slaves have attested to their Euro-American slaveholders using this devil-lore as a scare tactic intended to frighten them into further submission. One Mississippi ex-slave named Polly Cancer recalled this very thing. "Old Miss didn't teach me to read and write," she said, "but she did do this; she would read the Bible to us to tell us what the old bad man was going to do to us; she would show us the picture of him; he had a pitch fork in his hand and a long forked tail and a club foot and horns on his head; he would be dancing round pinching folks and sticking the pitch fork in them; . . . I sure was scared and I look for him to this day."[86] Because this kind of sensationalizing reached the enslaved through their captors, Polly Cancer, as her words illustrate, maintained a keen mindfulness of the "strong" presence of evil and the threat of hell. This probably meant she was a churchgoer, for where evil is perceived to be an imminent threat, people seek either religious or magical protection from it.

The evangelism of fear that terrified Polly Cancer emerged from the intense moral intimidation or "guiltification" that the clerics of early modern Europe imposed upon their parishioners to reinforce their authority, since the clerics believed that they alone could appropriately deal with the powers and proximity of evil and the dilemmas of death and damnation.[87] While on the one hand whites were gleaning this "guiltification" from their clerics and the preachers of the eighteenth-century Great Awakening,[88] they were, on the other hand, giving slaves like Polly Cancer the negative two-thirds of this "mortification"—the threats and the fears (minus the hopeful expectations). This "mortification" that intimidated, alienated, terrorized, and paralyzed the captives, further enslaved them in that having to think constantly about evil was spiritually and psychologically debilitating. These threats and fears were passed along to the descendants of the enslaved in the form of "devil tales," ballads, and blues lyrics. This is the reason black Chicagoan Charles Browning, in a feature article written for *The Chicago Defender* in 1934, would only qualify the problem of superstition in the black community with the complaint that this "supernatural dogmatism" was forced upon the enslaved by their white captors to keep them contented in their bondage.[89]

As a result of this "supernatural dogmatism" being forced upon enslaved Africans, the devil of early African-American depictions, reflecting the devil of early modern European lore and religious belief, often appeared as a "big black man" or a black "gentleman." Traditional black lore held that this gentleman, when moving about the earth sabotaging the good morals of the people, wore a frock coat and a high silk hat, beneath which laid an "ambrosial curl" that hid the single horn on his forehead.[90] His forked tail was hidden in his pants;[91] that is, if he had a tail, for other stories claimed he eventually lost his tail.[92] As one Alabama preacher explained to his congregation, the devil preferred the appearance of an average person, especially a churchgoer,[93] for if he looked like himself he could not easily do his evil. In fact, the devil was thought to be such a common-looking churchgoing "gentleman" that he was sometimes discernible only by his "evil eye," that cross-eyed stare or glance thought to cause harm if precautions were not taken.[94] The "evil eye" was what helped bluesman Freddie Spruell, as he told it in his "Low-Down Mississippi Bottom Man," identify a devilish, "sneaking and mistreating" "tomcat man" trying to seduce his wife and break up his marriage. He sang, "I don't trust that tomcat, he's got such an evil eye."

Taking on the appearance of a gentleman allowed the devil to function best as a "prowling man," who Skip James said never slept,[95] possibly, as one southern-born woman explained, because he was always trying to compete with (indeed beat) Jesus.[96] But the devil, according to black lore, was also believed to have prowled the earth as a rabbit, terrapin, serpent, bat, toad, grasshopper, housefly, blue jay, yellow dog, black billy goat, and especially a black cat.[97] Attiring himself in the skin of a black cat (his preferred animal form) allowed the "evil one" to prowl wherever he pleased and to overhear the secrets people share,[98] presumably secrets he could use to compete with Jesus and lead his victims astray. Even those who claimed not to be superstitious, like Howlin' Wolf, according to his rendition of "I Ain't Superstitious," seemed to convey a certain belief in the evils of the black cat. "Well I ain't superstitious," Howlin' Wolf sang, "[but a] black cat just crossed my trail." According to superstition, the devil, at night, often took the form of an owl because the bird's large eyes gave him good night vision.[99] He was also effective as a fly because he could move about more inconspicuously than as an animal or man and could walk "top side down" on ceilings and overhear information that would facilitate his evil pursuits.[100]

This devil-lore that developed among blacks in the rural South was maintained by those who emigrated first to the southern cities and then to northern cities. Blues singers, as the foregoing pages have begun to show, were among the tradition-bearers. For instance, Charley Patton's claim, in "Devil Sent the Rain," that the good Lord sends the sunshine while the devil sends the rain, was based on the lore that if it rained while the sun was shining then the devil was beating his wife.[101] The devil, of course, was not a monogamist, according to other blues singers. Whether he beat all of his wives, probably no blues singer said. But King Solomon Hill claimed, in "Whoopee Blues," that the devil certainly made "whoopee" with all his evil gals. The devil had ninety thousand women and needed only one more, Hill sang, and if his (Hill's) woman did not cease her infidelity she would be making "whoopee" with the devil in hell.

The bluesman whose woman was unfaithful (like Hill's woman) was usually said to be "no earthly good" and to belong to the devil. Washboard Sam illustrated this in his blues titled just so, "She Belongs to the Devil." Because his woman belonged to the devil, Sam "cried many a day." The woman was so "wicked," sang Sam, that he doubted if anyone could ever "change her ways." Eddie Burns, in his "Bad Woman Blues," similarly complained that his woman, who customarily went nowhere but to church and Sunday school, started "running around." It was nothing but the devil, he sang, that made her change her ways. If the women of Sam and Hill were not cautious, they would, according to the blues mythologies, end up like Papa Charlie Jackson's woman, whom Jackson sang about in his "The Cats Got the Measles." Jackson said he thought he heard a rumbling "deep down in the ground" and speculated that it was probably the devil chaining his "good gal" down. Jackson recorded this in 1925, and in 1938 Sonny Boy Williamson recorded a variation of Jackson's verse in a blues titled "Deep Down in the Ground." "You hear that rumbling deep down in the ground," sang Williamson, "now it must be the devil, you know, turning my womens around."

Lore such as the foregoing reflected and reinforced folk mythologies and had the tendency to cause some borderline believers (even some doubters) to wonder if it might not be true or at least contain elements of truth. After all, devil-stories were but myths in which Christian mythologies were carried to an extreme.[102] As folklorist James Aswell explained in his collection of Tennessee "liar's bench tales" published in 1940, the lore was probably comprised of elaborations on some kernels of belief that were modified as they were passed along in the oral tradition.[103] Aswell said further that liar's bench tales were intended solely to amuse storyteller and listener but that trained analysts could uncover unintended meanings. "Because his words will not be weighed, judged, and held against his morals or character, his stories are most apt to reveal what he really thinks about life and death, religion, and his fellow men than does his public attitude toward these things."[104] Thus, even satirical treatments of evil and the devil—for instance, where an individual outsmarts the devil[105]—could have expressed a "strong" belief in evil. Those who at times made light of the devil with humorous anecdotes really might have been terrified of the threat of evil and might have engaged in fun-making as a means of helping to ward off the terror of "the devil."[106]

Beliefs about evil and lore about the devil persisted in the city milieu and in city blues for about a generation after the great black migration. What an October 1931 advanced-release sheet from the American Record Company said to record dealers about Rev. Jordon Jones's two sermons on Oriole Records—"Black Cat Crossed Your Path" and "Hell and What It Is"—makes the point in a rather telling way: "This record will be bought by white people as well as negroes. The subject is true to negro superstition, they will like it and the white people will buy it for the kick they get out of it."[107] Blacks who were not so superstitious were sometimes described by the more "superstitious" as being "smart" like the whites.[108] After a generation or so, beliefs about evil and lore about the devil—such as the notion that blues singers play the "devil's instrument"—were subjugated into almost complete silence by the emerging middle class, who wanted to be smart like the whites and were trying to move toward social and cultural assimilation with that overculture.

PLAYING THE DEVIL'S INSTRUMENT

In contrast to what upwardly mobile blacks of the new North believed, church folks of the old South believed it was the devil who taught wayward Christians to play the "devil's instruments," instruments the evil one himself was thought to have played. Among early modern Britons, the "devil's instruments" included the flute, pipe, or cittern;[109] among Africans enslaved in America and their descendants, they were the guitar, banjo, and fiddle. Black men or women who played one of the these instruments were thought by some to be in actual communication with the devil and thus to be "devil's preachers." They were believed to have sold their souls to the devil, a notion that, as Paul Carus alluded, was a derivative of early modern British belief. Carus said, "The Devil, fighting with God for the possession of mankind, was supposed to have a special passion for catching souls. Being the prince of the world he could easily grant even the most extravagant wishes, and was sometimes willing to pay a high price when a man promised to be his for time and eternity. Thus originated the idea of making compacts with the Devil; and it is worthy of note that in these compacts the Devil is very careful to establish his title to the soul of man by a faultless legal document."[110] These beliefs explain why the church faithful, particularly of the Sanctified church (Holiness or Pentecostal), shunned the blues singer, as illustrated in an incident captured by the African-American writer Arna Bontemps:

> Just as sure as God had his heaven, the devil had his hell. And the box (guitar), as all the older folk know, has always been a special device of the devil's. I can remember what happened to one of these careless minstrels who made the mistake of wandering onto the church grounds during an intermission between services back in my childhood. The sisters of the church lit into him like a flock of mother hens attacking a garter snake. He protested. He was just fixing to play a couple of hymns, he explained. But this did not save him. He was obliged to leave in a hurry. The deaconesses knew from bitter experience, no doubt, that the church yard was no place for a box. They also knew that the songs with which the guitar was associated were not for the ears of children.[111]

The ambitious, daring, or desperate individual who wanted to learn the so-called "black art" of playing the blues was believed to have gone to the crossroads at midnight where and when he "took up" his instrument from the devil. This belief was a variation of the black lore regarding a person going to the crossroads to meet and talk with the devil for the purpose of attaining good luck throughout life.[112] All that was prerequisite for this trip to the crossroads was a "black cat bone," a special bone of that feared critter generally thought to be a witch, a woman who had sold her soul to the devil.[113] Derived from boiling or frying the flesh off of a black cat, this magical part of the cat anatomy could be identified by tasting all the bones until the bitter one was found.[114] The bone was then placed in a hoodoo sack and carried on one's person to the crossroads where a pact with the devil could then be made.

The belief that the newly adopted "child of the devil" could become invisible at will was possibly derived from early modern British belief that a witch could go anywhere invisibly while her body was at home in bed.[115] But the mythos of the crossroads and of meeting a man of magic there was unquestionably an African religious retention. In voodoo-hoodoo religious belief it was at the crossroads that one could find not the devil but Legba, the most powerful trickster-god of the Dahomean Fon's pantheon of deities. The confusion of these personages is easily explainable. Just as early Christian missionaries to the Fon taught their African converts that Legba was Satan, so did the semi-dualism of Christianity, imposed upon the holistic cosmology of the Africans brought to America as captives, force Legba (in the minds of the enslaved who remembered him) into the satanic role. Thus, in the lore surrounding blues singers learning their musical skills at the crossroads, the supernatural figure who showed up was not actually (or always) the devil; but he was called "the devil" even when his personality was more reminiscent of Legba's. Puckett documented one instance of the ritual selling of the soul as told him by a New Orleans conjurer:

> If you want to make a contact with the devil, first trim your finger nails as close as you possibly can. Take a black cat bone and a guitar and go to a lonely fork in the roads at midnight. Sit down there and play your best piece, thinking of and wishing for the devil all the while. By and by you will hear music, dim at first but growing louder and louder as the musician approaches nearer. Do not look around; just keep on playing your guitar. The unseen musician will finally sit down by you and play in unison with you. After a time you will feel something tugging at your instrument. Do not try to hold it. Let the devil take it and keep thumping along with your fingers as if you still had a guitar in your hands. Then the devil will hand

you his instrument to play and will accompany you on yours. After doing this for a time he will seize your fingers and trim the nails until they bleed, finally taking his guitar back and returning your own. Keep on playing; don't look around. His music will become fainter and fainter as he moves away. When all is quiet you may go home.[116]

The individual thus sold his eternal soul to "the devil," so that during his lifetime he would be able to do anything in the world he wanted, including playing whatever music he desired on the guitar.[117]

There were many similar stories about individuals taking up the fiddle or banjo from "the devil," but another one about the "git-fiddle" (the guitar) was told by former blues singer Rev. LaDell Johnson about his late brother, Mississippi blues singer Tommy Johnson. How could Tommy play anything he wanted, compose blues songs without anyone teaching him? LaDell asked the question rhetorically and answered:

Now if Tom was living, he'd tell you. He said the reason he knowed so much, said he sold hisself to the Devil. I asked him how. He said, "If you want to learn how to play anything you want to play and learn how to make songs yourself, you take your guitar and you go where a road crosses . . . , where a crossroad is. Get there, be sure to get there just a little 'fore twelve o'clock that night so you'll know you'll be there. You have your guitar and be playing a piece sitting there by yourself. You have to go by yourself and be sitting there playing a piece. A big black man will walk up there and take your guitar, and he'll tune it. And then he'll play a piece and hand it back to you.[118]

Not everyone who went to a crossroads felt certain they would actually meet the devil, and not everyone who caught sight of the devil saw Legba. That not all saw Legba might explain why not all who said they saw the devil dared to go through with the ritual selling of the soul. Willie Trice, born in rural North Carolina in the first decade of the new century, evidenced this in a story regarding his paternal uncle, Luther Trice, who probably was born around the later half of the nineteenth century. Trice's Uncle Luther had heard that if he were to go to the crossroads for nine consecutive mornings the devil would teach him to play the blues far better than he already could. In fact, Trice was told he would be able to play absolutely any music he desired. So he figured he would try. But on the Sunday morning Trice actually saw the devil, he by no means saw Legba. It was a beastly figure that had balls of fire coming from his mouth and red-hot eyes. Trice concluded that his uncle never sold his soul to the devil because he ran home as fast as he could.[119] It was this same devil of visible horror that frightened blues singer J. B. Lenoir's father into giving up the blues. When Lenoir asked his father why he stopped playing the blues, he answered: "Well son, I was laying down and that old devil got at me in my sleep—something with a bukka tail and a shape like a bull but he could talk—and when I spied him I started to run. But the devil he said, 'You can run, but you can't hide'; so that's the reason why I stopped playing the blues."[120]

The reaction of Luther Trice to seeing the devil of European depiction—running away "as fast as the devil"—was what most sensible folks expected of one who saw the approach of a vile-looking beast, particularly since this beast was perceived as not simply a moral menace but a mortal threat as well. Thus, if the devil of early African-American belief was always as hot, evil, and frightening as Trice and Lenoir's father portrayed him to be, then what blues singer in his right mind would dare sell his soul to the evil one?

THE DEVIL OF THE BLUES MYTHOS

Several possibilities might explain why some blues singers took the alleged risk of turning to "the devil" for the acquisition of magical powers and musical talent, an examination of which will help complete our composite portrait of the devil in the mythologies of the blues. Let it be said in advance that this composite picture will not only portray a devil that ultimately was weaker than God (semi-dualism), in part due to the implication of the Adamic myth, but a devil who generally was not the terror that he was in early modern European religious belief and lore.

Why did some blues singers take the alleged risk of turning to "the devil" for the acquisition of magical powers and musical talent? Given that blues singers embraced aspects of voodoo-hoodoo, there might have been a belief among some of them that "good hoodoo" could always steal souls back from the devil,[121] particularly in cases where the devil himself was seen as but a conjurer. Most blues singers, no doubt, interpreted this same possibility in the Christian terms of the "prodigal son" cycle, which I will detail in the next chapter. This cycle always allowed time for Jesus, himself sometimes seen as a conjurer, to win back souls from his evil adversary. For instance, a Mississippi ex-slave named Susan Snow described herself as a "prodigal" who once had been a drunkard and (descriptively speaking) "a devil" until she "got" religion.[122] Rev. LaDell Johnson, bluesman Tommy Johnson's brother, used similar language to describe his own former life as a blues musician, a life he called a "devil's life."[123] As sociologist Charles S. Johnson explained in the introduction to a collection of African-American conversion narratives, the Protestant faith expected conversion, provided a means for its ritual enactment, and even rewarded the convert with some status in that particular church.[124] In fact, it was not unusual or impermissible for an individual to revert repeatedly to the ways of the world before permanently settling down among the church faithful. This was exemplified in the conversion narrative of a man who was once a musician, probably a bluesman. "I was a great musician," the man said, "and at times, after I had spent seasons at fasting and praying, I would get tired of it and go back to the ways of the world. You see, the devil knows how to tempt a man. He always reminds him of the things he likes best, and in this way he can get his attention."[125] Even the heroic "badman," Devil Winston, who was said to have been possessed by the devil, was believed to have undergone a dramatic conversion.[126] If Winston's conversion was possible then Robert Johnson also could have renounced the blues on his deathbed as his mother claimed he did.[127]

The second reason some blues singers might have dared to sell their souls to "the devil" is that some of them were seemingly not that frightened of him.[128] One Christian said in a conversion narrative that even before God freed his soul he was never "hell-scared." "I just never did feel that my soul was made to burn in hell."[129] Carter G. Woodson, the great African-American historian, said the same thing about his father, who, before joining the church, had been a field slave. He never seemed worried about his soul going to hell, said Woodson.[130] As I will argue extensively in chapter 2, many (if not most) blues singers seemingly were not "hell-scared" because, for myriad reasons, they felt a sense of divine justification, among them being the fact that they were oppressed by whites and their songs told the truth about life. To this effect, bluesman Henry Townsend commented negatively about blues being referred to as "the devil's music":

"I don't think the Devil care for the truth, do you? . . . Because . . . the Devil is a terrible thing, so he wouldn't like nothing that was real or something that was nice. There's a lot of things is taught and told to us that we all have to disregard now because we find it not to be true. I've been told things even about the bible, and it's not in there. . . . So, the truth is, I guess I stick to my blues as the blues, and I'm not afraid to play them because I'm scared that I'm gonna go to the burning place, whatever it is. I'm not afraid of that!"[131]

Zora Neale Hurston recognized this spectrum of belief about the devil in her study of Florida folklore. While some of the African Americans she studied envisioned hell as a very real and harmful place—a flaming furnace inhabited by hellhounds that pursued dying souls[132]—others saw "the devil" as but a divine trickster who often competed successfully against God.[133] William E. Barton, compiler of *Old Plantation Hymns* (1895), drew the same conclusion about the portrayal of the devil in the spirituals. He described the devil as both a real terror and a source of mirth and enjoyment for blacks.[134] While Christ was often portrayed as a sort of master magician,[135] the devil was frequently depicted as a conjurer, as one black spiritual illustrates: "The devil is a liar and a conjurer too, if you don' look out he'll conjure you."[136]

Melville Herskovits was probably the precursor of the modern anthropologists who have argued that the use of the word "evil" in the context of reference to the devil or hell need not necessarily imply evil in the "strong sense"—mortally harmful evil.[137] Herskovits theorized that the perception African Americans held of the devil was different from that held by whites in their religious system, even by Protestant whites who most vigorously preached the doctrines of demonology and damnation.[138] The African-American perception of the devil, as he saw it, generally approximated the character of the African trickster-god; so that while blacks gleaned from Christianity their theological worldview, the process of readjustment in North America included the deity Legba surviving under a different name:[139]

That this Devil is far from the fallen angel of European dogma, the avenger who presides over the terrors of hell and holds the souls of the damned to their penalties, is apparent. So different is this tricksterlike creature from Satan as generally conceived, indeed, that he is almost a different being. To account for the difference, therefore, we turn again to that character in Dahomean-Yoruba mythology, the divine trickster and the god of accident known as "Legba." . . . It is of some importance to note that, in West Africa, this deity is identified with the Devil by missionaries. . . . It is thus understandable how, in the New World, where Protestantism placed special emphasis upon the difference between good and evil, the reinterpretation of this deity as the Devil was especially logical.[140]

In the African-American lore, Legba's synchronous duplicity was bifurcated by Christian dualism (or semi-dualism), though his personality as a trickster was maintained. He was no longer subhuman and super-human, male and female, profane and sacred, destructive and reconciling—no longer beyond good and evil; he was singularly superhuman, male, profane, destructive, and irreconcilably evil. On the other hand, though he was no longer loved, he was not direly feared. The contrast between the devil of African-American lore and the fallen angel of European dogma is clearly evident in a comparison of the devil in Virginia Frazer Boyle's *Devil Tales* (1900) and John Ashton's *The Devil in Britain and America* (1896). The devil of early modern Britons was the "master" of witches and sorcerers, while the devil of African Americans, as depicted in *Devil Tales*, was the "master" of hoodoo conjurers. The latter was not so much unequivocally evil as he was highly unpredictable. He was, for instance, the no-good city-slicker of Clara Smith's "Done Sold My Soul, Sold It to the Devil." Because her man quit her, leaving her "blue" and vulnerable, the devil slyly moved in on Smith, "grinning like an ole ches' cat." She took him up on his offer to make her happy and he gave her a lot of gold, but then, sang Smith, he would not leave her be: He trailed her "like a bloodhound" and was "slicker than a snake." He followed right behind her, she sang, "every crook and turn I make." Thus, the trickster-like "devil" of African-American lore of the old South (and country blues) was often portrayed as a conjurer; the trickster-like "devil" in the new North (and in city blues) was often portrayed as a pimp.

This is one of several reasons why blues singers took the alleged risk of turning to the devil for the acquisition of magical powers, specifically musical talent. But there still existed those like bluesman Luther Trice for whom the devil was neither a conjurer nor a pimp but an utter terror that would send any reasonable soul afoot. So there existed this spectrum of belief about the devil—an African depiction at one extreme end and a European depiction at the other. This is the reason it is difficult to infer a single, underlying explanation for evil as conceived in the mythologies of the blues, even though we have come close to drawing a composite picture of the devil's character(s) and nature(s). Additionally, as I will explain in my conclusion, as blues moved out of its "country" context into the "city" where it developed into a sophisticated "urban" art form, the devil became increasingly demystified and his threat less menacing.

Having completed this examination of the overarching mythologies of the blues, we will now look underneath this cosmological umbrella in order to identify the specifics of meaning that comprise the theologies of the blues. We will see that they are theologies just as rooted in black church orthodoxy as the blues mythologies.

CHAPTER TWO

THE THEOLOGIES
OF THE BLUES

Those who lived the life of the blues "behind the mule" were a "folk" people who tended to articulate their religious world outlook in lore and lyric rather than in scholarly discourse. As a result, blues scholars who had not immersed themselves in the whole of discourse about black culture were unable to recognize that the blues was authentically theological.

Among the first scholars to discover a bona fide theological aspect in the blues was Rod Gruver, in an article of 1970 titled "The Blues as a Secular Religion." Gruver perceived the blues as not simply a musical genre that was poetic and folkloric, but as the music of a "secular religion" that was presided over by blues-singing prophets and visionaries of the black poor.[1] This "secular religion" was comprised of both the dissolution of the puritan ethos that the enslaved Africans learned from their white captors and the evolution of a "new religion" constituted of mature self-reliance and independence of spirit[2]—namely, liberation from immature religious dependence that the nineteenth-century philosopher Ludwig Feuerbach said institutionalized religion tends to foster.[3] In this "new religion" of existentialism, women and men were gods, deified by means of lyrics that mythologized their sexuality.[4]

Owing much of its cosmology to the Judeo-Christian narratives and doctrines, early blues were in effect the spirituals of an "invisible" postbellum black religion that demystified Christianity and called into question some of its doctrinal tenets. What Gruver identified as fundamentally religious about the blues was not alone the deification of women and men, but its engendering of renewal, reunion, and "at-onement" for them.[5] It reconciled opposites—symbolized by the thematization of heterosexual love—and thus revealed the unity of all nature.[6] As it turns out, this "new" worldview was none but the old one—an Afrocentric, holistic perspective on the world and human personhood.

Two years after Gruver's article, there appeared an essay titled "The Ethos of the Blues" by Larry Neal, the late African-American poet, essayist, and literary critic. Neal defined the "ethos of the blues" as the "emotional archetype" that gave rise to the spirituals and their myriad sacred and secular musical offspring.[7] This "emotional archetype" was what he termed the "blues spirit,"[8] the spirit of that which, elsewhere, he called the "blues god." The "blues spirit" was mediated by the performer, who reflected on and responded to life's realities with a message undergirded by a "didactic and moralistic impulse."[9] Didactic, moralistic, spiritual, emotional—according to this language, Neal interpreted the blues as theological.

The same year Neal's article appeared there came *The Spirituals and the Blues* (1972) by James H. Cone, a black theologian beginning his academic career at the height of the black consciousness movement. Cone was the first scholar to write on the blues from the viewpoint of Christian theology, which I have already shown to be a major part of the mythologies of the blues. In the last chapter of his book, "The Blues: A Secular Spiritual," Cone claimed that the blues was theological because it manifested or activated the divine Spirit that moved people toward unity.[10] This was a Christian theologizing of Neal's notion of the "blues spirit" and Gruver's ideas regarding "reunion" and "at-onement." When Cone said the blues did not reject God but only ignored God in order to address the realities of life,[11] he was also touching on Gruver's contention that "blues people" engaged in an existential religion of mature self-reliance—liberation from immature dependence on institutionalized religion. Like Gruver, Cone also came to theological terms with the acting out of the repressed human instincts as regards sexual love. Cone said the blues rejected distinctions between the body and the soul, which meant, simply put, that there could be no wholeness without sex.[12] As a result of these insights, Cone made significant strides in revealing the false barrier between the blues and black religion. He concluded that the blues were by no means atheistic, profane, or immoral; they were, most aptly denoted, "secular spirituals."[13]

Paul Oliver used the existentialism of the blues in order to advance his argument that the blues were irreligious. He recognized that the blues singer was above all a "realist" who was not repulsed by the world's uglier side and was able to accept the evil with the good.[14] He said further that the blues singer was as deeply self-examining as the true philosopher, because he acknowledged his desires and faults and stated his thoughts with unabashed honesty.[15] But then Oliver turned the realism of the blues against the blues singer by concluding that what was revealed by that honesty was profane, thus evidencing the blues to be irreligious and evil.[16]

To the contrary, the fact that the blues spoke "the truth" and that "blues people" philosophically perceived truth to be the highest ethical value in the blues, made truth one of the orthodox elements in the theologies of the blues. Citing bluesman Henry Townsend's remark, "When I sing the blues I sing the truth," Cone inferred that the blues and truth were a single, inseparable reality. "There is," he asserted, "no attempt in blues to make philosophical distinction between divine and human truth."[17] Although David Evans chose not to reference Cone's theological understanding of this blues ethic, a theological interpretation nonetheless can be read into Evans's statement that truth-telling was the "essence" and "main aesthetic standard" of folk blues.[18] Thus, in terms of the folk blues, Albert Murray's claim that the performance of the blues emphasized aesthetics rather than ethics was like saying the performance of a black sermon emphasized aesthetics over ethics.[19] To the contrary, "preaching the blues," which I will try to establish as the main aesthetic standard of the blues performance, was indistinguishable from the ethic of telling the truth.

THE RELIGION OF THE BLUES

Paul Oliver said the blues was the song of people who turned their backs on religion.[20] However, almost all blues of the country and city genres made reference to God by means of such familiar interjections as "oh Lord," "good Lord," "Lordy, Lordy," "Lord have mercy," "the Good Lord above," "my God," "God knows," "for God's sake," "I declare to God," "so help me God," and "great God almighty!" According to bluesman J. D. "Jelly Jaw" Short, even Charlie Patton's guitar used to say "Lord have mercy." "Now that's what Charlie Patton'd make the guitar say," said Short.[21]

With reference to the "oh Lord" interpolation, blues scholar William Ferris recognized that blues singers often called on the Lord for support in their songs and that their audiences, in response, encouraged them to "preach the blues."[22] In spite of the obvious—that the blues was the only secular (non-church) music consistently and characteristically to petition the Lord—Oliver had already concluded that such colloquialisms were no more theological than one blues singer's interjection, "hell-o-mighty," as he boasted of the best gal he ever had.[23] Evans considered these interjections to be mere "apostrophes" for the simple sake of emphasis.[24] Agreeing with the concept, Garon used a lower-case "L" in the apostrophe— "lordy"—except when the Lord was actually being questioned or ridiculed.[25] Garon's double-standard draws on paradigms of European thought to support his claim that there is a denial of God and religion. Since the times of early modern Europe, the denial of God or religion was used as evidence to prove that one had "sold out" to the devil.[26]

The judgmental nature of these learned scholars is easily discernible by means of a simple query. Would Evans have said that bluesman Sonny Boy Williamson's last words to his wife—"Lord have mercy"—as he lay dying on his doorsteps from a mugging, an ice-pick stab wound to the head, were but an "apostrophe"? Would Garon have spelled Williamson's "Lord" with a lower-case "L"? What would they have had to say about James Son Thomas's illustration of how a blues verse can be changed into a religious one? We can take a line like "Lord, I ain't seen my baby since she been gone," said Thomas, and modify it to "Lord, come and see about me."[27] Whether petitioned by church folks in their spirituals or by "juke" folks in their blues, God was the reference source in times of trouble. Since the blues was about troubles, why the hesitance of critical thinkers to interpret the blues as being theological?

A reading of the blues where each text is considered in isolation will not work. The "oh Lord" interjection understood in the entire African-American historical and cultural context will prove it to be an abbreviation of the religious and ethical orientation that blues singers made explicit in various ways. Hambone Willie Newbern, in his "Shelby County Workhouse Blues," flushed out the meaning of one of the "oh Lord" permutations—"Lord have mercy"—when he sang, "Cast my eyes to the Lord say you please have mercy on poor me." Roosevelt Sykes, in "Poor Boy Blues," asked the Lord, "have mercy on me please," so he could give his heart just a little bit of "ease." Charley Patton, in his "Screamin' and Hollerin'

Blues," seemed to be extolling spiritual values when he sang, following the "Lord have mercy" interpolation, that he would not mistreat his woman for all his weight in gold. Otto Virgial, six years later in "Bad Notion Blues," seemed to have topped Patton in this respect, when he sang, "Oh Lord have mercy, . . . I wouldn't mistreat my woman for to save nobody's soul."

The lyrics of the blues tell us that "oh Lord" was a response to the "ultimate reality" that undergirded "blues life" in black America. The sounds of the blues—not the interpolations but the nonarticulations (moans and hums)—tell us that the whole being of the singer was engaged in deeply spiritual expression and confession that left the "blue" soul washed fresh at the blues altar. Larry Neal was correct that, "even though the blues may be about so-called hard times, people generally feel better after hearing them or seeing them. They tend to be ritually liberating in that sense."[28] Saturday nights in the "juke houses" were the sacred time and place for the communion of the blues,[29] which Albert Murray identified as "a ritual of purification and affirmation."[30] Leola Manning, in her blues titled "The Blues is All Wrong," sang something about the blues bringing "joy to our cry" and about the folks to whom she sang being "baptized with fire." This supports blueswoman Van Hunt's definition of the blues as "a sad thing and . . . a rejoicing thing."[31] "When I have troubles," confirmed Memphis Slim, "the blues is the only thing that helps me—I mean that's the only way to kind of ease my situation.[32] To this effect, Will Weldon sang in "Red Hot Blues" that "All you got to do is just swing and sway; when you're feeling low just dance these blues away." This "liturgy" in which barefaced "blues people" came face-to-face with the truth of human existence and the black experience, as "preached" to them in the blues, was a means of their discerning life's bare theological meaning.

In this rite and ritual of human discernment, the blues singer, according to blues scholar Julio Finn, assumed the role of a religious "elder" and the audience that of a ritual "initiate." The purpose of this "musical convocation," he said, was to invoke the "spirit of the blues"— namely, the spirit of black people—and thereby unite the ritual partici- pants.[33] In an essay on the blues as a form of Afrocentric communal therapy, Leonard Goines argued that the music functioned for blacks in the same way professional therapy functioned for whites. "The therapist is not there to propose solutions to problems but to ask questions so that the patient can clearly come to see and understand the nature of this problem. It is assumed that once a problem can be clearly and simply defined, solutions will follow. The blues functions in the same manner, as an analysis of the lyrics clearly demonstrates."[34] Given that black preaching has always functioned therapeutically in the black church, the notion of "preaching the blues" should come as no surprise.

PREACHING THE BLUES

There is a symbiotic relationship between the blues and gospel music, as Charles Keil recognized. With reference to the "sacred foundation" of the secular expression in the blues, Keil elaborated on the similar "sacred roles" played by the black preacher and the blues singer. Not only did they derive their "sermonic" material from the same intimate involvement in and knowledge of black reality, but the same person often filled both roles at different times in life, if not occasionally simultaneously.[35] Describing the blues event as a ritual overseen by the singer who plays a priestly "belief role" in the black community, Keil said:

> The word "ritual" seems more appropriate than "perfor-
> mance" when the audience is committed rather than apprecia-
> tive. And from this, it follows, perhaps, that blues singing is
> more of a belief role than a creative role—more priestly than
> artistic. The . . . discussion of bluesmen and preachers supports
> this shift in perspective, as does the Saturday-night and Sunday-
> morning pattern of the Negro weekend. Bluesmen and preach-
> ers both provide models and orientations; both give public
> expression to deeply felt private emotions; both promote
> catharsis—the bluesman through dance, the preacher through
> trance; both increase feelings of solidarity, boost morale,
> strengthen the consensus.[36]

Despite Keil's discovery of the "sacred foundation" of the blues's secular expression, he lost ground when he concluded that the blues was clearly a secular, if not actually a "profane," form of expression.[37]

Blues was indeed a secular music comprised of a synchronous duplicity—it was both sacred and profane—but to isolate one half of that duplicity and conclude that it was a "profane" form of expression was to devalue what blues singers meant by "preaching the blues." The similarities between the preaching of a minister and a blues singer were implied by Muddy Waters, who said of Son House that he could surely "preach the blues"—sit down and sing one song after another, he said, just like a preacher.[38] A former preacher turned blues singer, Son House expressed the urgency of carrying out this calling. With the whoop of a traditional black Baptist preacher, he said in his "Preachin' the Blues" that he had to stay on the job and had no time to lose; "I swear to God," he sang, "I got to preach these gospel blues." He went on to say that after he preached his "gospel blues" he would go ahead and sit down, but he insisted that when "the spirit" came the sisters should "jump straight up and down." Although the blues singer was the object of adoration and deification, as was his counterpart the black preacher, the spirit was as present when the women jumped straight up and down in the ritual of the blues as when they "shouted" (danced) in church. With Son House's "Preachin' the Blues" in mind, blues scholar Robert Palmer said blues singers were quite aware of the fact that their singing was comparable to a minister's preaching, not only in style but in its effect upon listeners.[39]

Son House's "Preachin' the Blues" was probably titled after Bessie Smith's "Preachin' the Blues" recorded three years earlier, in 1927, with piano rather than guitar accompaniment. Consistent with the ethic of blues preaching, Smith confessed in her sermonette to the "girls" that her intention was not to save their souls but rather to advise them practically as to how to preserve their "jellyrolls" (advice Jane Lucas gave three years later in her "Pussy Cat Blues"). Smith preached further from her cultural Bible in the mood of an existential biblicism, "Read on down to chapter ten, taking other women's men you are doin' a sin." Despite the claims of Oliver, the ethos of this "preaching" was serious, just as serious as the spoken sermonette with which Smith opened her recorded gospel song, "Moan, Mourners." Exhorting the "sisters and brothers" that they had gathered to discuss the serious business of "backbiting" that had been occurring among them, Smith said: "The thing I want to know is what bit me on mine, I mean, who bit me on my back."

Preaching the blues was unquestionably a highly valued religious experience and a skill that such Smith contemporaries as Ethel Waters and Billie Holiday had mastered. Ethel Waters, who by the mid to the late 1930s was among the most sought-after actresses on Broadway, never forgot the days she stood behind the blues podium. "I played the Hanna theatre in Decatur, 1931," she reminisced. "It was in Lew Leslie's

'Rhapsody in Black.' That was fun and we played to a good crowd, but I will never forget the days, long before that, when I poured everything I had into tunes set to rowdy lyrics."[40] What was it like when Waters poured everything out into the blues? In her 1937 edition of the "sepia stage review" titled "Swing Harlem Swing," Waters sang like she used to in those never-forgotten days and a reporter captured the spirit of sermonry. He wrote, "she . . . shouted 'Dinah' and vowed, 'I Aint Gonna Sin No Mo,' buried the gal for 'Messing Wid My Man,' advised her lover to 'Take It Where You Had It Last Night,' admonished the sisters, 'It Takes a Good Woman Now a Days to Keep a Good Man Home,' wondered 'Am I Blue?' [and] moaned in plaintive tones, 'Half of Me Wants to Be Good.'"[41] Another journalist captured Billie Holiday's blues preaching skills: "La Holiday, with her sultry blues-swinging voice, can quiet even the noisiest night club customers the moment she steps into the spotlight to sing a sophisticated torch song." Her stage presence, personality, and what she did with a song, the writer concluded, had a "soothing effect" on the wining and dining crowd.[42] Indeed, "Strange Fruit" and "God Bless the Child"—those were "preachin' blues."

The "classic" blueswomen generally had a more sophisticated touch to their blues preaching than the "country" or "city" blues singers. A made-up blues by a Texas field-hand thematized the Golden Rule in a way the audiences of La Holiday would have seen as somewhat crude. He sang, "I want all you women to treat me like I treats you; if I treats you dirty, you treats me dirty too."[43] City bluesman Sunnyland Slim executed some "fire and brimstone" preaching in his blues titled "The Devil Is a Busy Man." He said the devil has got power and no one ought think otherwise; if people are not mighty careful, he sang, the devil will lead them to their grave.[44] Big Bill Broonzy also engaged in some "fire and brimstone" blues preaching that he probably maintained from the days he both preached the gospel and sang the blues in order to make a living. When his father insisted that he stop "straddling the fence," Broonzy chose the blues,[45] but he did not cease "preaching." In his "Preaching the Blues," which followed in the Bessie Smith and Son House tradition, Broonzy said that women go to church just to show their "skirts" and men go just to hide their "dirt." He specifically warned the "brother" who occasionally had his way with married women that he had better get on his knees and pray both night and day because he could end up going to "hell" that way. There is a day coming, Broonzy exhorted, when Gabriel will blow his trumpet and judgment will come. "Brother what you gonna do?"

Oliver, coming from his Victorian perspective, contended that there was no religious or moral connotation intended by the theory and practice of "preaching the blues." Contrary to what I have illustrated, he insisted that Son House did not preach a blues counterpart to a sermon, and he called Bessie Smith's "Preachin' the Blues" a "mock sermon."[46] Only "occasionally," reasoned Oliver, did blues singers use their music to deliver a religious or (as he qualified it) "quasi-religious" message, the above piece by Broonzy being, he said, "quite rare."[47] Attempting to discredit once and for all the notion that "preaching the blues" involved a moralistic impulse, Oliver said that in content and sentiment the blues was the creation of people who set themselves apart from the church and accepted "worldly values" that they expressed "seldom with any ethical or moral consider-ations."[48] But given all the evidence to the contrary, how could Oliver erect such a thick barrier between the so-called profane and the sacred, between Bessie Smith's preaching in her blues and in her recorded religious songs, such as "Moan, Mourners" and "On Revival Day?" According to one of Smith's musicians, the two were inseparable, in that her blues perfor-mances evoked the mood and fervor of southern black worship. "She was real close to God, very religious," he said. "She always mentioned the Lord's name. That's why her blues seemed almost like hymns."[49]

While gospel singers and preachers extolled the glories of heaven, blues singers—as marginal Christians—explored present reality rarely with reference to Jesus Christ. "This is not atheism," argued Cone, "rather it is believing that *transcendence* will only be meaningful when it is made real in and through the limits of historical experience."[50] As Blind James Brewer figured, "you got to live down here just like you got to make preparations to go up there. You can't go there until you get there; that is you can't cross the bridge until you get to it."[51] "Preaching the blues" was coming to grips with the religious meaning of living "down here."

THE BLUES AND THE SPIRITUALS

When Oliver explained that some blues singers also recorded religious music, he did not account for the fluid relationship between the spirituals and the blues, as Richard Wright briefly did in *12 Million Black Voices* (1941) and James Cone in *The Spirituals and the Blues* (1972).[52] We were told by Oliver that, unlike the spirituals, the blues were "worldly" and lacked "spiritual values."[53] Neither did Oliver account for how blues singers themselves perceived the connection between the spirituals and the blues, information that was available in the interviews that comprised his own book, *Conversation with the Blues* (1965). In that book are interviews Oliver had with musicians such as Willie Thomas and Teddy Roosevelt "Blind" Darby, both of whom preached and sang blues; musicians such as Blind James Brewer, who played blues and gospel; and musicians such as John Lee Hooker, who, like Brewer, saw the spirituals and the blues as based on the same mood and ethos.[54] Oliver himself said in his introduction to the book that many blues singers pointed out this close connection,[55] but obviously he was unwilling to give any credence to their views and cultural self-understanding.

Religious songs, in general, were not only borrowed from thematically, they were sometimes referenced in a narrative context; such as when Hi Henry Brown sang in "Titanic Blues" that as the ship was sinking in the "deep blues sea" a band was playing "Nearer My God to Thee." Mississippi Bracey's blues, "I'll Overcome Some Day," was apparently intentionally titled after the popular hymn of Charles Albert Tindley, the black Methodist Episcopal minister of Philadelphia. Of all the religious songs borrowed from thematically, the spirituals were foremost among them. Of all the spirituals, "Nobody Knows the Trouble I've Seen" and "Sometimes I Feel Like a Motherless Child" were favorites, particularly "Nobody Knows":

> *Nobody knows the trouble I've seen,*
>
> *Nobody knows my sorrow.*
>
> *Nobody knows the trouble I've seen,*
>
> *Glory Hallelujah!*

Eurreal Montgomery, in "Pleading Blues," used the language of "Nobody Knows" to express how he felt when his gal mistreated him. He sang to his audience, "You don't know how worried must I be," concluding that, "Nobody knows but the good Lord and me." For the same reason—being treated like a "lowdown" by his woman—Red Nelson sang in "Crying Mother Blues" that, "Nobody knows my troubles but myself and the good Lord." As illustrated in Montgomery's and Nelson's blues, and further evidenced in Otis Spann's "Nobody Knows My Troubles," blues singers were generally more explicit about the "troubles" they had seen. Spann had specific troubles—money troubles and woman troubles—

and he found nothing "glorious" about this reality. He claimed that nobody knows the trouble he had seen, complaining that he had lost all his money and his woman treated him so "mean." Trixie Smith, in her "Praying Blues," also had troubles, namely, man troubles. She prayed about it in her blues but found glory wanting. She said to the "folks" to whom she sang that they did not know half the trouble she had seen; "nobody knows," she crooned, "but the good Lord and me." Smith continued with her behest, that the Lord kindly hear her plea and send her a man who wanted "nobody else but me." Sara Martin, in "A Green Gal Can't Catch On," similarly sang, "Lordy, Lordy, Lordy, look what trouble I've seen." What was her trouble?—thousands of other gals "taking my man from me."

Urban blues was no different with regard to the singers giving the specifics of their troubles, except that it often omitted reference to "the Lord"; or, as I said in my introduction, the "oh Lord" interjection seemed less religiously convincing. Based on the argument in my conclusion—that the "urban" style was a blues denatured of explicit references to the mythologies, theologies, and theodicies of country and city blues—it is not surprising that Jimmy Rushing's "Nobody Knows," sung with the Count Basie Orchestra in 1939, replaced the Lord's name with that of "baby." Regarding the reason the woman Rushing loved was so far away from him, Rushing sang, "Nobody knows but my baby and me." Replacing the Lord's name with "baby" was a practice that became common in the emerging rhythm and blues of the 1940s. This might have been what W. C. Handy was thinking about when he wrote (significantly in 1940) that the phrase "oh Lordy" was equivalent to the "impromptu embellishment" "oh baby," both being similar to jazz "fills."[56]

The use of the spiritual "Sometimes I Feel Like a Motherless Child" also illustrates what the blues singer meant when he said the spirituals were born on the blues side,[57] or what Thomas Dorsey meant when he said there were "moaning blues" that were used in the spirituals and "moaning spirituals" that were used in the blues.[58] Washboard Sam, in "I've Been Treated Wrong," borrowed from the mood and words of both "Motherless Child" and "Nobody Knows." He said he did not know his real name or where he was born and that he had such "troubles" it seemed like he was raised in an orphan's home. It seemed so, he sang, because his mother died and left him when he was only two years old and the number of "troubles" he had been having "the good Lord only knows." Akin to Robert Pete

Williams in "Motherless Children Have a Hard Time" and Barbecue Bob in "Motherless Child Blues," Bill Jazz Gillum paraphrased the "Motherless Child" spiritual in "Got to Reap What You Sow." He said he was a poor boy a "great long way from home" and that he had no one to teach him the difference between right and wrong. Bukka White, in "The Panama Limited," came close to singing the original words of the spiritual. "I'm a motherless child," he sang, "I'm a long ways from home."

What do these blues songs say about the claim of David Evans, obviously entrenched in the thought of Oliver, that there is no theological connection between the spirituals and the blues? Perhaps alluding to Cone, Evans commented that, "Some writers have . . . tried to make a case for the influence of spirituals on the blues. . . . There is a similar degree of emotional depth in the best blues and spiritual singing, but the actual influence of the spirituals on the blues could have been of only the most general sort."[59] Like Oliver, Evans did not give much credence to blues singers' own words about the spirituals being "born on the blues side."[60] Thus, neither of them could see that the "oh Lord" interjection and its myriad permutations were more than mere apostrophes, that they were spirit-filled interpolations. For instance, Archie Edwards's response to those who did not think the blues were spiritually "deep" was that the blues were the next deep thing to the spirituals.[61] John Cephas said essentially the same thing. If you could sing the spirituals, he explained, then all you needed to sing the blues was to be able to play the guitar to accompany yourself, because the two were so "closely related."[62] Adding deeper reflection to his claim, Cephas also said that in both church music and the blues the singer sang about something that inspired them in their life. "Something happened in life to cause a guy to write about his life with the blues. It's all life stories in song. It's very profound, you know. It's actually telling a story, true-to-life stories from out of the black community."[63] To the contrary of Oliver's and Evans's outsider perspective, Alberta Hunter said it all when she remarked that the blues are "like spirituals, almost sacred."[64]

BLUES AND PRAYER

Often when prayer was mentioned in the blues, the blues singer commented on how "having the blues" drove the spirit of prayer away. This was the kind of thing Garon pointed to in an attempt to argue, with his Europeanist reasoning, that the blues denied God and therefore was completely beyond connection with the religion of blues singers' upbringing.[65] Bluesman James Platt, in projecting himself into the position of one about to be executed in "the chair," said he had neither the heart to send a message home nor the heart to pray. I will discuss other instances of this in the next chapter in the context of the "theodicy problem," but only need now to point out that often there were times when blues singers did pray, as illustrated in Blind Lemon Jefferson's song about a flood, "Risin' High Water Blues." Because the water was rising and coming in his windows and doors, "I leave with a prayer in my heart," sang Jefferson: "Backwater won't rise no more." Maggie Jones, in "Thunderstorm Blues," shared her fear of thunder and lightning and confessed her call for divine comfort. With the devil "a-groaning" and the "wicked"-sounding wind howling, not to mention that Jones was all alone and "scared to death," there was only one thing left for the poor woman to do: "I'll start in praying," she sang, "till the storm is through." Jones did not wish to die in a violent thunderstorm; she wanted to see another year come and go, as Charlie Patton said he did in his "34 Blues." Though the new year may bring sorrows or may bring tears, sang Patton, "oh Lord, oh Lord, let me see your brand new year."

Such so-called "occasional" references to religion were to Oliver "half-hearted" and only temporary in the most literal sense, which he concluded about the prayer Lightnin' Hopkins uttered in response to the threat of a deadly hurricane.[66] Hopkins said he was sitting in his kitchen looking out across the waves (perhaps the waves of cotton), and when he saw a "mean" twister coming he started to pray. He fell down on his knees, and these were the words he said: "Oh Lord, have mercy and help us in our wicked ways." He prayed on, "Lord, Lord what shall we do? Yes, there ain't no other help I know, oh Lord, but you." Had blues singers actually been on their knees when uttering some of these verses, even the likes of Oliver might have thought they were genuine black prayers.

Blues singers not only prayed in moments of "instant religion," which was perhaps the real test of fundamental religious belief (one's feeling of extra-dependency), but they also spoke theologically in the aftermath of tragedy. Uncountable blues singers bemoaned their loss of a lover and the pain of going to the funeral or burial, and they did so in lyrics that tended to show agreement with the ritual traditions of the church. When the woman Robert Wilkins "did love and like" passed away, Wilkins sang in his "I'll Go with Her Blues" that he dressed himself in black so he could show the world he indeed wanted her even though he could not get her back. Oliver himself cited an example of a blues Buddy Moss moaned at the wake of his woman. It was a blues (and there were many like it) that also calls into question Oliver's claim that the blues did not look forward to life after death.[67] "Lord, Lord, Lord," Moss sang, bemoaning that the woman he loved was dead and "never more to roam"; "she was a kind black woman and she'll make heaven her happy home." In their daily existence, "blues people" were concerned with coming to grips with living "down here," but in the aftermath of tragedy they were clearly concerned with the eternal well-being of their deceased loved ones.

"The Natchez Fire," by Gene Gilmore, was an even greater contradiction to perceptions of the blues as irreligious. It was a blues sung to the survivors of the approximately two hundred black victims of a dance-club fire in Natchez, Mississippi, in April 1940. The media took the sensationalistic perspective, saying that it was "the greatest holocaust to hit the country in many years," leaving in its wake a "mass of human flesh."[68] The mayor of the city perceived it from the practical perspective and gave a proclamation calling for all the citizens of Natchez and Adams County to donate money to help bury the dead and assist the injured.[69] Oliver, the worst of all, pulled together the historical pieces to this event and recognized it to be a tragedy of great significance to blacks and of little consequence to whites, and then identified Gilmore's blues as a mere "epitaph" that tried to offer, he said, "a *little* comfort to the bereaved."[70] It was not an "epitaph," it was a eulogy, and of all who spoke—the media, the mayor, the historian—it was the blues singer who gave black Mississippians and black America their much-needed eulogy in documentary form for all history. Gilmore sang, "Lord, I know, I know how you Natchez people feel today; some of them thinking of the fire that took their children's life away." He said it was late one Tuesday night and people had come from miles around; they were enjoying their lives, he sang, when the Rhythm Club went down. He said there was sadness and misery when the hearses began to "roll"—over two hundred dead and gone, he sang, "Lord, and they can't come here no more." Gilmore wound up his eulogy telling all the people to listen to what he had to say; "don't be uneasy 'bout your children," he sang, "because they are all at rest today."

Gilmore's "The Natchez Fire," like the Bronzeville Five's eulogies in their recordings "Natchez Mississippi Blues" and "Mississippi Fire Blues," was sung for all who lost friends and loved ones among the two hundred victims. There were also eulogistic blues that were personal in nature, such as Joe Williams's "Brother James." Williams storied about brother James dying under surgery after an automobile accident that resulted from his drinking "bad whiskey." Concerned that brother James died drunk and might not have had time to utter a final prayer, Williams said this eulogistic prayer for his old friend: "Sleep on brother James, well I'll meet you resurrection day." In his farewell, Williams also said he would see his buddy again some day; he would be sitting at the official table when brother James came that way. Other eulogies in the blues repertoire included the memorial recording to the tragic death of Blind Lemon Jefferson, "Wasn't It Sad About Lemon," by the duo known as Walter and Byrd. Brownie McGhee also eulogized a great bluesman in "The Death of Blind Boy Fuller."

Given the foregoing kinds of blues expressions—preaching, prayer, eulogy (not "mock sermons" and "epitaphs")—it is quite obvious why the transition between being a blues singer and becoming a Christian preacher was so fluid and why this "conversion" was so typical in the early days of the blues. What we will turn to now is a detailing of some of the other kinds of theological concerns that blues singers articulated.

THEOLOGICAL POLEMICS IN THE BLUES

It is helpful to interpret explanations of good and evil as contested concepts, since such explanations continuously take form in ongoing dialectic between opposing views.[71] The theologies of the blues were shaped in just such a dialectic with doctrinal Christianity, a dialectical oppugnancy I will detail further in the next chapter in the context of the theodicies of the blues. Engaged in this perpetual dialectic, blues singers, taking their texts from the cultural bible of their "peripheral religion," produced such songs as Hi Henry Brown's "Preacher Blues," Joe McCoy's "Preachers Blues," and Luke Jordan's "Church Bell Blues," in which church folks (especially the black preacher) were not simply joked about but resolutely disparaged for their moral hypocrisy and self-righteousness.

Blues singers borrowed some of their critical language about the preacher's hypocrisy and insatiable carnal appetite for food, drink, and sex from the religious jokelore of the South. One such tale portraying the black preacher in just this light began with a preacher calling a meeting after his first service at a new church.[72] Using the meeting as an opportunity for himself and the congregation to get to know and understand one another, the preacher asked everyone who loved the Lord to sit on one side of the church and everyone who loved wine and women to sit on the other side (assuming, apparently, that all the women loved the Lord). One man did not budge but looked rather puzzled. When the preacher inquired as to the problem, the congregant explained that he did not know on what side to sit because he loved both the Lord and the carnal pleasures. The preacher responded—and this was the joke's clincher—"Well, son, you just come up here in the pulpit with me. You've been called to preach."

Some of the blues singer's criticisms of the church were influenced by this kind of southern jokelore, but Oliver placed all such material under the rubric of minstrelsy and vaudeville, a claim he said was supported by the fact that blues singers seldom criticized anything worthy of comment—religious doctrine, church authority, or religious worship.[73] But who is to determine what is worthy or unworthy of criticism and in what form that criticism should come? Mainline Protestants, for example, long criticized the Holiness and Pentecostal groups that broke away from them because the mainliners perceived their moral concerns—dancing, card playing, wearing make-up, and so forth—as petty. Also (though I will wait to explicate this in the next chapter where it is more significant), blues singers knew how to produce the familiar "sounds" of minstrelsy in order to mask the seriousness of their protest. As we are coming to understand, it was simply Oliver's Europeanist moral bias against the black blues that tainted the music. He would not have made the same claim against gospel singer Washington Phillips, whose "country" blues–sounding gospel song, "Denomination Blues," had verses essentially indistinct from those of Bo Carter's and Walter Vincson's blues, "He Calls That Religion." One of Phillips's verses in part two of his gospel song of 1929 said that a lot of preachers are preaching and think they are doing well when "all they want is your money and you can go to hell." Carter's and Vincson's (the Mississippi Sheiks') "He Calls that Religion" said the preacher used to preach to try to save people's souls but then he began to preach just so he could buy some "jellyroll." In the refrain they twice repeated "He calls that religion," then gave the single resolution, "but I know he's going to hell when he dies."

If the blues verses that criticized the preacher and church folks had been considered in the context of blues narratives—autobiographies, biographies, interviews, and the "blues school of literature" (such as

Ellison's *Invisible Man*)—it would have been extremely difficult for Oliver to have maintained that their detractions were meaningless minstrelsy. For instance, Son Thomas said, "Now you take just a lots of people in church today. They'll drink more whiskey than me. They'll drink more beer than me. And they'll do a lot more things than I'd do but still they belong to the church and I don't."[74] John Cephas, whose father was a Baptist minister, said church people were in effect hypocrites because they frowned on Saturday night house parties at which the blues was played and yet they themselves met at one another's homes on weekend nights to drink corn liquor.[75] What was especially hypocritical, he said, was when his parents had friends to their home on weekend nights and asked him to entertain them with the very music they accused of ill effect.[76] These brief narrative pieces actually call into question Oliver's claim that the blues singers' criticisms of the church were not as strong as churchgoers' criticisms of the blues.[77] Church folks simply called blues singers "sinners" and perhaps said they were playing "devil's music," and nothing more needed to be said because everyone understood the implications of that. Blues singers, true to their concise realism and directness, posited a myriad of observations about church folks' hypocrisy and self-righteousness and did so in a variety of moods ranging from the comic to the sardonic to the dogmatic.

Given Oliver's Victorian world outlook, it is not surprising that he conjectured that the pleasures of the flesh, so often thematized in the blues, were regarded with abhorrence by church folks.[78] To the churched, particularly the Sanctified churched, singing "Lordy baby" was blasphemous. It was not obeying God; it was following the devil, doing evil. Thus, a second means by which the blues stood in opposition to church doctrine was its rootedness in an ethos of eros. Gruver, in his article titled "The Blues as Secular Religion," gave this exposition of the conflict:

> Woman had been nearly forgotten in the Christian doctrine of a male-dominated trinity. The Christian fathers blamed woman for the sensual depravity that helped wreck ancient Rome, and her infamous deed in the Garden of Eden has not been forgotten yet. . . . Under Christianity her sexual appeal became a pagan snare, her essential humanity, a heathen delusion. . . .
>
> The Christian fear of woman is evident in a medieval couplet by Cardinal Hugues de St. Cher: "Woman pollutes the

body, drains the resources, kills the soul, uproots the strength, blinds the eye, and embitters the voice." The Cardinal's hatred of woman contrasts sharply with Sonny Boy Williamson's exaltation of her and the good she does: "Every time she starts to lovin' she brings eyesight to the blind." Sonny Boy's Woman not only brings eyesight to the blind, but she makes the dumb talk, the deaf to hear and the lame to walk.[79]

Paul Garon went further, redressing those who claimed blues singers were preoccupied with sex. He said, "let us point out that all *humanity* is preoccupied with sexuality, albeit most often in a repressive way; the blues singers, by establishing their art on a relatively nonrepressive level, strip the 'civilised' disguise from humanity's preoccupation, thus allowing the content to stand as it really is: eroticism as the source of happiness."[80] Garon was seemingly drawing on the thought of the late French philosopher Michel Foucault, who said in his history of sexuality that if sex is repressed and condemned to prohibition then the person who holds forth in such language, with seeming intentionality, moves, to a certain degree, beyond the reach of power and upsets established law.[81] Sex also might have been a means for "blues people" to feel potent in an oppressive society that made them feel socially and economically impotent, especially since sexuality inside the black community was one area that was free from the restraints of "the law" and the lynch mob. To be restrained socially and economically and then forced to live pietistically was what blues ethnomusicologist Alan Lomax designated "the double burden of Calvinist conflict and racial degradation."[82] It was simply more than some men and women (not all of them "blues people") could tolerate when they got from "behind the mule" at sundown on Saturday.

The third form of evil that blues singers objected to was "Jim Crow ethics" and the political quietism of the church, which I will discuss in the next chapter as their rejection of the eschatological or otherworldly theodicies. Not only was the psychoanalyst and African nationalist Frantz Fanon correct that without oppression and racism there would be no blues,[83] but without church music being so politically quietistic there would be no distinct music known as the blues. Without masking his disdain of racialism with thoughts of future reward or assuaging them in a gospel song, Huddie Ledbitter (Leadbelly) recounted the "Jim Crow" he and his wife encountered in the nation's capital. Unable to find a room in any of the black-owned hotels, they were forced to spend the night in the apartment of a white acquaintance. The following morning they overheard the landlord chastising the tenant about their presence. Later Leadbelly composed his famous "Bourgeoisie Blues": "Home of the brave, land of the free, I don't want to be mistreated by no bourgeoisie; Lord it's a bourgeois town." Without covering up her pain with praise, Bessie Smith, in "Poor Man Blues," petitioned the "Mister rich man" to open up his heart and mind and give the poor man a chance by helping to stop hard times. If hard times persist too long, she pleaded, even an honest person will do things that are wrong. Another blues singer protested even more acrimoniously, in a way no church song ever dared do: "They say we are the Lawd's children, I don't say that ain't true; but if we are the same like each other, why do they treat me like they do?"[84] J. B. Lenoir, in his "urban"-styled "Everybody Wants to Know," warned the "rich people," with a tinge of threat, that they had better listen "real deep"; when the poor people get real hungry, he sang, "we gonna take some food to eat."

These three themes—the disdain of church hypocrisy, pietism, and political quietism—comprise a part of the theologies of the blues that were shaped in the protracted polemic the "juke" folks had with the church folks. What lay at the root of the tension between the church and the blues was, if we have to pinpoint it, the priestly office of the church, which held the prerogative not only to fix the parameters of evil and the identification of evildoers but the limits of acceptable religious behavior that led to hypocrisy, pietism, and quietism. What we will discover now is that, because the priestly office of the black church could discredit dissident interpretations of good and evil derived situationally or in pursuit of individual interests and that office persisted in identifying blues as evil, some blues singers actually found themselves echoing this anti-blues legalism of the church. Most of all, all blues singers seemed to have maintained a distinct consciousness of sin.

THE CONSCIOUSNESS OF SIN

When Sippie Wallace returned to the church in her senior years to serve as a musician while continuing to sing the blues professionally,[85] her concern about violating church doctrine obviously evidenced a consciousness of sin. Her concern certainly was not simple guilt, which can be a substitute for the feeling of sin. Guilt is the internalization of anticipated chastisement by the priestly office, an internalized chastisement that, in a completely solitary experience, weighs heavily upon the consciousness prior to actual penalty.[86] The guilty conscience, then, makes itself its own tormentor.[87] Based on the Oliverian presuppositions, Oliver, Garon, Evans, and their like would have had to argue that guilt substituted for the feeling of sin in the consciousness of "blues people" because of their seeming lack of concern with the objective sacrilege of standing "before" the divine measure. Clearly, the feeling of guilt could have displaced the consciousness of sin if one was a radical secularist who emphasized the "I" more than the "before thee."[88] But just at the moment one might have been led to believe that the "before thee" was forgotten by a blues singer's alleged unreligious consciousness and that guilt was substituting for the religious feeling of sin, we hear the interjection, "oh Lord." This implies that the petitioner was not at all irreligious, as scholars might have been led to believe, and that a consciousness of sin was present. Paul Ricoeur explained that "The vocative—O God—which expresses the invocation of the petitioner, puts the moment of rupture back within the bond of participation; if God were Wholly Other, he would no longer be invoked. . . . In the moment of invocation the sinner becomes fully the subject of sin."[89]

Because I have argued that the "oh Lord" interpolation in the blues was not a theologically meaningless apostrophe, I maintain that it and its myriad permutations kept the conscience of the blues singer fully the subject of sin and not merely of guilt. Doctor Clayton, for instance, was conscious of sin, as evidenced in his blues, "Angels in Heaven." He sang, "I know why blues singers don't go to heaven 'cause Gabriel bawls them out." Little Son Jackson commented in "Evil Blues" that his father was a preacher and his mother was sanctified; "well now you know I must've been born the devil," he sang, "because I didn't want to be baptized." In order to be certain that these rhymed lyrics were not mere play, we need only turn to the blues narratives. Explaining why it was a sin to sing the blues, Little Son Jackson said:

> Whether a man sing the blues or ballads or what have you, there's no way in the world that he can get around and not make a sin of it in some way . . . because it's on the wrong side. It's a two-sided road and you on the wrong side all the time. A man who's singin' the blues—I think it's sin because it cause other people to sin. But church music is from the Lord and I never knowed anybody to sin over that. I don't think it's sinful

to sing of a wrong done to you, but it's the way you do it. I mean you could sing it in a spiritual form. . . . If a man feel hurt within side and he sing a church song then he's askin' God for help . . . but I think if a man sing the blues it's more or less out of himself. . . . He's not askin' no one for help.[90]

Son Thomas also reflected a consciousness of sin that he obviously learned from the church. He believed firmly that playing blues on Saturday night and going to church on Sunday morning was "goin' too far wrong." He warned, "Now I'd be afraid to do that 'cause somethin' bad can happen to ya. . . . You can't serve the Lord and the devil too."[91] "Classic" blues singer Chippie Hill similarly stated that she would never sing a hymn in a nightclub. "Now that's wrong. You can't play with God in a nightclub: if you do He'll put an affliction on you." Hill continued, "As long as I work for the Devil, I better continue with him. You got to sing for the Devil or go to Church."[92] It was Son House's consciousness of sin that made him choose between preaching the gospel and singing the blues when he had been doing both. "I can't hold God in one hand and the Devil in the other," he decided. "Them two guys don't get along together too well. I got to turn one of 'em loose. So I got out of the pulpit."[93]

It was orthodox "blues belief" that those who chose to sing the blues were gambling away their chance to reap the eternal bounty and would reap what they sowed. Blueswoman Flora Molton told this illustrative story: "I never forget, I was just singing 'I got the world in a jug, stopper in my hand, and if you want me, got to come under my command.' I didn't know my husband was nowhere around, I looked around and he was standing behind me. I said, 'Oh, you scared me.' He said, 'That's the way death's going to slip up on you.' And for a long time I didn't sing no blues."[94] Playing the blues—"Well, it's just the chance you take," confessed Son Thomas.[95] "When Gabriel sound that trumpet and everybody rise, you gonna burn if you ain't right."[96] This very worldview is what led Oliver to conclude that Robert Johnson's "Me and the Devil Blues" was not a hint to having made a pact with the devil but an expression of guilt that reflected the strict moral teachings of the church.[97] Given the blues lyrics and narratives we have heard thus far, the notion is quite feasible, except that Johnson's disposition likely would have been not "guilt" but a genuine consciousness of sin. After all, blues lyrics were replete with references to sin. In Robert Johnson's "Drunken Hearted Man," Johnson blamed his drunken-hearted state on "sin," which he said was "the cause of it all," adding that "the day you get weak for no-good women that's the day that you surely fall." His language about "no-good women," "falling," and "sin" was an intentional reference to the Edenic temptation and transgression and the doctrine of "original sin."

Just as in the biblical text when the man blames the woman upon God's interrogation of them in the garden, so has bluesman "Adam" long placed much of the burden of his sin on blueswoman "Eve." Occasionally this was an implicit reference, but it was most certainly intended because of the predominance of the Adamic myth, as illustrated in the last chapter. For instance, Furry Lewis, in his "Mistreatin' Mama," and two years later Son House with about the same words in "Preachin' the Blues" (part one), said they could get religion any day except that the women and the whiskey would not let them pray. A few years later, Louie Laskie, in "How You Want Your Rollin' Done," blamed women for his being unchurched, a sinner. He said he too could get religion "most any day," but the women and gambling would not let him pray. Sonny Boy Williamson created a narrative around this theme in "The Right Kind of Life," in which he demonstrated a strong consciousness of sin that resulted from the influence of his mother. His mother, who functioned as a mediator between him and the ultimate standard, often sat him down to discuss his being so "wild," in fear that women and whiskey would be the ruin of her "only child." Someday, he sang to his audience, he was going to "change his mind" and stop chasing women and staying drunk all the time. Regarding his having been married twice, Williamson also said that "people know by that, Lord, that I ain't been living the right life." Lightnin' Hopkins, in "Unkind Blues," said his mother was a Christian and had been begging him to join the church too; "babe, but how can I join the church," he sang, "and always bother with you?"

Deeply embedded in the Adamic mythology of the blues and its attendant theology of sin (even "original sin"), blues singers did not simply internalize sin so that they experienced only guilt resulting from self-adjudication by their conscience. Guilt indeed can be a substitute for the feeling of sin, but the lyrics of the blues illustrate that blues singers were conscious of standing before the divine measure, particularly when a "no-good" woman or a "no-good" man prevented them from measuring up.

JUSTIFICATION IN THE BLUES

"Supposing truth is a woman—what then?"[98] This query opening Friedrich Nietzsche's *Beyond Good and Evil* (1886) raised a question that has confused scholars about the place of woman in the morality of blues and as regards the blues singer's consciousness of sin. If truth were a woman then man would be "justified" in loving her so, despite the opposing mandates (or misconceptions) of Christianity. But woman was not "truth," she was the one about whom the truth was told in the blues, and this seemed to give female "blues people" some degree of affirmation. That women felt affirmed in blues sung by men is the most reasonable way to explain why they were generally so supportive of the blues. Memphis Slim, an avowed protégé of Bessie Smith, confirmed this when he said, "The only people that ever really supported blues and are still supporting blues now, the only black people that are not ashamed of the blues is our black women. They always supported the blues, and if it don't be for black women the blues would have been dead a long long time ago."[99] Perhaps women felt affirmed because, as Son Thomas claimed, "It ain't very many blues made that ain't made up about a woman."[100]

But affirmation for the woman was not necessarily "justification" for the man. What functioned as justification was the good she did for him. A "no-good" woman was disrespected and sometimes blamed for sin; otherwise, woman—the bluesman's wife or lover—was held in high esteem. Sonny Boy Williamson told the world in "Eyesight to the Blind" that every time his woman started loving she brought eyesight to the blind. Sonny Boy Williamson No. 2 (Rice Miller) sang similarly in "Western Union Man," a blues about a woman who "brought life back to the dead." Robert Wilkins, in "Long Train Blues," said his women would not write or call, which made him think that she might have been dead. He sang, "if I had wings baby like Noah's dove, I would raise and fly God knows where my lover was." Washboard Sam, in "Gonna Hit the Highway," was also in search of his lover. He wanted to find her and prayed to the good Lord that he did not fail; for if he did not find her, he sang, "Lord, I'll be forever on her trail." Walter Davis said to his woman, in "Lifeboat Blues," "I will stick closer to you than Jesus did the cross." Amos Easton sang in "No Woman No Nickel" that he just wanted one friend to keep him from feeling so sad, thus petitioning, "Lord, you know I want a friend like the one that Adam had."

All of the bluesmen were justified in their love of their woman because they were "good" women; but even had they not been justified, there was an old saying that Funny Papa Smith sang about in "Howling Wolf Blues" (part one). "Now the preacher told me that God will forgive a black man most anything he do," sang Smith, "I ain't black but I'm dark-complexioned, look like he ought to forgive me too." These waggish words conceivably rang true to most "blues people," so true that John Lee Hooker echoed them eighteen years later in his "Black Man Blues" (after all, it was axiomatic that "blessed are those who mourn"). "Tell me God forgive a black man most anything he do," he sang. The source of Smith's and Hooker's theological interpretation of the Sermon on the Mount probably lay in the colloquialism that "God takes care of old folks and fools," a saying that Smith was skeptical about in "Fool's Blues." Smith said that he was told that "God takes care of old folks and fools" but that since he had been born God must have changed his rules. He said that until about six months ago he had not prayed a prayer "since God knows when"; "now" he sang, "I'm asking God every day to please forgive me for my sin." With continued skepticism regarding God taking care of old folks and fools, Smith said that it must be the devil he was serving, that it could not be Jesus Christ, because he asked Jesus to save him but it looked like he was trying to take his life. In addition to all of these troubles, Smith's health was gone and he was left with the "sickness blues," so it did not appear to him that God took care of old folks and fools.

The explanation of this kind of "justification" given by folklorists Howard Odum and Guy Johnson approximates the point I am trying to make. "There seems to be a tendency for the despondent or blues singer to use the technique of the martyr to draw from others a reaction of sympathy. Psychologically speaking, the technique consists of rationalization, by which process the singer not only excuses his shortcomings, but attracts the attention and sympathy of others—in imagination, at least—to his hard lot."[101] Odum's and Johnson's perceptions were insightful, except that the way they stated the insight allowed it to apply only in the instance of guilt. Based on my foregoing argument that fault had not been fully internalized by blues singers to the degree that it displaced the feeling of sin with that of guilt, it is necessary to conclude that it was the quest for divine justification and not simply the escape of self-adjudication that was evidenced in Smith's blues.

The blues singers' principle of truth was similar. It too seemed to offer them not escape from guilt but actual divine justification. "Some people think that the blues is something that is evil—I don't," said Henry

Townsend. "If the blues is delivered in the truth, which most of them are, . . . if I sing the blues and tell the truth, what have I done? What have I committed? I haven't lied."[102] Townsend was seemingly on the verge of giving the Sermon on the Mount its ultimate blues interpretation by articulating, connotatively, the meaning of truth, the highest value in the blues. This interpretation would have been that, not only did God "forgive a black man most anything he do" and "take care of old folks and fools," but blessed are those who bear no false witness and bare the truth. That from their blues podium singers preached and confessed the truth appears to have provided them with a sense of divine justification.

Despite the attempts of blues singers to use the persona of the martyr in order to assure themselves of partial (if not total) divine justification, the beliefs and maxims from their cultural bible were ultimately unconvincing even to themselves. To illustrate, by way of "Fool's Blues," Smith said he was told that "God takes care of old folks and fools" but that since he had been born God must have changed his rules. No matter how radically blues singers criticized churchgoers for their hypocrisy and self-righteousness, they could not escape their own Christian indoctrination resulting from having been raised in the church and having received continued criticism from church folks regarding the blues being evil. Externally the blues ethic of truth was axiomatic, but the eye of the high God, embodied in Christian doctrine, turned out to be the ultimate source of measuring evil.

Given the overbearance of Christian doctrine and indoctrination in blues singers' lives, it is not surprising that Blind Lemon Jefferson derived some justification from his maintenance of a kind of churchly morality. Jefferson, as Rubin Lacy recalled it, refused to play his guitar on Sunday, no matter how much money he was offered. "I seed a fellow offer him $20 to play him one song one morning," said Lacy. "Shook his head . . . he say, 'I couldn' play it if you gave me $200. I need the money, but I couldn't play it. My mother always taught me not to play on Sunday for nobody.'" Lacy, obviously feeling justified for other reasons, volunteered: "I'll play it. I might as well play it on a Sunday as play it on a Monday."[103] It was evidently this rule that Jefferson sang about in his "Chock House Blues." He said he had a woman for every night of the work week but saved Saturday to "sweeten up" and Sunday to take his woman to Sunday school. "She's a fine looking fair brown," he sang, "but she ain't never learned Lemon's rule." Dinah Washington once maintained such a rule, as reported in a newspaper piece titled "New Dinah Washington: She Sings Sundays Now":

Washington—Dinah Washington, dynamic delineator of songs and unchallenged "Queen of the juke boxes," broke with her oldest personal tradition [when] she agreed to open a one-week engagement at Lou and Alex night club here Sunday night.

The objection to Sunday openings on Dinah's part originally stemmed from her years as a gospel singer with the famed Roberta Martin group. As she put it, "There was just something in me that rebelled at the thought of a Sunday opening, with all its attendant thrills, even though I often have to work on Sunday in the theatres and night clubs."

As a result of this feeling the singer has steadfastly side-stepped Sunday openings until it has become an obsession almost amounting to superstition.[104]

The sincere effort of Jefferson and Washington not to sing the blues on Sunday, not to "serve two masters" (even if it meant choosing the blues over the church), seemed to offer them some sense of divine justification.

Blues singers probably were not cognizant of the psychological conflict they experienced in trying to balance their blues justifications and church indoctrination, so they went on confidently positing their exonerative beliefs and maxims, such as "Blues ain't nothin' but a good man feelin' bad" or "Blues ain't nothing but the facts of life." The justification here, elaborated on by blues singer Van Hunt, was that the blues and singing the blues were natural, unpreventable, and justifiable occurrences. "The blues is something," said Hunt. "Oh, Lord, you don't care, you get to the point, you give up and don't care for nothing. Right along in there, you got the blues. . . . The blues is a feeling that can't nobody do nothing with, it's a thing that will get on you. . . . It's a good feeling and it's a sad feeling and it's a sort of low down feeling. Now that's deep, deep inward, see, and it's got to—you can't push it or you can't shove it—it's got to die down itself for you just to feel like normal again. And it's a striking thing, it will strike you when you are not thinking of it or nothing of the kind."[105]

Occasionally a preacher, particularly one like Rubin Lacy who was once a blues singer, loaned some theological validity to the blues justifications. Lacy claimed to have had more blues since he had been preaching than he ever had when he was playing the blues.[106] "What is the blues? Who has the blues?" asked Lacy. He answered, "Sometimes the best Christian in the world have the blues quicker than a sinner do, 'cause the average sinner ain't got nothing to worry about. . . . But a Christian is obliged to certain things and obligated not to do certain things. That sometimes cause a Christian to take the blues. What is the blues, then? It's a worried mind."[107] Thus, Willie Thomas, believing blues to be in no way contradictory to the nature of God, contended that when church folk sang "Lord, have mercy, save poor me," they were actually singing the blues—in church![108] Similarly, John Lee Hooker concluded that when the spirituals were created they were created "on the blues side." It was due to their kinship, said Hooker, that he quit singing spirituals and started singing the blues.[109] John Cephas said of his grandfather, who was not a blues singer but who loved the blues, that had he not had some favor in God's eyes he would not have been "elected" to live to the age of one hundred and two.[110]

Another exonerative belief fashioned in the face of church folks' accusations was that God was the bearer of the blues singers' musical gifts. Van Hunt perceived her ability to sing blues to be a gift from God.[111] Blind James Brewer similarly claimed that, "God give me this talent and he knew before I came into this world what I was goin' to make out of this talent."[112] Archie Edwards recalled that the first prayer he ever prayed was, "Lord, let me play the guitar like these old-timers"; and the Lord delivered, he said.[113] Willie Thomas further justified playing the blues by suggesting that the talent was one God gave to blacks, because of their oppression, and not to whites. "The white man could get education and he could learn to read a note, and the Negro couldn't," said Thomas. "All he had to get for his music what God give him in his heart. . . . And he didn't get that from the white man; God give it to him."[114] The same justification was implied in saxophonist Earl Bostic's decision to stick with music rather than enter the ministry, despite the disparaging letter he received from his former professor at Langston University criticizing his new hit blues, "Barfly Baby." When he first entered the Oklahoma college, Bostic was planning on a preaching career, but abandoned it after it was clear that his special talent was in the area of music.[115]

Neither was there anything inherently evil about the music of the blues. Blues singers understood well that gospel music—for instance the songs of Thomas Dorsey and Robert Wilkins—were little more than religious lyrics set to blues music. Flora Molton actually recalled a woman bishop in a Holiness church who gave blues songs new words. "It's Tight Like That," she exemplified, became "He Was Done Like That."[116] "Blues is so close to religious music that you can play a blues in the church now and they think's one of them good old swingin' hymns," said bluesman Lowell Fulson. "All you have to do is just keep out 'baby,' and that other sweet stuff you put in there."[117] In fact, the blues was so closely related to religious music that many blues singers also sang spirituals and gospel songs—Bessie Smith, Memphis Minnie, Josh White, and many more. Two excellent examples are Son House's recording of the spiritual "John the Revelator" and Brownie McGhee's and Sonny Terry's recording of the spiritual "Twelve Gates to the City."

Even after he had given up the blues to become a preacher, Robert Wilkins offered some justification for playing the blues. He said that when playing the blues he never lived a fast life, that blues was just a way of earning a living.[118] No doubt it was a justification used by other blues singers as well. It was reported in 1944 by the *State Press*, a black-owned newspaper published in Little Rock, Arkansas, that blues singer Miss Rhapsody was upset with the portrayal of blues musicians as "fast." The article said, "the race conscious lady freezes when people 'type' blues singers as vulgar, cheap, cussing pistol packing mamas who live the lives off stage of women they sing about." It went on, "She hopes that presently the public will give an artist her recognition when she chirps blues notes at the mike and let her walk off the stage into her other private life, without being 'classed' for the song she has just sung."[119] Clyde Bernhardt, one of the musicians in Ma Rainey's band, wanted the blues mother to be remembered in this way. He said she never cursed and was always more of a spiritual person who was very active in church work than a person in show business.[120]

Although Ma Rainey, like so many other blues singers, probably felt "justified" in singing the blues, the fact remains that she re-joined the church just before her death. As church folk would say, she became "converted." If blues singers did not actually feel that something was missing from their lives due to their consciousness of sin, then often they succumbed to the pressures of the church faithful, who looked disparagingly on the blues and "blues life." As Elizabeth Cotten, of North Carolina, explained: "When I learned how to play my guitar, I began to play, as my deacon used to call then, the worldly songs—the blues.... Then I joined

the church, and they told me I couldn't play those worldly songs and serve
God. I had to serve God or the devil, one. . . . I decided to stop playing the
worldly songs."[121]

The proof that there existed a conflict within blues singers regarding
the good or evil nature of the blues was documented in the stories they
told. The conversion of Thomas Dorsey was one of many narratives about
singers whose reasoning discerned nothing disapproving about the blues,
but whose consciousness of sin along with pressures from the church
faithful steered them back "home." Dorsey admitted, on the one hand,
that he started writing gospel songs due to "a definite spiritual change." On
the other hand, he claimed never to have harbored inner discordance when
he sang the blues. Even following his return to the church, he still
considered blues to be "good music." "I'm a good church man," he said,
"but I don't put the blues away." Convinced that blues had just as good
a message as gospel, Dorsey remained in the gospel music profession, he
said, only because of his success.[122] His statement to the musicians gathered
in Cincinnati for the 1951 annual National Convention of Gospel Choirs
and Choruses subtly illustrated this ambiguity in that, as the closing
sentence alludes, he was making a good living off of gospel. Regarding
performers "jazzing and swinging" the religious music he helped popular-
ize, Dorsey said: "If the words are not clearly heard, much of today's
gospel music can be confused with the 'blues.' We sincerely hope that this
bad practice will cease now. Let us always, please, keep our gospel music
as it was intended—a music of reverence and worship. Gospel music has
had greater increase in usage than any other music during the last ten
years."[123] That Dorsey stopped singing the blues, contrary to what he said
about singing gospel for only financial reasons, was evidence that some
indwelling struggle had in fact existed and was resolved only by means of
his conversion. "I know why they stop singing the blues," unriddled Little
Jr. Parker, "their conscience troubles them."[124] Their consciousness of sin,
resulting from their religious indoctrination, convicts them.

THE BLUES SINGER AS A PRODIGAL

After all that has been said about the theologies of the blues, if there
remains a single reason with which the Oliverians could persist in saying
that blues was devoid of spiritual values and lay beyond the enclave of
Christian influence, the response was stated by James Baldwin. "It is not
too much to say that whoever wishes to become a truly moral human being

. . . must first divorce himself from all the prohibitions, crimes, and hypocrisies of the Christian church."[125] Brought up in the church and having divorced themselves from it, later to return, the prodigal sons and daughters of the blues were on a moral sojourn during which they carried on their own rite and ritual recollecting their religious upbringing. To understand that "blues life" was narrative in this way and to view that narrative as a process of moral maturity, is to emancipate the blues from the accusation of being evil. The narrative "process" of the blues was *beyond* good and evil.

St. Clair Drake and Horace Cayton said, in a section of their 1945 study of black Chicago titled "Prodigal Sons and Daughters," that most African Americans were familiar with this theological scheme and the ritual requirements for salvation.[126] Keil also recognized that there was a "strong prodigal-son pattern" that allowed people to move from a secular role to the sacred role without any difficulty.[127] Jeff Titon agreed, saying that many blues singers went on to become preachers, thus "acting out the parable of the Prodigal Son."[128] Within the "prodigal" cycle, conversion was always an option. As Little Hat Jones sang in "Little Hat Blues," one year he may get tired of singing "Our Father kingdom come," but another year he just might be heard singing "Lord let thy will be done." Gatemouth Moore, speaking as a preacher and former blues singer, noted this very thing. "I've seen it through the years, the same people that heard me sing the blues go to church to hear me preach. I see the same faces. I know them, for they used to hear me sing blues, now they're in church with me. . . . And just time makes the difference, that's all."[129]

That this ethic of "blues life" (an ethic of survival turned ethic of redemption) was narrative in nature was quite natural, for African people have always been a storied people. As practicing preachers and gospel singers, former blues singers undoubtedly turned to their life experiences to tell the story of their repentance and redemption. One such narrative was lived out by Charley "Papa" Patton. Raised in a church where his father was a religious elder, Patton remained marginally involved in the church during his entire blues life. Even though he occasionally preached, performed spirituals in the church, and recorded religious songs alongside the blues, he made a decisive turn to the church when he sensed his encroaching death in 1934. According to his niece, he began preaching all week and died not long afterwards.[130]

As the "prodigal son" story was lived out in the black community, often the blues singer returned "home" to become a preacher. Robert Wilkins, for instance, left for Memphis in 1915 where he played blues with the likes of Patton and Son House. Although Wilkins never lived a fast life, he chose not to raise his children up under the "blues life"; so he returned to the church and in 1950 was ordained a minister in the Church of God in Christ.[131] To illustrate the point, following his conversion, Wilkins's blues "That's No Way to Get Along" (recorded in Memphis in 1928) was reworded and recorded in 1964 under the title "The Prodigal Son."

Blues singer Tommy Johnson did not live long enough to complete his cycle and tell his story, but his brother, Rev. LaDell Johnson, did. Tired of living a "devil's life," Johnson decided to stop playing the blues and return to the church, even though he had just bought a new guitar two weeks earlier. Recalling the last night he played the blues, Johnson said he returned home, hung his guitar against the wall, and got in bed to go to sleep; but the devil kept awakening him with the sound of that last blues he played. This worried him so much that he got up and put his guitar face-up on the floor so he could see from where the sound was coming. Only after he fell asleep again did the music recommence, sounding just like that last blues he played. This time when he awoke he turned the guitar face-down on its strings. But when the music woke him up again the guitar had been turned face up. Frustrated, he pushed the instrument under his bed again. When he arose that morning he told his wife that he had given up the blues. He was so serious about his decision that he sold that two-week-old seventy-five-dollar guitar for a mere five dollars just to get rid of it. That was around 1918. His calling to preach did not come until about six years later, when one day he was out laying his beans. He said the Holy Spirit came to him and he heard a voice commanding him to go and preach the holy word. He became a Sanctified preacher in Jackson, Mississippi, in 1924.[132]

The narratives of this cultural bible were uncountable. Moody Jones's story was another example. He broke with the blues to become a pastor of a Sanctified church as early as 1955.[133] J. B. Lenoir became a preacher like his father and brother in Monticello, Mississippi,[134] and Blind Willie McTell renounced the blues around 1957 to answer the call to preach.[135] Flora Molton, raised the daughter of a Virginia preacher, later relinquished the blues to preach in a Holiness church.[136] Nehemiah "Skip" James, son of a Baptist preacher, eventually returned to the church to become an ordained minister in 1942. He put down his blues guitar and picked up gospel singing, accompanying himself on the piano.[137] South Carolinian Gary Davis, who returned to the church an ordained minister in 1933, sang religious songs up until his death in 1972.[138] Lizzie Miles did not become a preacher when she stopped singing the classic blues in 1959, but she did, true to her Catholic upbringing, become somewhat of a religious recluse. "I have chosen to live a life of a nun," said Miles, "not a modern one, but an old-fashioned Godly one and have given up the outside world. I take part in nothing. I only attend church and spend the rest of my time in prayers for these troubled times all over the world, making penance for my sins and trying to serve God as I should. It is my way of thanking Him for all His wonderful blessings."[139]

In the African-American religious tradition, the prodigal son or daughter returned home was not only expected to tell the story of their sojourn but to authenticate their conversion by telling their "story within the story." In the real-life narratives of former "blues people," the correlative "story within the story" was often a dramatic conversion experience. When former blues musician Gatemouth Moore returned to the church a preacher in 1949, he told the "story within the story" that centered around his having been a longtime featured attraction at a Chicago nightclub. One night, Moore proceeded to the stage to sing but when he opened his mouth there was silence. Again, he storied, he went to the stage to sing but not a sound could be made. A third time he went to the stage and this time, to his own surprise, there issued forth a church song. "I was converted in a nightclub," he confessed.[140]

Often the dramatic conversion experience of former "blues people" transpired on the brink of personal, near fatal, tragedy, as was the case with Rubin Lacy, the son of an African Methodist Episcopal minister. During his "blues life," Lacy criticized religious hypocrisy, such as in "Ham Hound Crave," in which he attacked the "dirty deacon" for taking his gal. But all that changed when he returned to the church. In 1932, he said, he was working at a sawmill in Mississippi and was seriously injured. Upon striking the ground he heard a voice warning him that the next time he would die. When he recovered from his injury, he proceeded to the nearby Missionary Baptist church and professed his calling to preach. He traded away his blues guitar for a ministry of pastoring and preaching throughout Mississippi.[141]

Jack Harp relinquished his "blues life" to return to the church around 1958. Conversion for him commenced with his giving up cigarettes, which he evidently believed were killing him. Several times a day Harp went out onto his porch for a smoke, until one day he heard a voice decreeing, "You smoked your last cigarette." From that time onward, he and his wife held prayer meetings in their home on Wednesday and Friday nights, until on one Sunday he was "saved." He testified as to having seen the Holy Spirit descending from atop their Christmas tree amidst its silver twinkle. Then and there he received Spirit baptism, and he later went on to become a minister. No longer could he sing the blues, Harp said. "If I'm saved and sanctified and sing the blues, I'm not clean."[142]

Most prodigal "blues people" who had not yet returned home to share their stories and the stories within their stories, eventually would; for the church was the place of their upbringing and (according to the cultural expectations) their fate. Tommy McClennan, in "I'm a Guitar King," said he was going to sing the blues everywhere he went until he got back in the "territory'." That he was speaking of returning to the church was evident when he said his mother warned him that he was "'most too old" and not to forget that he had a soul. Shaky Jake had promised that he would retire from singing the blues to become a preacher,[143] while Son Thomas only hinted as to his eventual return. "Well I hadn't made up my mind to join a church," said Thomas, "I always say when I join the church, I would lay all them blues aside. Probably quit playing the guitar period because if you playing spirituals and used to play blues, the next thing you know the devil git in you and you gonna start right back playing the blues. I always say if I ever join the church, I'm gonna let all that go."[144] Thomas also claimed to have known a forty-year-old bluesman who said he was going to "juke" for forty more years and then he was going to join the church.[145]

Former blues singers who became preachers or gospel singers acquiesced the vantage point of privity into the process of moral maturity. Living the life of the blues taught them to come to grips with the reality of existence in their black and blue cosmos. Now privy to what they perceived to be a greater truth, none other than the former blues singer could "tell the story" of their own prodigality and reveal the prodigality (the hypocrisy and self-righteousness) of the church faithful. "I used to be a famous blues singer," Rev. Lacy exhorted his congregation, "and I told more truth in my blues than the average person tells in his church songs."[146]

CHAPTER THREE

THE THEODICIES
OF THE BLUES

nvironmental disruptions were not perceived as being "evil" until they adversely affected human interests, particularly the interests of the oppressed who already faced the preponderance of moral evil in the world. For some people, personal sickness might have been more of a theodical problem than suffering caused by natural disasters,[1] but not among peoples of African descent for whom life evolved around community as much or more than around the individual. When black sharecroppers and migrant workers of the postbellum South witnessed the great damage spring floods caused their community's meager dwellings, they were often moved to croon the blues like Sippie Wallace in "The Flood Blues." Feeling that there was no other choice but to call on the good Lord, Wallace said that the water was rising and "people" were fleeing for the hills; "Lord, the water will obey," she sang, "if you just say 'be still'." Lonnie Johnson, in "St. Louis Cyclone Blues," also implied that the Lord was an all-knowing and all-powerful good God. He said the shack in which they were living reeled and rocked but never fell, and that the way they were spared "nobody but the Lord can tell." Thus, in the light of the existence of an all-powerful, all-knowing, and all-good God, who could have simply spoken to the waters and they would have obeyed, why the suffering of the oppressed was not arrested or at least lessened created the "problem of evil" that lead to the discourse of "theodicy" in the blues—provisional answers to the question of how an all-knowing and all-powerful good God permitted evil and suffering to exist in God's created world.

Now that I have shown that there were mythologies of the blues, beneath which rubric were theologies of the blues, I will demonstrate that blues singers reflected both on the cause of evil and on the nature of suffering and that, as a musical response to these kinds of reflections, the blues owes much of its religious nature to its discourse of theodicy. To discover and document the theodicies of the blues—explanations for the existence of evil in a world created by the good Lord—is to show that the blues was theistic rather than atheistic and that the ethos of blues was thoroughly religious. Blues singers' theodicies were essentially demonstrations of their religious belief, functioning for the purpose of self-reassurance that the existence of evil did not negate the existence of God.

Theologian James Cone seemed to think that the blues was not created to address the theodicy problem. "What is the explanation of black suffering in the blues?" he asked. "It is important to observe that the blues, like the spirituals, were not written or sung for the purpose of answering the 'problem of evil.' They merely describe the reality of black suffering without seeking to devise philosophical solutions for the problem of absurdity."[2] I am arguing that the blues were sung in part to answer the "problem of evil," and Lawrence Levine made an observation that helps support my perspective. Levine recognized that within the blues gathering, as within the black church gathering, "common problems" were enunciated and understood and often the "seeds of a solution" were suggested.[3] In carrying this observation further, I am identifying the paramount "common problem" addressed in blues as the "theodicy problem" and contending that seeds of solution to this problem were in fact suggested. These solutions were suggested in the context of a community of "blues people" that helped absorb the grief of its members through the rite and ritual of the gathering. Thus, "blues people" did more than merely describe the reality of black suffering; they actually devised provisional philosophical solutions to render evil and suffering comprehensible.

While Cone and I at least agree that the blues is theological, Paul Garon's surrealist reading of the blues, as I detailed in the last chapter, stands in the greatest tension with our perspective, insofar as he saw "blues people" as not only abandoning the church but religion altogether.[4] Cone's claim that the blues was theological at least would allow him to reconsider the possibility of blues being theodical. Garon's contention that blues was not even theological amounted to his unquestionable claim that blues was anti-theodical:

> The blues critique, emphatically materialist, is directed not against the heavenly abstractions (God, Jesus, the Holy Ghost) but against the hypocrisy and pretention of the pompous self-appointed "representatives" of God on earth. Nothing would be more false, however, than to suggest that the blues is therefore not opposed to religion as such, but only to this or that organized religious institution, or (still worse) to suggest that the blues itself is some sort of "secular religion." . . . The blues does not intervene on the theological plane with the obsolete tools of rationalism or in the name of some empty "humanism." On the contrary, it enters the fray wholeheart-edly *on the side of Evil*. The "Devil's music" is the denunciation of everything religion stands for and the glorification of everything religion condemns. . . . The blues is uncompromis-ingly atheistic. It has no interest in the systems of divine reward or punishment: it holds out for "paradise now."[5]

As I said in my introduction, for Garon to call the blues "devil's music" and then to celebrate it was seemingly an attempt to use the designation in a metaphorical sense, where the principle of evil is viewed as the motive force of historical progress. But his attempt to use the blues as such a metaphor was fuddled by his failure to recognize the so-called "atheism" of the blues as nothing more than a polemical moment for "blues people" to stand in opposition to a history of oppression by white "theists" (Christians), a polemical moment that by no means precluded blues being religious and possibly theodical. Contrary to Garon's claims, the blues critique was theological (doubtless rational), was certainly critical of the heavenly abstractions, and was specifically critical of the institution of Christianity. Blues was critical of these and yet remained theistic. Blues may have entered the fray, as Garon argued, "on the side of evil," but in no other way than in the metaphorical sense. As I will explain, using Jungian analysis, "blues people" sought wholeness that was attained through imperfection. Neither was blues the "devil's music" (a designa-tion of the "sanctified" of the Holiness-Pentecostal movement), and it was by no means irreligious. As I illustrated in the last chapter and will continue to demonstrate, "blues people" were naught but victims and pilgrims.

Blues might have been "atheistic," as Garon also argued, but again not in the way that he was thinking. Rather, the "problem of evil" partly resulted in "blues people" ignoring the God they perceive ignored them and fashioning a new god. This "new god" had something to do with what the late African-American literary critic Larry Neal aptly named the "blues god." Neal said, "The blues god is an attempt to isolate the blues element as an ancestral force, as the major ancestral force of the Afro-American. What I always say about the blues god is that it was the god that survived the middle passage."[6]

THE BLUES GOD

Persons who protest against God because the world neglects to manifest God's work both materially in their lives and historically as human life unfolds, existentialist Albert Camus called "metaphysical rebels"[7] and philosophical theologian Kenneth Surin "protest atheists."[8] Simultaneously rejecting their own mortality while refusing to recognize the God that compels them to subsist in the condition of suffering and evil, these rebels are not atheists in the conventional sense, said Camus; they are inevitably blasphemers in the pursuit of discovering a "new god."[9] Paul Oliver unknowingly stumbled on blues singers' prayerful petitions to this "new god" when analyzing Victoria Spivey's "Christmas Mornin' Blues." Spivey asked Santa Claus to please hear her plea and bring her nothing but, she sang, "my daddy back to me." Oliver's comment was that Spivey's plea was, in effect, a prayer directed not to God but to "a deity personified by Santa Claus."[10] After citing several other blues lyrics that thematized Christmas, Oliver concluded that Santa Claus was "a God-substitute."[11] This "God-substitute," this "new god"—the "blues god"—was not the intolerant God of Protestant puritanism that paradoxically tolerated racial oppression and ecclesial hypocrisy, states of affairs against which the "protest atheists" of the blues rebelled.

The thought of Carl Jung on "the Self"—the archetype of wholeness whose nature it is to unite opposites—is very useful in trying to comprehend why "blues people" found it necessary to discover a "new god." This is especially the case since Jung's theories were closely aligned with the African worldview because of his attempt to comprehend the holistic nature of the cosmos,[12] an effort that led him to analyze the mythological figure of the trickster-god.[13] Jungian scholar John Sanford explained that the traditional Christian attitude, as mediated through the church, has been too intolerant. "It has refused to accept the shadow side of the personality and has rejected the dark side of the Self. It has insisted upon an impossible standard of perfection and has not acknowledged the necessity, even value, of a wholeness that comes about through imperfection, not through perfection."[14] In other words, there must be an attempt to integrate into the human consciousness all (including "evil") belonging to its essential wholeness that has been rejected and repressed.[15] While folklorist Newbell Niles Puckett did not have this insight, he did recognize its effect, which was especially true of "blues people." He said that blacks generally accepted the doctrines of Christianity while continuing to live according to conflicting secular mores and that sometimes they expanded the activities of God to explain certain phenomena not specifically addressed in the Bible.[16] Puckett also commented, obviously about "blues people," that biblical personages were summoned through conjuration to help in daily "petty" and even "unholy" affairs.[17] Like Oliver, who spoke of a God-substitute, Puckett neglected to realize that this god of expanded activities was a god that more closely approximated the integration of good and evil.

Even though overshadowed by the dualism or semi-dualism implied by the Adamic myth, the "blues god" approached monism, the integration of good and evil, for a fairly obvious reason. The "blues god" and the devil of African-American depictions were, in personality, the African trickster-god bifurcated. As a result, the "blues god" was not all good and the devil was not all bad. To this extent, Zora Neale Hurston was correct that "the Negro has not been christianized as extensively as is generally believed. The great masses are still standing before their pagan altars and calling old gods by a new name."[18] The "blues god" came close to being that old god, Legba, called by a new name, but the dualism of Christianity seemed to have left its deep impression. "The Lord," as petitioned by the blues singer, was also an amalgamation of the *loas*. As LeRoi Jones (Amiri Baraka) commented, "Social demeanor as a basic indication of spiritual worth is not everybody's idea. Sexual intercourse, for instance, is not thought filthy by a great many gods. It was possible to be quite promiscuous, if it came to that, and still be a person capable of 'being moved by the spirit.' But in postbellum Negro society, Christianity did begin to assume the spirituality of the social register; the Church became an institution through which, quite sophisticatedly, secular distinction was bestowed."[19] "Blues people" leaned toward monism where the "blues god" has much of the character of the

African trickster, whose synchronous duplicity made him responsible for good and evil; but they tended toward dualism by still shifting blame onto the devil—in personality, the frightful side of the bifurcated trickster-god.

Because the unity of opposites (such as good and evil) was an essential aspect of wholeness to the African psyche and worldview, the exclusion of so-called "evil," according to Jung, meant that it had to be manifested elsewhere.[20] Due to the repression of "evil" in the Christian religion, evil was typically manifested as sensuality and sexuality in worship itself. Cone keenly recognized that those who did not experience the free acceptance of sexuality in the blues gathering on Saturday nights expressed it subliminally in the context of song and sermon on Sunday mornings.[21] Albert Murray concurred in identifying similarities between the most lascivious dance movements associated with the blues gathering and the movements that occur when church worshipers "shout" until possessed by the Holy Spirit.[22] Blues singers themselves astutely distinguished this, which is why they returned criticism at church folks' suggestion that the blues was evil because of its "dancing." As Charlie Nickerson pointed out in his blues "Round and Round," a preacher will stand in the pulpit "bobbing up and down" and sisters will be in the "amen corner" singing "let's go round and round."

The moral dichotomy of good and evil was too reductive. Restoring wholeness and balance in the lives of the disinherited was the work of the "blues god," as evidenced by the success the blues has had in blurring the psychically unhealthy boundaries between the sacred and the nonsacred. Josh White could sing "some black snake's been suckin' my rider's tongue" and move right into "just a closer walk with thee" with no contradiction, wrote Don McLean. "The cigarette tucked behind his ear could curl a set of satan's horns or a blue halo over Josh's head, and they both seemed to belong."[23] Little Hat Jones sang in "Hurry Blues" that sometimes you will hear him singing "Nearer My God to Thee" and other times "Sweet Atlanta Blues."

"The Self does include 'the devil' as the personification for what has hitherto been rejected," explained Sanford, "but can ultimately belong to the whole."[24] Once integrated into the wholeness of the Self, what may otherwise be evil is evil no longer.[25] One moves beyond good and evil. Hence, if the blues entered the fray "on the side of evil," as Garon contended, it was only as the Self attempted to attain wholeness that was achieved through imperfection rather than through perfection. Because the church refused to accept the shadow side of God, which was the permissive side of God's personality, "blues people" had to fashion a "new god"—the "blues god," whose personality was the positive element of the bifurcated African trickster-god. Had the "blues god" actually been the old god Legba with a new name—"Lord"—the integration of good and evil would have precluded the theodicy question. But because of the omnipresence of the Adamic myth, this "God-substitute" (as Oliver called him) was still a good God; and why evil and suffering still existed when he could simply speak to the waters and they would obey, preserved the "problem of evil" and the discourse of theodicy in the blues.

THE THEODICIES OF THE BLUES

Like all theodicies,[26] the theodicies of the blues were fundamentally historic because they comprised a synthesis of (1) the introspection of personal narrative reflections, (2) the experience of historical reality that evidenced the problem of evil and suffering, and (3) the sacred history of biblical narratives learned from the church. A brief examination of each of these will reveal more about the character of the "blues god" as a "new god" with deep historical roots—more about, as Zora Neale Hurston put it, an essentially old god called by a new name.

The personal narrative reflections of blues singers were social, as were their theodicies, so that the "I" in the blues was communal. Universally, from the moment a movement of rebellion commences, explained Albert Camus, the experience of suffering was seen as collective: "*I* rebel—therefore *we* exist."[27] The collectivism of this individual experience was further illuminated in blues singer John Lee Hooker's philosophy of the blues, which put to rest Oliver's claim that blues singers spoke for themselves and did not identify with others.[28] Hooker said, "It's not the manner that I had the hardships that a lot of people had throughout the South and other cities throughout the country, but I do know what they went through. My mother, my daddy and my stepfather, they told me these things and I know that they must have went through those things themselves. And so when you gets the feelin[g] it's not only what happened to you—it's what happened to your fore-parents and other people. And that's what makes the blues."[29] This explains how St. Louis Jimmy actually composed blues based on the experiences of his peers. "I looked at other people's troubles and I writes from that," he said, "and I writes from my own troubles."[30] The historical nature of the blues mood was also recognized by Boogie Woogie Red, who said that "blues have been goin' on for centuries and centuries," concluding that, "they was always here."[31] Blues as a historical continuum stemming back centuries and centuries is what Houston Baker defined as "blues' awesome genealogy," his definition of Neal's "blues god"—that "ancestral force" Neal said survived the middle passage.[32]

Regarding the second historical element in the theodicies of the blues—historical reality that evidences the "problem of evil"—Baker is again helpful. He brought the blues concretely into historical context by equating them with the size and arrangement of the homes in which the disinherited of southern black communities have traditionally dwelled. He suggested that these homes signify the "economics of slavery"—the continuing impoverishment of black people in this country. "The nonmonetary, 'mythical' dimensions that arise from the size and arrangements of black homes are supplied by an Afro-American expressiveness that can be succinctly denoted as 'blues'."[33] In fact, the "economics of slavery," as symbolized by the meager size and crowded arrangement of black dwellings, was specifically alluded to in the blues, as were the difficulties the impoverished had with the "rent man" when unable to pay their bills. In "Hard Time Blues" Francis Scrapper Blackwell complained about it. He said that times had gotten so hard that he could not find a job and every morning the rent man was grabbing his doorknob. Leroy Carr, Blackwell's longtime blues partner, also knew about impoverishment and the irateness of the "rent man." In "Tight Time Blues" he said he had no shoes or clothes and that the "house rent man" had thrown his belongings outdoors.

The theodicies of the blues were historical, thirdly, in that they were biblically derived. Foremost were the "reap what you sow" and "work of the devil" theodicies. The blues tended not to advance the "otherworldly" or "end-of-time" (eschatological) theodicies prevalent in the black church— for instance, "the harder the cross the brighter the crown" and "the first shall be last" theodicies. Peetie Wheatstraw's use of the latter phrase in his "First and Last Blues," which he said he got from the "good book," was an experiential and not an eschatological formula and thus was not used as theodicy. For instance, in "The First Shall Be Last and the Last Shall Be First," Wheatstraw said, after singing that title phrase, that all he was trying to do was figure out which woman treated him the worst. The blues tended not to advance the eschatological theodicies because "blues people" either found the possibility of future reward not to be comforting in their present situation of suffering or they simply distrusted the promise of future reward, given the severe contradictions of ecclesial hypocrisy, racial oppression, and unrealized biblical assurances.

The "work of the devil" theodicy in the blues was characteristically biblical and non-eschatological. In retort to those who have claimed that the blues was atheistic, this demonology implied theism, namely, religious dualism. It also implied its own "theodicy question": "Why does God not kill the devil?" William Barton, compiler of *Old Plantation Hymns* (1895), suggested that blacks would not have wanted the devil dead even if God could have killed him. "Satan is a decided convenience," he said. "It is always possible to load upon him what else must be a weight upon the conscience."[34] Barton was equating African Americans' use of the devil with Christians' use of the doctrine of "original sin" as a last-resort explanation for all that goes wrong in the world. Since moral evil, as opposed to natural evil (environmental cataclysms), was the paramount theodical concern of "blues people," the devil was a convenient and customary means for them to explain the existence of certain kinds of travail in their lives.

Thus, one answer to the "problem of evil," as bluesman Peg Leg Howell proved, was to posit an evil god. Believing in an evil god that coexisted with a good god meant that evil did not have to be justified as the work of the God worshipped, even though the consequence was the undermining of the notion of God's omnipotence. Unsure of the real reasons for his hardships, Howell considered bad luck and divine retribution as possible explanations before blaming all of his problems on the devil. First he blamed "fate." He said he was just a worried "old rounder" with a troubled mind and that his being "bundled up from hardship" was because fate had been unkind. Then Howell blamed himself, alluding to the "reap what you sow" theodicy that we will discuss shortly. He said it was because he would not listen to the advice of his mother or his dad that his "reckless living" had put him in bad. Finally, the devil became the decided convenience. Howell said he could not shun the devil because he stayed right by his side; "there is no way to cheat him," he sang, "I'm so dissatisfied."

For the above three reasons—the historicity of personal reflection, of reality evidencing the "problem of evil," and of biblical orthodoxy—the most favored of the blues theodicies was also fundamentally historic. It was the "reap what you sow" theodicy.

THE "REAP WHAT YOU SOW" THEODICY

There was an old saying uttered by a Mississippi ex-slave that, "what goes over the devil's backbone is bound to pass under his stomach."[35] However, church folks, with whom "blues people" engaged in constant polemic, generally disagreed with the "blues belief" that the devil occasionally caused their ill-fated suffering. As blues scholar Albert Murray explained, they insisted that the misfortunes blues singers had were none other than divine retribution for their living outside God's protection as mediated through the church.[36] In this church-blues polemic, the extent to which the blues succumbed to the theological beliefs of the church and to which "blues life" subsisted in its shadow was evidenced by the prevalence of the biblical "reap what you sow" theodicy in blues lyrics. Blues scholar Robert Palmer did not call it a theodicy, but he did recognize the phrase to be a "biblical injunction."[37] Regardless of whether this "injunction" was actually a theodicy as used in the Bible, it was often used as a theodicy in the blues. By means of this theodicy, blues singers explained numerous of their afflictions as resulting essentially from the very sins the church accused them of: drinking, gambling, womanizing, and generally living a life of reckless abandon.

Despite the biblical teachings in the gospels that disallowed the equating of misfortune and sin,[38] it was apparent in numerous blues, such as Jimmy Oden's "Going Down Slow," that the "reap what you sow" theodicy was closely connected to the belief that "sin is sickness." It is because human beings enter the world of ethical concern and discourse through a juridical and penal view of history, where violated interdicts are expected to be satisfied only by punishment (revenge or suffering), that suffering can take on the role of a symptom of sin.[39] It is in this respect that we can understand Oden in "Going Down Slow." With his health failing him after living a life of "fun," Oden asked someone to please write his mother and tell her the shape he was in and to pray for him and forgive him for his sin. Tell her not to send a doctor, he sang, "doctor can't do no good; it's all my fault, didn't do things I should." Associating sin with the evil of sickness, as Oden did, was a rationalization that often resulted from the human attempt to exonerate God from responsibility for suffering and evil. Consequently, it was believed that to avoid suffering, even suffering accrued from just punishment, sin had to be avoided through ritual pardon—purification, justification, or mercy.[40] Rituals of purification were principally viewed as falling within the domain of the church, although the most diverse justifications were posited, as I illustrated in the previous chapter, in the theologies of the blues. Pleas for mercy were common in both the church and the blues, but in Oden's blues it was his mother who was asked to mediate between the blues and the church.

No matter in what language the aphorism "sin is sickness" was couched, that human beings "reap what they sow" was probably the most typical of the blues theodicies. For example, Big Bill Broonzy, in his "Key to the Highway," poetically pictured himself riding off into a Texas sunset in order to inquire of the creator what sin begot his troubles. He said he was going to west Texas, "down behind the sun," to ask the good Lord, "What evil have I done?"

Although the "reap" theodicy was often indirectly implied, as in Broonzy's blues, it was just as frequently stated explicitly, a quite poignant example being Skip James's "Cypress Grove Blues." Reflecting on death and the balmy place of burial, James said that the old people had told him what he "never did know": "The good book declares we got to reap just what we sow." In "Dirty Deal Blues," Robert Wilkins (who later became a preacher) identified the "reap" theodicy as a universal law inherent to God's creation. He said he was so glad that the "whole round world" did know that "every living creature" has to reap just what they sow. Tommy Johnson, in "Bye-Bye Blues," confidently exhorted that those who did not reap what they sowed at present would eventually pay the price for their transgressions. The good book says "You reap just what you sow; going to reap it now," he sang, "or baby reap it by-and-by." Maggie Jones, in "Never Drive a Beggar from Your Door," waxed churchy as she preached a moralistic interpretation of the "reap" theodicy. She said that anyone who sees a blind man on the street should remember that he too has to eat. "No one ever knows what the future has in store," she sang; "never drive a beggar from your door."

The "reap what you sow" theodicy often appeared in the blues of those who had been or shortly would be brought before the county judge for possible sentencing and imprisonment. In Washboard Sam's "I'm On My Way Blues," the theodicy of "reaping" was paraphrased with language correlative to Sam's brush with the law. Arrested, sentenced, and imprisoned, Sam said that even though he was not a bad fellow the judge sent him away. Vowing never to forget that day, Sam sang, "Yeah the good book do tell you that crime do not pay." Similarly worried over going to the courthouse in the morning where he might be given a prison term (or "the chair!"), Jesse James sang from experience, in "Lonesome Day Blues," when he warned others of the *law* of "reaping." Having traveled widely "around the territor'," James sang: "You hear me talking to you, you got to reap what you sow."

Often the phrase "You're going to reap what you sow" was not theodicy but threat; at least, it was not fully theodicy in that it was principally threat. This was true not only in the blues but in the spirituals as well—for instance, the spiritual "You're Going to Reap Just What You Sow." Generally, when the blues singer was speaking about herself or himself—"I am reaping"—it was theodicy; when warning a lover who was mistreating them—"You will reap"—it was almost always threat. In connection with the latter, when the blues singer was explaining past or existent suffering, it was theodicy; when forecasting suffering, it was generally threat. Alberta Hunter, in "Down Hearted Blues," clearly expressed more threat than theodicy. She said to her man, after he mistreated her and drove her away from his "door," that the good book says "You've got to reap just what you sow." Eddie Jones (Guitar Slim) essentially repeated this threat to his woman in his "Reap What You Sow" of 1953, as did Clifford Gibson in "Stop Your Rambling" and Frank Stokes in "Mistreatin' Blues."

That this "biblical injunction" was used as threat in the foregoing instances is evidenced even better in its paraphrase in Jimmy Reed's "Bright Lights, Big City" of 1961. Reed said to his "pretty baby" that she was going to need his help some day and that she was going to wish she had listened to "some of those things I say." Robert Johnson's "If I Had Possession Over Judgment Day" illustrated that it was the "I" of threat (and guilt) and not the "before thee" of theodicy (and the consciousness of sin) that characterized these verses. He said that if he had possession over judgment day his woman would not even have the moral right to pray. He would pass that judgment, he said, because upon peering into the future as far as he could see, he saw that another man got his woman "and lonesome blues got me." Alluding to the biblical injunction regarding the behavior of his woman, Johnson said to himself as he walked away, "your trouble going to come some day."

Trixie Smith, in "Love Me Like You Used To," couched her threat in "honey." She pleaded with her man for him to come back and love her like he used to because she thought about him everyday. Then she warned,

"You reap just what you sow in the sweet by-and-by and be sorry that you went away." Otis Rush's "Reap What You Sow" of 1969 was similar. His warning to his woman that "There was going to be judgment in the morning," and that "it will all come back on you" was threat, not theodicy, despite his positing of the "reap" injunction. "You're gonna be mournin' in the morning," he sang, "'cause you made your bed that way." Tampa Red, in "Crying Won't Help You," also warned his woman to "watch those seeds you scatter," because everything would "come back home" and she would reap just what she sowed. Joe McCoy, in "Evil Devil Woman Blues," also warned, "it's coming home to you," because his woman threw him outdoors when he had done so much for her. Hattie McDaniel, in her classic blues, "I Thought I'd Do It," sang the same thing. In thinking about her man's "evil deeds," his sowing "all them evil seeds," she decided he might as well not whimper and whine because she had accepted him back for the last time. "So as ye sow," she sang, "so shall ye reap." These threats, clearly not theodicies, were indistinct from Sonny Boy Williamson saying to his woman, in "Your Funeral and My Trial," that she had better treat him better or it would be her funeral and his trial. Lucille Bogan was just as bold in "You Got to Die Some Day!" She said to her man that he may be beautiful but he has got to die some day; "and you going to reap what you sow for treating me this a-way."

Blues singers also cited the "reap" theodicy as a warning to their lovers to remain faithful to them. In his "Pea Vine Blues," Charley "Papa" Patton (who both sang blues and preached) cautioned his woman in one verse about what the good book said about "reaping" in order to, in the next verse, exhort her to behave as a good woman should: "Stop your way of living and you won't have to cry no more." Blind Boy Fuller, in "Rag, Mama, Rag," similarly recollected the disloyalty of his ex-sweetheart. He said he would not have thought his "baby" would have treated him so, but she let another man sneak in her back door. "Mind mama what you sow," he sang, "you got to reap just what you sow." In "Wild Cow Blues," Joe Williams only alluded to the "reap" theodicy, but his admonition to his "wild cow" was unambiguous as he pleaded for her to cease her infidelity. He said she could read out of her hymn book and her Bible too and could fall down on her knees, he sang, "ask the good Lord to help you." She was going to need his help some day, he sang; "you won't quit your running around woman, please quit your lowdown ways." The above lines in Williams's blues could have been theodicy, but a similar verse by Blind

Willie McTell, in "Southern Can Mama," was clearly threat. McTell said to his woman that she could read her Bible "from Revelation back to Genesee," but that if she got "crooked," he sang, "your southern can belongs to me."

The difference between Williams's "Wild Cow Blues" and McTell's "Southern Can Mama" is that Williams seemed emotionally hurt while McTell seemed angry. Charlie Patton also seemed hurt and not angry in "Pea Vine Blues." He said he cried all night and was not going to cry anymore. Then, putting judgment outside of himself, he sang that "the good book tell us you got to reap just what you sow." The most poignant and prayerful use of the "reap" theodicy, more touching than Patton's plea, actually was posited in the form of a loving warning. Robert Wilkins, in his "Dirty Deal Blues," could not help from crying because he had to let his pretty woman go. He said he was so glad that the whole round world knows that every living creature "reap just what they sow." But his woman acted as though she did not know this, which was the reason Wilkins was crying to the Lord to let her "reap no bad seed." "Please God," he pleaded, "make my woman reap righteous seed."

In contrast to Wilkins's poignant positing of the "reap" theodicy, its most riveting expression came in the last verse of Bertha Henderson's "Lead Hearted Blues," where she alluded that having the blues was itself a "reaping." "Lord, Lord," she sang, "can't rest no place I go; blues is driving me crazy, must be reaping what I sow." Washboard Sam's "Evil Blues" implied a similar notion. The worst feeling Sam ever had was those "old evil blues" that treated him "awful bad." Having had the blues all night, Sam said he would be glad when morning came so he could have a talk with a gypsy to see what evil he had done.

Crimes, infidelity, a life of reckless abandon—these were some of the transgressions for which "blues people," due to a consciousness of sin, believed they reaped divine retribution. Suffering was justifiable to them for reasons of divine retribution, not, as in the church, for redemption or pedagogy. What was never manifested in the blues was the use of the "reap" theodicy to explain the evil heaped upon black people for their alleged crime of being black. This significantly undermines Oliver's contention that the number of blues oriented toward protest is relatively small because of black people's naive acceptance of their racial stereotypes.[41]

THE QUESTION OF DIVINE RACISM

Pursuant to the question raised by William R. Jones in *Is God a White Racist?* (1973), Oliver, really to substantiate his claim that blacks accepted their racial stereotypes, would have to show logically that "blues people" believed God to be a "white racist." This was the subtle implication in his claim that "blues people" perceived blacks to be evil because their color was the basis of their troubles. "He begins to resent the colour of his people," said Oliver, "the colour of his own skin which he feels is burned to the depths of his very being, to his black soul."[42] There are actually very few blues that Oliver could possibly cite to make such a notion hold. Alice Moore's "Black and Evil Blues" might be one. Moore could be interpreted as equating blackness with evil when seemingly questioning why the good Lord would create her black if black was evil. "I'm black and I'm evil and I did not make myself," she declared. Though Moore was merely complaining that whenever she got a man a "no-good woman" stole him away, Oliver could have taken literally her grievance, "I believe to my soul the Lord has got a curse on me."

However, for every blues Oliver could possibly cite to argue that "blues people" submissively accepted their racial stereotypes and, by implication, their destitute lot in life, there were many more verses repudiating his claim. Both Leroy Carr, in "Good Woman Blues," and Lucille Bogan, in "Pig Iron Sally," resorted to humor to contest such notions. "*They* say black is evil and *they* don't mean you no good," sang Carr; "but I would not quit my black woman baby if I could." Bogan, with her own comic logic, discredited the moot point that good or evil was in any respect correlated to racial hue. "*Some folks* say black is evil but I will tell the world *they're* wrong," she sang; "because I'm a sealskin brown and I been evil ever since I been born."

Even folklorist Newbell Niles Puckett, whose work was fraught with racial biases, recognized the humor in lyrics that seemed to reveal a lack of race pride: "Although the Negro in his rhymes sometimes declares definitely, 'I wouldn' marry a black gal,' he also sings, 'I wouldn' marry that yellow Nigger gal,' or 'I wouldn' marry that white Nigger gal,' and decides with emphasis, 'I'd rather be a Nigger than a po' white man,' showing clearly that race-pride had not been completely blanched."[43] Indeed, before "blues people" would accept the idea that "black is evil," they would, without really (or outwardly) passing judgment on the good Lord, redress him regarding the obvious imbalance in justice. The most comfortable means for them to raise this "theodicy question" (for which, I have said, no answer was ever given) was to mask their queries in the garb of wit and waggery. This was an epitomizing of the old adage, "We laugh to keep from crying"—or, as Lonnie Lomax put it in "Laplegged Drunk Again," "I smile to keep from crying."

What Puckett attempted to explain, Houston Baker called the "mastery of form"—the masterful manipulation of the minstrel mask that commenced a tradition of discursive modernism apart from the traditional suppression of black personhood.[44] While whites were hearing and loving the stereotypic sounds they expected from blacks, what was really "sounding" from behind the mask was a voice that was beginning to challenge the traditional discourse of lordship and bondage controlled by the "master."[45] Oliver was misled, duped, as were all whites who heard the familiar sounds of minstrelsy and feared not that "the blacks" were getting out of "place."[46]

When whites heard blacks laughing—those familiar minstrel sounds— they were also comforted that blacks were happy-go-lucky folks who accepted their racial stereotypes. But black people laughed, as the old blues adage was stated, because "we have learned to swallow our tears and live on the salt." Oliver should have known that the correlate to "When you see me laughing, I'm laughing to keep from crying" was "When you think I'm laughing, I'm crying all the time."[47] This was what Langston Hughes was trying to get at when he said the blues always impressed him as being sadder than the spirituals because their sadness was not softened with tears but was hardened with laughter.[48]

Perhaps no blues singer learned to laugh while living on the salt of his tears better than J. T. "Funny Papa" Smith. Because Smith was commenting on a propagation made by a preacher (the whipping boy of the blues singer's polemics), his "Howling Wolf Blues" was likely a questioning and denial of "divine racism" rather than an acceptance of racial stereotypes. Smith said the preacher told him that God would forgive a black man "most anything he do"; "I ain't black but I'm dark-complexioned," he sang, "look like he ought to forgive me too." But God, it seemed, did not treat him as though he were "humankind," but wanted him to be a "prowler" and a "howling wolf" all the time. Again, in "Fool's Blues," Smith seemed to employ buffoonery not simply to blame God for failing him, as Oliver claimed,[49] but to mask his solemn pondering of the "problem of evil." He said that some people told him "God takes care of old folks and fools" but that since he had been born God must have changed his rules. "I used to ask a question then answer that question myself," he sang, "about when I was born wonder was there any more mercy left." Then came a most powerful resolution to that "question of evil," masked with familiar minstrel sounds. Smith said that it must be the devil he was serving, that it could not be Jesus Christ, because he asked Jesus to "save" him and yet it looked like Christ was trying to take his life.

In light of the malignity mercilessly heaped upon the black disinherited, Sam Chatman also found it more palatable to flow with the spirit of the "blues god" and laugh in order to keep from crying. He said God made us all, some he made at night, which was why he did not take time to make us all white. When God made him, he continued, the moon was giving light and he was so sorry God did not finish him up white. When God made people he did "pretty well," concluded Chatman; but when God made a "jet black nigger," he sang, he made some "hell." The seriousness of these verses was further masked by the familiar minstrel sounds of the chorus that separated them: "I'm bound to change my name, I have to paint my face so I won't be kin to that Ethiopian race."

This last piece, in particular, raised the controversial issue regarding the theatrical performance of the blues. Concluding that there was something repugnant about blues singers publicly parading modified versions of their integral selves for the entertainment of their oppressors, Baker initially likened such theatricality to blacks donning the minstrel mask.[50] Later he seemed to have resolved that this was but the "mastery of form"— the manipulation of the minstrel mask for the purpose of challenging the traditional discourse of lordship and bondage controlled by the "master." Under the cover of stereotypic "sounds," blues singers such as Chatman and Smith laughed away notions of "divine racism." The question "Is God a white racist?" was never a question of theodicy.

THE BLUES INSURRECTION AGAINST THE HEAVENS

While "blues people" drunkenly laughed away notions of "divine racism," they often engaged in sober insurrection against the heavens. Son House's insurrection against his condition of oppression, as illustrated in his denial of the otherworldly abstractions, is exemplary. There "ain't" no heaven and "ain't" no burning hell, he sang; and where he will be going when he dies, "can't nobody tell." John Lee Hooker borrowed this verse from Son House's "My Black Mama" (part one) in his "Burnin' Hell." Everybody was talking about the burning hell, he sang; "when I die, where I go, can't nobody tell."

Can this apparent insurrection against the heavens really be considered "sober" since there was an obvious symbiotic relationship between the blues and jokelore? For instance, in Frank Stokes's popular blues, "You Shall," the humorous adaptation of the Lord's Prayer was strikingly similar to its use in an old southern joke. Stokes sang, "Oh well it's our Father who art in heaven; the preacher owed me ten dollars, he paid me seven." He concluded, "Thy kingdom come, thy will be done; if I hadn't took the seven Lord I wouldn't have gotten none." Compared to the identical use of the Lord's Prayer in a comic tale of the African-American tradition,[51] how can we be certain there was an "insurrection" and that the insurrection was "sober?"

In this southern tale, a rich man, who was ill and approaching his last days, was telling his wife Jennie how he remained so affluent, and how she, after his passing, could remain so by shrewdly withholding a fraction of servant John's pay. The rich man said, "the prayer I'm gonna teach you, Jenny, is the Lord's Prayer that I live by, I pay my servants by; and they always was pleased." He said, "Our Father which art in heaven, if ya owe John ten dollars, don't pay him but seven. Thy Kingdom come, let thy will be done; if he don't take that, Jenny, don't give him none." Blues singer Nolan Welsh, in "St. Peter Blues," seemed also to be joking when he said that when he got to heaven he was going to sit down in St. Peter's chair and ask him, "Look a-here St. Peter, you got any white lightning here?"

So, how serious were many of the blues singers about this insurrection against the heavens? Obviously they were serious enough for Garon, Oliver, and other blues scholars (who were lulled into a stupor by the familiar minstrel sounds) to conclude that the blues was an atheistic denial of the "heavenly abstractions." However, that which might have appeared to be complete denial of the "heavenly abstractions" was actually, according to Albert Camus, defiance. "The rebel defies more than he denies," said the existentialist philosopher. "Originally, at least, he does not suppress God; he merely talks to Him as an equal. But it is not polite dialogue. It is a polemic animated by the desire to conquer. . . . His insurrection against his condition becomes an unlimited campaign against the heavens."[52] Garon and Oliver were unable to see beneath the mask of minstrelsy and realize that this laughing was, as Hughes put it, tears hardened by laughter. It was a mask that veiled their sober pondering of the "problem of evil."

Typically the blues defiance of the heavens resolved to disbelief in the biblical "kingdom on earth as in heaven" idea (which also could be at the root of Stokes's "You Shall"). Jesse James enunciated a complete distrust in the "kingdom come" prayer in light of the immensity of suffering he had witnessed among his people throughout the land. He sang, in "Lonesome Day Blues," that he had been all throughout the nation and around "the territor'" but he found no heaven on earth, he sang, "Lord nowhere I go."

Though Skip James was born the son of a Baptist preacher and would one day become a preacher himself, he nonetheless recognized, in "Hard Time Killin' Floor Blues," that life for black people was unpredictable. He said people were just drifting from door to door; they could find no heaven, he sang, "I don't care where they go." When blues singers said people could not find any heaven anywhere they went, it rang true to "blues people," because having the blues was the antithesis of what heaven represented. Having the blues was "hell." Sara Martin sang, in her "Death Sting Me Blues," that "Blues is like the devil, they'll have me hell-bound too." Lonnie Johnson, in "Devil's Got the Blues," said the blues is like the devil because it comes on you "like a spell"; it will leave a heart full of trouble and a mind full of "hell."

Blues singers' defiant denial of the "heaven" and "kingdom come" abstractions (which accounted for the absence of eschatological theodicies in the blues) was typically followed by a search to acquire or construct a heaven of their own—a heaven where the spirit of the "blues god" could reign. To this end, Texas Alexander was wistful in "Yellow Girl Blues." In order to gather a cluster of brown-skinned women around his throne, he decided to get himself a "heaven kingdom" of his own. Henry Thomas, in "Texas Worried Blues," was no less ambitious in desiring to procure the salvific glories of the "heaven" and "kingdom come" ideas *now,* in an eschatological present. In order to give all "good-time women" a home, Thomas decided, like Alexander, that he was going to build himself a heaven of his own. Bessie Smith sang the same thing from a female perspective in her "Workhouse Blues," except that she produced more constructive sounds from behind the mask. She wished she had a heaven of her own so she could give all the "poor girls" a long happy home.

Although Smith's wish was not really humorous, Oliver saw beneath

Alexander's and Thomas's mask of wit and waggery long enough to conclude that blues singers' sardonic treatment of heaven was disregard for the beliefs, prayers, symbols, and rituals of the church.[53] However, he did not see beneath the mask deeply enough to recognize that the defiant denial of a transcendent heaven did not account for the atheism he was arguing for. The denial of a transcendent heaven only accounted for the rejection of the eschatological "harder the cross/brighter the crown" theodicy, and the reality of a living hell only accounted for the repudiation of the "kingdom come" theodicy.

While many "blues people" dreamed about having a heaven of their own where people of the opposite sex would cluster around their thrones, most considered themselves to be blessed by the "blues god" just to have one good woman or one good man. While a "no-good" woman could cause a man to "fall," as Robert Johnson sang in "Drunken Hearted Man," a good woman, according to Louie Lasky, was "salvation" to a weary soul.

In "Teasin' Brown Blues," Lasky confessed that he was crazy about his woman's "jellyroll" because, he sang, "I know you got something will send salvation to your soul." Bessie Smith also implied that as long as one's lover was a "good soul" then sexual love was open to be healing and salvific. In "Take Me for a Buggy Ride," she said to her man that he was no "creature" but a good old soul who "done sent salvation," she sang, "to my very soul." Charlie Spand sang praises about his supposed "salvation" in "Back to the Woods Blues." "Just as sure as the good Lord sits in the heaven above," he sang, "now your life ain't all pleasure unless you be with that one you love." Amos Easton's "No Woman No Nickel" was similar, in that he requested of the "blues god" a good woman just like Eve to help resurrect him once again. He petitioned the "Lord" to look down on him and pity his "worried cares" and to help him to "rise once more," under the condition that he change his "free-hearted ways." Making the Adam and Eve narrative into a paradigm of moral sexual companionship (monogamy), Easton continued his prayer to the permissive "blues god," asking for just one friend to keep him from feeling so sad. "Lord," he said, "you know I want a friend like the one that Adam had." Louise Johnson alluded, in "Long Way From Home," that the bestowal of divine mercy was the gift of a "good man," let us presume, a man like Adam. She awoke one morning with the blues all round her bed because, she said, she never had a good man to ease her "worried head." She moaned, "Lord have mercy on me . . . , mercy's all I need." Praying to the "blues god" in her

"Praying Blues," Trixie Smith also pleaded for mercy. "Lord, Lord, kindly hear my pleas, please send me a man that wants nobody else but me."

While Easton made the Adam and Eve narrative into a paradigm of moral sexual companionship, George Torey transformed the platonic love of Protestant puritanism into a sexual love sacralized by the more tolerant "blues god." In "Lonesome Man Blues," Torey, using biblical language in a poetry of erotic love, said that if he had wings he would heist those wings and fly like Noah's dove and light on the woman he loved.

Without referring directly to the Adam and Eve narrative, many other blues singers alluded to the idea that Eve was good (rather than evil) and that sexual love was a salvific gift of the "blues god" capable of driving the blues away. In his meditative "Talking to Myself," Blind Willie McTell negotiated with the "blues god" about just such "salvation." McTell sang, "Good Lord, good Lord, send me an angel down"; and the "blues god" responded, "Can't spare you no angel but I'll swear I'll send you a teasing brown." In "Broke Down Engine Blues," McTell prayed to the "blues god" for the return of his "good gal," his Eve. He said he went to his "praying ground" and fell on his bended knees; "I ain't crying for no religion," he sang, "Lordy give me back my good gal please." McTell concluded that, if the Lord would give him back his woman, he would not worry him "no more." Henry Townsend, in "Henry's Worried Blues," asked the Lord for the same "favor"; but Texas Alexander, in "Justice Blues," was even more impolite in his dialogue. Alexander said that he cried, "Lord, my father, Lord, [thy] kingdom come," insisting that the Lord should send his woman back and then (and only then) "thy will be done." The Georgia Pine Boy negotiated similarly. He said he was going up to heaven to talk with "the good Lord above" and that if the good Lord would not give him an angel then he would settle for the return of the one he loved. Will Batts, in "Highway No. 61 Blues" (later recorded by Jack Kelly in 1933), was quite serious when he said he was going home to sit down and read his Bible and then ask the good Lord, "Give me back my baby, if you please." Louie Laskie had the audacity to say that he was going to ask the good Lord to send him an angel down, but that if she was not a good one he would keep his "teasing brown." Walter Vincson told his male listeners that if they had a woman that "don't do kind" they should pray to the good Lord to get her off their minds.

The "blues god" knows what a good man and a good woman need to be resurrected from the "hell" of the blues brought on by moral evil. In the words of Tommie Bradley, they needed to "shake that thing." As long as one's lover was a "good old sole" then as far as the permissive and merciful "blues god" was concerned—as far as "the Lord," the *loas* was/were concerned—sexual love was open to be salvific. While "blues people" responded to the "problem of evil" by denying the "heaven" and "king-dom come" abstractions and seeking to construct a heaven of their own where the spirit of the "blues god" could reign, their actual rebellion against the oppressive conditions of evil involved equally impolite criticism of the white oppressor and the church, and flight from both.

THE BLUES REBELLION AGAINST OPPRESSION

We previously observed a few instances in which having the blues was consequential of divine retribution—"reaping what you sow." However, as Ma Rainey's "Slave to the Blues" illustrates, having the blues was homologous to being "chained to the blues," which was an imagery correlative to the definition of the blues as "secular spirituals" (slave songs) and the definition of the economic system that produced the blues as postbellum slavery. Personifying the blues as the oppressor, Rainey asked if she, a good-hearted woman, would have to die a slave. "Do you hear me screaming," she sang, "you're going to take me to my grave." Other blues singers, in their "secular spirituals," likewise likened their institutionalized disinheritance unto slavery. Walter Davis sang in "Travelin' This Lone-some Road" that, "The racket that I am now in, Lord, it make [for] white slavery." Migrant worker Washboard Sam sang, in his "I've Been Treated Wrong," that he had been "treated like an orphan and . . . worked like a slave."

Blues singers often referred to the cultural evil of racial discrimina-tion and poverty (evils of helplessness, depravity, and separation) by using the code word "bad luck"—that linguistic minstrel mask that deceptively implied mere superstition. The "bad luck" faced by blacks of this era was essentially the continued legacy of slavery. Whether one was a sharecrop-per, tenant farmer, or migrant worker on the logging or turpentine camps, or whether one was working in the cotton fields, sugar plantations, or coal mines in the convict lease system, the black laborer was essentially a legal slave, a live tool. Although the convict lease system was outlawed by Congress in 1887, it and other forms of peonage continued in the form of the chain gangs and prison farms. One of myriad kinds and cases, discovered in 1947, involved a black woman held in slavery for twenty-nine years by a missionary school teacher. The teacher befriended the black youth when she was the missionary's fifteen-year-old maid in Athens, Alabama. Because of an indiscretion the young maid was involved in, no doubt at the initiation of the woman's husband, the missionary teacher (turned slave mistress) threatened to expose the "sin" and institutionalize the youth.[54]

This kind of "bad luck" was so distressing to blues singer Eddie Boyd that he, like novelist James Baldwin, eventually left the country, settling in Sweden. Tired of unjust, selective prosecution, Boyd could take no more. He had been accused of peeping even though he could not see, begging though he could not raise his hand, avoiding his tax payments though he had no money, dodging child support though he had no children, murdering someone though he never harmed a soul, and forgery though he could not write his name. "Bad luck, bad luck is killin' me," he sang; "I just can't stand no more of this third degree."

In the blues, reference to the white oppressor was typically masked by referring to them generically as "they." In our earlier discussion of the question of "divine racism," the oppressor was the "they" and "some folk" that Leroy Carr and Lucille Bogan reproached when singing, "*They* say black is evil" (Carr) and "*Some folk* say black is evil" (Bogan). *They* were also the "they" that a blues theodicist redressed in this verse: "*They* say we are the Lord's children, I don't say that ain't true; but if we are the same like each other, . . . why do *they* treat me like *they* do?"[55]

That the suffering caused by the "they" was evil and to be resisted was implied in the system of retaliation instituted by the victims of antebellum slavery and maintained by the hostages of postbellum peonage. Masking their racial concerns behind economic and class ones, by referring to the *they* as "you rich people," J. B. Lenoir, in "Everybody Wants to Know," warned that the poor would get their labor's just reward by whatever means necessary. "You rich people listen," he sang, "you better listen real deep; we poor peoples get hungry, we gonna get some food to eat." Leroy Carr was even more vehement and vengeful than Lenoir in "Tight Time Blues," vowing to "get even" with the landlord who evicted him and discarded his belongings outdoors.

As previously illustrated in our discussion of the "reap what you sow" theodicy, there were various types of suffering that "blues people" willingly endured, in that they assumed sole responsibility for their transgressions and divine retribution. However, an isolated examination of such protest blues as the above by Boyd, Bogan, Carr, and Lenoir leads us to believe that "blues people" instinctively rejected racial oppression without positing any theodicy to exonerate God of the potential accusation of being a "white racist." In reproaching racial oppression, then, it appeared that "blues people" stumbled into an epistemological crisis where their conventional biblical theodicies gave way to a secular theodicy, a crisis where the means by which "blues people" distinguished between suffering that should be personally endured or divinely eliminated was reduced to a secular decision. This "secular theodicy"[56] was what William R. Jones called "humanocentric theism" in his book *Is God a White Racist?*[57] For "blues people" to be secular theodicists or humanocentric theists was for them to believe that the created, rather than the creator, were the ultimate arbiters of what was morally good or evil in the world, a possibility that roughly coincides with Paul Ricoeur's notion of "man the measure," who not only self-adjudicates through the internalization of sin (which is guilt) but who turns those internalized standards outward and, while still ignoring God, adjudicates the evil of the other. In humanocentric theism, God is exonerated of any moral evil because God's sovereignty is separated from human history. This invalidates "divine racism" and any theological attempts of the oppressors to justify racialism.[58] It thus appeared that blues made theodicy a secular problem, as illustrated in Pleasant Joe's "Sawmill Blues." Here, "Cousin Joe" was not accusing God of creating a world in which moral and natural evil prevailed; rather (without theological explication), he was reviling the oppressor for constructing a "civilization" in which one race of people suffered the preponderance of moral evil. How else could he have so audaciously sung, "I didn't build this world but I sure can tear it down?"[59]

To our surprise, however, a close reading of the expanse of blues lyrics reveals, after all, a possible biblical theodicy for the evil of racial oppression—that is, an explanation that exonerated God from the possible accusation of being a "white racist." It was a theodicy in which the white oppressor was perceived as being the devil, who made life for black people a living hell. Mississippi ex-slave Charlie Davenport said the Ku Klux Klan was "sure enough devils walking the earth seeking what they could devour."[60] Another Mississippi ex-slave, James Lucas, similarly claimed, "Them Ku Kluxes was the devil,"[61] the same thing another ex-slave said about a particular slave master—"a devil on earth."[62] Another ex-slave said the

KKK were "raising the devil on every hand."[63] Still another said, "Yes, in them days it was hell without fires. This is one reason why I believe in a hell. I don't believe a just God is going to take no such man as that into his kingdom."[64]

Even when "blues people" caused suffering in their own families and communities by venting their anxieties therein, they often pointed to the demonic oppression of Kluxism, Nordism, Bilboism (whatever name one wants to call the white supremacist ideology) as largely responsible. Blues singer John Sellers attested to this in his psychology of "hard times," which identified such problems as alcohol and drug abuse and family and community violence as the result of the poverty in which blacks were enslaved. "Now take most blues singers—they have lived rough lives, or have been rough in their lives . . . because hard struggles and hard times—it makes people hard and mean towards each other regardless of who they are," said Sellers. "If you have poverty you must have hard times and roughness—because if you come up a rough way it makes you tough. . . . Poverty makes you rough . . . and that's part of the blues."[65] This was what Lonnie Johnson seemed to be alluding to in "Devil's Got the Blues," when he sang about the adverse social effects of having the blues. "The blues," he sang, "will drive you to drink and murder and spend the rest of your life in jail." As the victim of such mistreatment by her man, Minnie Wallace realized that it was the oppressive world that caused him to vent pent-up frustrations in a way that was destructive to his loved ones. In her blues titled "The Cockeyed World," she sang: "This old cockeyed world will make your good man treat you mean." This notion of the oppressor-devil possibly sheds some light on the meaning of similar verses in Joe Williams's "Mr. Devil Blues" and Robert Johnson's "Me and the Devil Blues." Williams blamed the "mean old devil" for causing him to leave his family and his happy home, and Johnson alluded that it was "the devil" that caused him to beat his woman until he was "satisfied."

That the oppression resulting in adverse social behavior among the oppressed was neither to be blamed on God nor patiently endured but eliminated was further evident in blues that thematized the idea of *escape*. Oppressive racialism together with repressive puritanism drove blues singers to flight. Reflecting on the "road" motif in such blues by Floyd Jones as "Dark Road" and "On the Road Again," Justin O'Brien defined the flight of being "on the road" as both a frame of mind and a fate that at different times represented both exile and refuge.[66] Crooning wearily his

"C and A Blues," Peetie Wheatstraw knew just how the blues could drive a man away. He said the blues usually made a woman just "hang her head and cry" while it made a man "catch him a train and ride." While some bluesmen also claimed to have hung their heads and cried, Texan Maggie Jones, in her "North Bound Blues," demonstrated that blueswomen also caught trains to ride. She herself decided to go north where she could be free, free of hardships such as those in Tennessee; north, she sang, where there were no Jim Crow laws like down in Arkansas. Complaining about the bigotry of the Jim Crow South, perhaps in his home state of Alabama, Cow Cow Davenport planned to join his kindred exiles and refugees in northward flight. "I'm tired of this . . . Jim Crow town," he sang; "doggone my black soul, I'm sweet Chicago bound."[67]

The most spiritually pernicious aspect of the postbellum slave system was not that it caused exiled "blues people" to take refuge in northward flight or that it caused a community to turn destructively upon itself, but that the inconsistency between the teachings of the church and its actual involvement in promoting evil and suffering in the world was capable of driving the spirit of prayer into "exile." Son House sermonized in his "Preachin' the Blues" that, when up in his room he bowed down to pray, the blues came along and drove his spirit away. In "Catfish Blues," Robert Petway avowed to this very occurrence in a similar verse, but he was down at the church when he was unexpectedly called on to pray. He got on his knees and "didn't know not a word to say"—the identical experience Texas Alexander sang about in "Sittin' on a Log." Lightnin' Hopkins, in "Baby," said that though his mother told him never to forget to pray, when he did fall down on his knees he forgot just what to say and said, "Baby!"

To drive one's spirit of prayer into "exile"—which was the "theodicy problem" responsible for the evolution of the blues and its ethos of insurrection—was perhaps the most blasphemous form of evil. Taking refuge in a retreat to the periphery of Christianity, the "protest atheists" of the blues engaged in a polemic of power with the church, which was a co-conspirator of the slave system partly through the propagation of eschatological theodicy.

THE BLUES BROADSIDE UPON THE CHURCH

Akin to the absurdity of racial oppression was the perceived evil of ecclesial hypocrisy, which was also responsible for the prominence of the "problem of evil" in the minds and songs of "blues people." Oliver argued that only occasionally did the blues express belief that the church or God had failed "blues people."[68] This was true about the latter, due to their positing theodicies that exonerated God from responsibility for evil; but it was not true of the church, because blues singers did not directly equate God and the church, as Oliver obviously did. For instance, Peetie Wheatstraw, in "The Good Lawd's Children," said some of the good Lord's children are not any good; they are "the devil" because they would not help you even if they could. Some of the good Lord's children, he continued, actually kneel upon their knees and pray but serve the devil at night and the Lord at day.

Verse upon verse of blues easily could be cited to illustrate the prevalent theme of ecclesial hypocrisy. But there is a more pressing matter: the revolt of the blues against the repressiveness of Christianity and the consequential enthronement of the "blues god." Because of the lack of range in the personality and permissiveness of the God of Protestant orthodoxy, the naturally repressive nature of Christianity was an especially potent opiate insofar as it stymied the spirit of revolt in a people already abjectly oppressed. Garon was especially passionate about this matter: "The black church, in attempting to incorporate the more 'civilising' aspects of Christianity, has served the purposes of the ruling class by attempting to crush the spirit of revolt, replacing it with the doctrine of accommodation."[69] The doctrine of accommodation was essentially a theodicy that lead to quietism, which was why Garon categorically placed the black church alongside the pre-judicial southern "law." Having listened to Nietzsche—"You say you believe in the necessity of religion. Be sincere! You believe in the necessity of the police!"—Garon said that so often the institutions of the church and the law worked hand in hand in creating repressive categories in the mind and society that it is necessary to discuss them concurrently.[70]

That the hypocrisy and repression of the church drove "blues people" to take flight from these perceived evils helps substantiate my contention that they were marginal Christians "on the road"—which was both a frame of mind and a fate. During this flight, "blues people" worked through the "problem of evil" by reconstructing, in the light of their specific circumstances, certain of the biblical theodicies. Kenneth Surin would probably disagree with the latter part of my claim because of the impossibility he sees in creating a Christian account of evil without the symbols of the cross and resurrection, symbols that were absent in the blues theodicies. Claiming that conversion to faith in Christ is the sole means of solving the "problem of evil," Surin said: "Without conversion, the very *process* of seeking an answer to the question 'whence is evil?' will be undermined by the distorted thinking of a crippled intellect. For the perversion of the human will is complemented by a perversion of the memory and the intellect . . . ; and so evil . . . comes to be yet more deeply entrenched in the unconverted person's attempts to find a solution to the 'problem.'"[71] Paul Avis alluded to the same point in maintaining that the question of theodicy cannot be tackled apart from the question of atonement, nor the question of atonement apart from that of theodicy.[72]

Major Jones, author of *The Color of God* (1987), probably would agree with Surin and Avis theoretically. However, Jones's comment that no black person can "see God in clear perspective" without eventually confronting the serious questions of personhood related to being black in America[73] leads me to believe that the antithesis of Surin's and Avis's conviction might be true for those who are oppressed by the church (and the law). In terms of Avis's formulation of the atonement-theodicy problem, what Jones's comment says to me is that first and foremost the question of atonement cannot be tackled apart from the question of theodicy, and that only later, retrospectively, is an understanding of the atonement needed to bring the (still unresolved) question of theodicy into focus. To use the thought of James Cone, the position of Major Jones suggests that when the white oppressor performs evil acts against black people in God's name there may come a time when it is necessary to renounce *claims* to that "faith" in order to affirm authentic faith.[74] I contend, then, that for "blues people" the process of conversion to authentic faith comprised the type of break with "faith" that created the blues, but that "break" by no means interrupted the knowledge "blues people" had of the existence of God or Jesus Christ. I also maintain that it was from this periphery of Christianity (where *claims* to faith could be safely renounced) that the intellects of "blues people" were freed from the "perversion of the memory and intellect" of the church, enabling them to seek, out of their own unpredictable reality, an answer to the "ultimate concern" of evil's cause. This prioritizing was "idolatry," perhaps, and "blasphemy" perhaps too (from the perspective of the church), but in the words of Camus, "With rebellion, awareness is born."[75] How else could one ever arrive at the point of truly comprehending the atonement—God emptying God's self into the world to be a human being as disinherited and despised as "blues people?"

Far more than the religious songs of the church (which themselves often crippled the intellect by distorting reality), the blues addressed the truth of empirical life and caused the oppressed to acknowledge their lack of control in a world full of hard times and troubles. Former bluesman Rev. Rubin Lacy, to this effect, admonished his congregation:

> Sometimes I preach now and I get up and tell the people now that . . . I used to be a famous blues singer and I told more truth in my blues than the average person tells in his church songs. . . . The blues is just more truer than a whole lot of the church songs that people sing. Sometimes I think the average person sings a church song just for the tune, not for the words. . . . But the blues is sung not for the tune. It's sung for the words mostly. . . . Now you get out here to sing a church song about "When I take my vacation in Heaven." That couldn't be the truth. That's a lie in the church, because a vacation means to go and come. You don't take a vacation in heaven. But now if you're playing the blues, you say "I never missed my water 'til my well went dry." That's the truth. . . . That's the difference in a church song and the blues.[76]

When former "blues people," such as Rev. Lacy, made their dramatic turn toward a face-to-face relation with Christ and a vision of the atonement, the conversion of these prodigal sons and daughters had come full circle. For the abjectly oppressed, it might have been that this was the only way that their conversion could have been made complete. When former "blues people" finally turned to say "God is here with us suffering," then the turning to and facing of the atonement was imbued with the truth of life's unpredictability for the oppressed. Homage had been paid to the "blues god," the keeper of the gates, and access had been gained to the Christian high God.

SEEING GOD IN CLEAR PERSPECTIVE

The idea that the blues brought the victimized to the point where they could "see God in clear perspective" was fictionalized in Ralph Ellison's *Invisible Man*. In this "blues" novel, the protagonist, sharecropper and blues singer Jim Trueblood, awakened one morning from a salacious dream to find himself sexually atop his daughter Matty Lou, who laid asleep between her parents. The wife, Kate, roused and was as outraged as Trueblood was himself astonished and ashamed. Wounded by her physically violent reaction, Trueblood staggered from his home, hurt and humiliated, searching for a means to redemption through the local preacher. But the preacher caustically chastised him for his crime (as preachers have always chastised and rejected blues singers) and reprimanded him to go and make peace with the Lord. Unable to eat, drink, sleep, even pray (his prayers driven away by the absurdities of life), Trueblood's means to redemption came to him late one night in the form of song. Irrespective of conscious distinctions between secular and sacred musical genres, Trueblood, without moral friction, as Ellison's story went, moved fluently from singing a church song to crooning the blues:

> Finally, one night, way early in the mornin', I looks up and sees the stars and I starts singin'. I don't mean to, I didn't think 'bout it, just start singin'. I don't know what it was, some kinda church song, I guess. All I know is I *ends up* singin' the blues. I sings me some blues that night ain't never been sang before, and while I'm singin' them blues I makes up my mind that I ain't nobody but myself and ain't nothin' I can do but let whatever is gonna happen, happen. I made up my mind that I was goin' back home and face Kate; yeah, and face Matty Lou too.[77]

For literary critic Houston Baker, this passage took on dogmatic meaning. "The first unpremeditated expression that Trueblood summons is a religious song," said Baker. "But the religious system that gives birth to the song is, presumably, one in which the term 'incest' carries pejorative force. Hence, the sharecropper moves on, spontaneously, to blues."[78] From my theodical line of reasoning, the night Trueblood looked up to the stars, the mythical spirit of the "blues god" induced him to sing impulsively a blues song of archetypal dimensions: "I sings me some blues that night ain't never been sang before," he said. In his singing, Trueblood was awakened to existence: "I ain't nobody but myself." He was roused to a recognition of life's unpredictability: "ain't nothin' I can do but let whatever is gonna happen, happen." Trueblood's return home to face his wife and daughter therefore fictionalized the idea that in singing the blues—which Rev. Lacy said "is just more truer than a whole lot of the church songs"—evil may in fact become less deeply entrenched in the "unconverted" person's efforts to discover an answer to the "problem of evil."

The same thing that happened to Trueblood—being led impulsively to sing the blues—happened to Tennessee blueswoman Van Hunt. Hunt said, recalling her youthful years, "I would rather sing church songs, then I'd wind up singing what you call the blues of the day." Declared Hunt, "I didn't know at the time. I just thought, you know, I was just singing."[79] Even as an adult she used to "rest her bones" by singing and was unaware that she was into the blues. "Old man told me, say, 'Listen,' say, 'What is it you call yourself doing?' I told him, and he said, 'Well you ain't got nothing but the blues. You singing the blues. You ain't got nothing but the blues!' I said, 'What is the blues?'"[80]

This was the stubborn fact of life for black people subsisting in the hostile world of the postbellum South: life was one in which "ain't nothin' I can do but let whatever is gonna happen, happen." Only as a blues singer was Little Buddy Doyle free to come to this realization. In his "Hard Scufflin' Blues" he sang, "Good book trying to tell us where there's a will there's a way, but it seem like the many ways draining out of me more and more every day." Little Hat Jones also knew all too well, as evidenced in his "New Two Sixteen Blues": "I want somebody to tell me what 'Lord have mercy' means, so if it means anything, well Lord have mercy on me." James "Stump" Johnson similarly said that all the world was crying "mercy," but "what does mercy mean?" His old boss man, sang Johnson, "didn't have no mercy on me."

The question implied by "blues people" was not whether evil and suffering were intolerable things that ought to disprove the existence of God but that "Lord have mercy" was, given life's unpredictability, a powerless prayer and "why?" "Why?" *was* the paramount query—*the* "theodicy question." In the final analysis, "blues people" were the great forerunners of all who would later speak to the "blues god" through secular musical genres in genuine pursuit of an answer to the "question of evil": "I want somebody to tell me what 'Lord have mercy' means."

CONCLUSION

ow that I have shown that there were mythologies, theologies, and theodicies of the blues, why is it that when we listen to contemporary urban blues this rural residue of religion is essentially no longer present? This conclusion answers that question by tracing the movement of the blues from the rural South ("country blues") to the urban North ("city blues") and explaining the diminishing of the rural residue of religion in "city blues" as it evolved into modern "urban blues." I will argue that the rural folkways that were part and parcel of country blues were at first modified in the new "city" setting, subsequently subjugated and sublimated in the modern "urban" context, and then increasingly (though never fully) forgotten by succeeding generations. Essentially, I will assert, alongside the blues poet Sterling Brown, that in the city the rural folk became a "submerged proletariat" whose folk culture was suppressed in part by commercialism.[1] Thus, city and urban blues (as the offspring of country blues) reflected the conditioning of the South's rural emigrants to the city's new universe of experience: city blues represented the African American's transition from the relinquishment of old folkways to the appropriation of the new progressive mentality; and urban blues, especially from the black progressive's perspective of reading old-time religion as suppressive of intellectual Race progress, represented the liberation of African Americans from the alleged tyranny of superstition.

The paradigmatic case study for the examination of this blues continuum, country blues → city blues → urban blues, is the movement of the blues from its southern capstone and spiritual home, the Mississippi Delta, to Chicago, the blues capital of the urban North during the great black migration and beyond. To understand that the great black migration was viewed as a religious "exodus" by its northern initiators and the southern emigrants is to glean a further perspective on the traditional religious cosmology reflected in country and city blues. Concurrently, to comprehend the dynamics of the country-to-city diaspora, as examined in the Mississippi-to-Chicago migration, will be to understand why and how the rural residue of religion (mythologies, theologies, and theodicies) diminished in city and urban blues in other cities as well—Memphis, St. Louis, Detroit, Pittsburgh, New York, and so forth. Thus, before examining why country blues's residue of religion in city blues diminished as city blues developed into its urban successor, we will begin by examining the great black migration (1915–30), because the culture-shock of the new city life commenced upon the country-to-city diaspora.

THE GREAT BLACK MIGRATION

A black community has existed in Chicago since the late 1840s; the "Windy City" was a major terminus of southern blacks migrating northward, especially from Mississippi (often with stop-off points in Memphis and St. Louis). It was not until wartime, however, that the black migration from the South became a full-fledged diaspora. The variables that made it a successful dispersal of over one million blacks from the southern states northward between approximately 1915 and 1930 were myriad, but the impetus seized by the Moses of the exodus (whom, shortly, I will identify and discuss) was that social conditions and economic opportunities had deteriorated for blacks in the South between the 1880s and 1916 and a pernicious "Jim Crow" had flourished.

Of all the southern states, Jim Crow's regime was especially iniquitous and unscrupulous in the most "race-haunted" of the states, Mississippi, during the epoch Roy Wilkins termed the "lynching era" (1889–1945). The master-slave institution, hardly affected by the Civil War or Reconstruction, had reemerged on the postbellum plantation as systemic peonage for the principal purpose of economic exploitation. In an article of July 1924 published in *The Chicago Defender*, "Other Causes of Migration from Dixie," William Offord recognized that "The battle between freedom and slavery was not ended by the Emancipation Proclamation—only the method and form of slavery as a formal state of society was ended, but as a force, a power, a moral element, it was and has remained a thing to be desired by the South as much as ever. . . . The former masters have remained lords of the soil and dominate the former slaves and hold them in what is in effect abject serfdom."[2] In order for the former masters to remain lords of the soil, the Siamese twins of the southern slavocracy—Social Darwinism and Jim Crow—were called upon to find reason and means to keeping the former slaves in a state of serfdom: to relegating them to an inferior education, to denying them the vote, to restricting them to travel in the railroad "nigger cars" and the steamboat "Jim Crow stalls" and seating in the cinema "Buzzard roosts," and to sustenance in the "niggertown slums." The "niggertowns" or "darktown slums" were always located in the worst sections of town, typically the low-lying, flood-prone areas near rivers or drainage ditches. These areas, where the religious cosmology of the blues was indigenous, had minimal public services—no sewage and water systems and no paved streets, sidewalks, or lighting—services generally found in the white residential areas. As Langston Hughes concluded, "Poverty and Jim Crow are sisters under the skin."[3]

The residents of these depressed black neighborhoods were ruled by the terroristic "negro law," whose antecedent lay in the antebellum "slave code." Offord, in the above article on causes of the Dixie diaspora, explained that this "law" was intended to "maintain an attitude toward our Race which tends to and does generally preserve the relationship of master and slave as it existed in antebellum days."[4] This illegitimate form of "law" differentiated between "justice" applied to whites and to blacks. While white-on-black and black-on-black crime was neither real crime nor really punishable, black-on-white crime was viewed by whites as an unforgivable offense. Often, blacks were convicted of crimes basically because of their race. In a political cartoon published in the *Defender,* to illustrate, a white judge representing the "American Courts" was looking down at a black man and saying, "I find you guilty! First, because you were born black, and secondly because of your crime."[5]

In part for economic reasons, the most menial crimes committed by blacks (including the crime of being black) were punishable by extradition to the convict leasing system. When wealthy white landowners felt the ill effects of the dwindling labor market resulting from the great migration and there were insufficient convicts to be leased to them (in effect as slaves), all that was required to remedy the shortage was a monetary bribe and innocent black men were convicted and sentenced to a number of days or months at hard labor.[6] Still existent in many southern states during the 1920s, the convict leasing system partly explained why numerous blues lyrics reflected a fear of "the law," and why many of these particular lyrics raised the "theodicy question."

Left unarticulated, at least in recorded blues, was the utter dread of conviction in the court of "Judge Lynch," the unjust "justice" system administered by white vigilantes with the popular consent of their white communities. The most frequent verdict given by "Judge Lynch" was, as his name implied, lynching, the "white death," that which Billie Holiday sang about in her poignant "Strange Fruit." Not uncommon between 1900 and 1940 was an even more masochistic means of murder—terminal torture by public burning "at the stake." Known by whites as "negro barbecues," these "celebrations" continued until there was no more flesh left on the charred bones of the black victims.

In order to avoid these forms of "cannibalism," blacks (and blues singers) had to maintain Dixie's protocol of always deferring to whites, showing them respect and obedience even in the face of disrespect and disdain. The mask of humility, which was reflected in the lyrics (the text) of recorded country blues (but not in its texture), helped blacks to survive under this regime that at every turn severely penalized them for manifestations of racial dignity or achievement. Whites moved down the social and economic ladder, resulting in blacks being driven deeper into "the blues," but attempts by the oppressed to move up any other ladder than "Jacob's" (toward a "nigger" or "kitchen heaven") involved paramount risk.[7] Giving black children a decent education was disallowed by whites in fear that the disinherited might become discontented with their assigned "place." Likewise, it was literally life-threatening for the "ex-slaves" to be caught with publications that advocated their education and betterment—Chicago's *Defender* and the NAACP's *Crisis,* for example. One blues singer commented thus to other blues singers in a "rap session" set up by ethnomusicologist Alan Lomax in the late 1940s:

> Speakin' of the *Chicago Defender,* . . . I were in a place once
> they called Marigold, Mississippi. They had a restaurant there
> and in the back they had a room with a peephole in the door.
> I thought it was a crap game goin' on back there and I went
> back to see. . . .

And you know what they were doin' back there? They were readin' the *Chicago Defender* and had a lookout man on the door. If a white man had come in the restaurant, they'd stick the *Defender* in the stove. Burn it up. And start playin' checkers. . . . That's the way they had to smuggle the *Defender* down there. Now if they'd caught this fellow that *brought* the *Defender,* they'd have called him a bad nigger.[8]

In sum, throughout the Darwinian "Jim" era, one of the greatest influences on the country blues was that blacks were systematically relegated to this state of peonage: the overall prevention of black intellectual growth helped conserve the traditional black cosmology, which constituted the religious nature of the blues.

In addition to Darwinian "Jim" flourishing in the South and maintaining the system of share tenancy and crop liens that prevented black farmers from profiting, further impetus for the great exodus resulted from the Mexican boll weevil's assault on the South's crops. When coupled with the annual problem of spring floods, the agricultural industry suffered immense deprivation, resulting in the loss of jobs. At the other end, up North, because the war in Europe had cut off the labor of immigrants from southern, central, and eastern Europe, vacant positions in Chicago's mass production industries were just waiting to be filled by a migrating black populace. As explained by Alexander L. Jackson, columnist for *The Chicago Defender* at the time of the great migration: "The brother in the South is hearing the call of spring up North and the call seems to be irresistible. They are packing up their duds and boarding the trains from all parts of the South. The restrictions on immigration from Europe coupled with good business has brought about a scarcity of labor everywhere. The South is the only part of the country that has just raw labor, untrained and unappreciated. Northern producing centers, therefore, will be compelled to use this labor whether they prefer it or not until some change is made in the immigration law."[9]

White southerners initially saw the mass migration of blacks as a resolution to their "race problem" but soon realized that their labor pool was being drained, stolen. A political cartoon in the *Defender,* carrying the caption "Great Scot! What Have I Done," pictured a white southerner with "The South" stamped on his shirt, "The Lyncher's Rope" hung across his arm, and a newspaper in his hand bearing the headline: "Negro

Migration to the North in Full Swing. 150,000 Negro Workers Leave Southern States in Year! Cotton Supply Imperiled!"[10] While the *Defender* was encouraging the black exodus, Dixie whites attempted, with no success, to terminate it. Under the caption "Exodus Continues from South by Thousands," a staff correspondent for the *Defender* wrote: "With no hope, those of Color who have sought 'to better their condition' are bound for the 'promised land.' Resolutions passed by meeting of white men, promises and the like, many come and go—the exodus continues."[11] In a *Defender* piece titled "Why More Folks Go North," the writer explained that the southern white man wants a "beast" in the form of a man. He concluded, "No wonder the North continues to beckon and no wonder you and your sons and daughters heed the call."[12] One writer to the *Defender* in May of 1917, from Lexington, Mississippi, said that whites cared less for blacks than they did the "vilest beast."[13] The words reflected the very thoughts of blues singers, which gave impetus to their singing the blues. As one bluesman put it in the late 1940s, "Fact of the business, back not long ago, a Negro didn't mean no more to a white man *than* a mule."[14] The jazz musician Jelly Roll Morton was reputed to have said that, as whites see it, it takes ten blacks to equal one dog.[15] This was the very reason yet another Mississippian, from Greenville, wrote to the *Defender* about his desire to emigrate to Chicago: "Dear Sir," began his letter of May 1917, "I want to get my famely [family] out of this cursed southland[.] [D]own here a negro man is not good as a white man's dog."[16] Not only were whites unsuccessful at keeping blacks in the South, they were also unsuccessful at luring them back to Dixie once they had already emigrated north. During the early twenties, for instance, the Mississippi promoters of the "back to Dixie" campaign failed to lead a station full of blacks back "home" on the train that the black sophisticates of Chicago dubbed the "Plantation Special."[17]

Southern whites did not stop trying to refurbish their slave-labor pool but mobilized Dixie's journalists to counter the influence of the *Defender*. One means they employed was the political drawing, which typically contrasted the balmy and "friendly" old South with the cold and costly new North. But the editor of the *Defender* was a shrewd Race man. He had these pieces collected and reprinted in his paper for the purpose of disgracing them. One political drawing taken from the *New Orleans States,* carrying the caption "Good Times North a Myth Colored Man Finds," collapsed beneath the weighty critique of the *Defender*. To the left of the two-picture drawing was a black man relaxing on the bank of a pond, fishing and drinking brew. To the right a distressed black city-dweller was reading a newspaper, "The Chicago Pretender," containing advertisements of overpriced commodities. The unforgiving critique of the *Defender* commenced with the caption, "This Picture, Paid for by 'Blood Money' of Southerners, is Lure to Oppress You." Below the picture, an article warned African Americans to ignore the deceit of "Mr. Charlie." It read, "You know that the white man's idea of a decent, God-fearing Race man is one who does as he is told and submits to the slightest wish of a white man because he is white, and not for any good reason." It continued, "If that Southern white man could get along without you he would not be spending his money for these special messages to you. He needs you now because you are making yourself scarce. . . . Let him do the praying for once, while you rest a while and look on."[18] To this effect, another *Defender* headline appropriately read, "South Bending Knees in Plea to Halt Exodus."[19] The *Defender* also counterattacked the political cartoons printed in southern white newspapers by publishing their own drawings. One of these had a southern white writing a letter to "The Black Man Up North." It read, "Dear Sir, Come back South. We will educate you, give you plenty of work in the cotton fields and a good cabin for you and your family. Come back South. [Signed] Southern White Man." The reply to "The White Man, Down South" read, "Dear Sir:—Give me my right to vote; stop lynching; take off the Jim Crow cars; open the doors of all industries to me and treat me like a man, and I'll come back—Maybe! [Signed] The Black Man."[20]

The foregoing evidence proves that Arna Bontemps and Jack Conroy, in their book, *They Seek a City* (1945), were incorrect in claiming that the great black migration had no Moses, that it was leaderless and spontaneous.[21] If the migration was so spontaneous and leaderless, then why did blacks wait so long to leave the land of oppression? The North was no mirage to them; Chicago had long been known, especially because of the mail-order catalog of the city's Sears and Roebuck Company. Blues musicians knew the city too, if for no other reason than that the Sears catalog was advertising more than a page of guitars as early as 1897.[22] Blacks waited so long to leave the land of oppression because social movements, such as the great migration, tended not to occur spontaneously and succeed. They resulted from the availability of resources and the kind of organizational structuring that the *Defender* created at that historical moment.

Although labor agents of the railroads and steel companies recruited in the South, and personal letters from emigrants to the folks back home spoke highly of the city, it was the *Defender* that elaborated on the South's ills, articulated the goals of migration, and helped open the lines of communication between southern blacks and the North and between country bluesmen and the city's recording industry. Indeed, the *Defender* not only described itself as the defender of Race welfare and advancement,[23] it claimed outright to have initiated the great migration.[24] As a matter of fact, the *Defender* gained national prominence and circulation with its advocacy of the "Great Northern Drive" beginning around the First World War. As a result, the newspaper received uncountable letters from southern blacks desiring to emigrate to the North. One correspondent from Marcek, Mississippi, in a letter of October 1917, wrote this, following the salutation "Dear Sir": "I am a reader of your paper the Chicago Defender. After reading your writing ever[y] wek [week] I am compell[ed] & persuade[d] to say that I know you are a real man of color. . . . I wants to come to Chicago to live."[25] Another correspondent from Greenville, Mississippi, said in his letter of May 1917 that he had been reading the weekly issue of the *Defender* for five months and had decided he wanted to move to Chicago.[26]

The *Defender* was the movement's Moses, personified in its editor, Robert S. Abbott, who founded it on May 5, 1905. In the twenty-fifth anniversary issue of the *Defender,* which included an autobiographical piece by Abbott, a page-long portrait of the founder carried the caption, "Twentieth Century Moses." To this effect, Abbott wrote, "I have faithfully and diligently striven to make known and alleviate the suffering of my people. . . . I have not yielded to sentiment nor to the wishes of the pacifist, but have endeavored, by the help of God, to serve aright as He gave me the ability to see the right."[27] Though Abbott had no respect for the blues, in part because it represented the system of slavery out of which his foreparents came, he was the Moses of blues singers and would-be blues singers as well.

From the beginning, the great migration was given a religious interpretation by the movement's Moses, who saw it as an "exodus" from Pharaoh's land of oppression. Some Dixie whites were also able to interpret thus the meaning of the signs and plagues of the southern cotton plains that seemed to warn of some impending crisis. In an article titled "Why Jim Crow Is Flying North," reprinted in the *Defender* from *Collier's Weekly,* a white man named W. O. Saunders recalled hearing a black "boy" from Georgia singing this blues:

> *Boll weevil here, boll weevil there*
>
> *Boll weevil everywhere,*
>
> *Oh, Lordy, ain't I glad!*

That this blues seemed to Saunders to be a song of emancipation haunted him for years until he came to associate its singer with the masses of blacks making their exodus to the North. Essentially characterizing the boll weevil as the animal trickster of black folklore, Saunders explained: "To millions of hungry and oppressed blacks laboring for a mere subsistence on the cotton plantations of the South the invasion of the Mexican boll weevil, laying waste the acres of the plantation owners, was nothing less than an act of Providence. To these blacks, who read the Bible and believe every word of it, the plague of the boll weevil was but the hand of God laid heavily upon their taskmasters."[28] Following through with his religious reading of the great migration, Saunders concluded that compared to the homes blacks owned in the South the squalid tenements of the northern blackbelts were "very mansions in the skies."[29]

Actually, the social system in the North was not so radically different from that in the South as to denature the blues immediately of its "blue" hue and thus its attendant mythologies, theologies, and theodicies. Black migrants found that the "promised land" of the North offered them neither economic nor social equality. What the white literati of the Chicago Renaissance discovered and documented about the dour realities faced by Chicago's European-immigrant poor—its slums, severe working conditions, and anti-immigrant inclination—was even worse for the black emigrants in the years leading up to the symptomatic race riot of 1919. The novel *An Eye for an Eye* (1905), by the white lawyer Clarence Darrow—protégé of abolitionist John Brown, friend of Robert Abbott, and "defender of the man who is down"[30]—examined the favoritism the affluent received over the indigent in the judicial system; no doubt the novel signaled an even worse treatment awaiting the masses of blacks from the South. When blacks began arriving en masse in 1916, some trade unions were closed to them. The factory jobs they were able to procure during the wartime boom were still the least desirable (unskilled) positions, opportunities for advancement were nearly null, and periodic layoffs had to be contended with since blacks were always the last hired and the first fired. This might have been Big Bill Broonzy's complaint in his "Starvation Blues," recorded in Chicago in 1928, in which he complained about not having a job, money, or food. Because there was no food in his kitchen and there was a rent sign on his door, Broonzy concluded that if his luck did not improve he would be unable to stay at his home "anymore." Walter Davis drew the significant conclusion in his "Howling Wind Blues," recorded in the Windy City in 1931. He sang, "Poor people are like prisoners but they just ain't got on a ball and chain," concluding, "I do swear it's all the same." African Americans also paid higher prices for homes and rental properties than their white class-counterparts, and white landlords allowed blackbelt properties to deteriorate since the residents were essentially locked inside its color line. As an article in the *Defender* summarily put it, "Jim Crow," the southern field hand, had become the sophisticated city-dweller "James Crow."[31]

The city might have been a symbol of hope, but the bottom line was that "James Crow" made blacks sing the blues just about as quick as "Jim" did in the South. This was perhaps what blues scholar Charles Keil was alluding to when he said the characteristics of Delta blues—the heavy sound and rough intensity of drones and moans—only intensified in "citified" country blues.[32] Keil gave a further hint as to what city life was probably like for those blues singers who just arrived from the South when he said, "a bluesman in the country or for the first time coming to grips with city life sings primarily to ease his worried mind, to get things out of his system, to feel better; it is of secondary importance whether or not others are present and deriving similar satisfactions from his music."[33] It should not be surprising, then, that when Mississippi-born Sunnyland Slim moved to Chicago in 1943 he still found good reason to sing the blues: "I had a reason to go to Chicago to be on record. That's really the most reason I come there. I could make good money down in the roadhouses, in all those clubs, but I wanted to be on a record. . . . I don't say I like Chicago, it's dirty and cold and it's got all that politics, but I just come up to Chicago anyway."[34] In addition to the cold, filth, dirty politics, poor working conditions, long hours, low wages, exclusion from labor unions, and so on, black emigrants faced hostility from Irish, Polish, and Italian immigrant workers when they answered employers' calls for strike-breakers. It was the increasing hostility of European immigrants toward blacks plus the resultant politics of "James Crow" that forced African Americans into the isolated community on Chicago's "South Side" and that eventually exploded into the city's race riot of 1919.

Despite the long Darwinian arm of "James Crow," life was still better for African Americans in the North than under the regime of James's older brother "Jim" in the South. There was racial discrimination in employment and housing, but blacks in the North otherwise had a livable measure of political capacity, economic autonomy, and defendable rights. A journalist for the *Defender* made this point in his severe criticism of a political drawing intended to frighten southern blacks away from the North. Addressing his southern black readership, the journalist wrote that the "lying pictures" were being printed in southern white papers "to hand you a little taffy to keep you in slavery." He concluded, "Tell the South that . . . it is better to die free than to live the slave of any man or government. In the North you at least are free. And life without freedom is death."[35] Chicago novelist Richard Wright later captured this sentiment when he spoke these words in behalf of all Mississippi emigrants: "We'd rather be a lamppost in Chicago than the president of Dixie!"[36]

On the South Side—in the "lamppost" district—blacks built their own churches, businesses, civic and welfare institutions, and, in general, adopted Booker T. Washington's pragmatic philosophy of self-help. There was also a kind of Du Boisian intellectualism inherent to Chicago's black metropolis, a "talented-tenth" progressivism largely promoted through the black press, *The Chicago Defender*. This mindset was one that, as we will see, helped to diminish country blues's rural residue of religion in city blues as it developed into its "urban" offspring.

THE MILIEU OF THE METROPOLIS

In an introduction to St. Clair Drake's and Horace Cayton's monumental study of black Chicago, *Black Metropolis* (1945), Richard Wright asked, "What would life on Chicago's South Side look like when seen through the eyes of a Freud, a Joyce, a Proust, a Pavlov, a Kierkegaard?"[37] The closest we can come to an answer to his question is to observe the commentary of Edgar Lee Masters in his *Tale of Chicago* (1933). Through the eyes of this Chicago writer of European orientation, life on the South Side looked anarchic, indulgent; its music sounded riotous. It looked like a city that "rioted in the feelings of youth and strength and liberty" as it "danced itself toward the Great War."[38] As early as 1911, continued Masters, Chicago as a whole was "the most dramatic and tumultuous, laughing and pleasure-seeking city of the land."[39] The "anarchy of Chicago," which not even the city's clergy could control, was partially the consequence of injustice in the courts and exploitation in the factories and stores, not to mention the gambling, prostitution, and organized crime.[40]

Drake and Cayton similarly concluded that the Midwest Metropolis was "notorious for its secular emphasis."[41] This prevailing secularism, which Wright called a "new worldliness,"[42] was partly responsible for denaturing the blues of its rural residue of religion, since the wings of religion were increasingly weighed down by a capitalist-based secularism. In a literary study of Chicagoan Sherwood Anderson, Kenny Williams, herself a native of the "Windy Burg," brought this insight:

> There was no attempt to mask the distinctly commercial goals with the vagueness of the "protestant ethic" or with the religious premise that related one's "calling" with the degree of visible success achieved. God or His will may have played an integral part in the destiny of seventeenth-century New England, but Chicago reinforced the eighteenth-century deistic idea that man himself could be divine. Whereas the city's creators may have harbored delusions of grandeur, the legends finally admitted that Chicago was a place . . . where brute force frequently manifested itself through the evident demoralization and dehumanization of those who worked incessantly for material things.[43]

The music that best reflected this demoralization and dehumanization was the blues, according to the likes of Masters (middle-class whites) and Wright (upwardly mobile blacks). Masters never even called the music by name but only referred to it as "riotous music." He said, "Tenderloin restaurants like Fred Wing's and Buxbaum's on South State Street, where the negroes were numerous, entertained with good food and riotous music the sons of the night life."[44] Although Masters viewed all of Chicago's "dancing" and "laughing" to be but the exterior of the city's dualistic make-up of defiled body and sanctified "inner life,"[45] he failed to recognize that the "riotous music" he spoke of was similarly comprised of a synchronous duplicity—crude, perhaps, in its externals of language and sound but inclusive of an inner sanctity, its religious "residue."

Further evidence of the city's "new worldliness," which led to the diminishing of blues's inner residual sanctity, was that the church lost the status and influence it once had in the South's rural areas and small towns.[46] Of the four components that comprised individual and community life for black city-dwellers—staying alive, advancing the race, praising God, and having fun—new emphasis was placed on fun-making by the "lower-class," said Drake and Cayton, as a means of releasing social and economic tensions:[47] "In the face of this wide range of alternative interests, religion ceases to be the focus of lower-class life. The vast majority organize their behavior around 'good-timing,' fixing the attention on the cheaper forms of commercial recreation. . . . Some cling to the church as a subsidiary center of interest. Others drop their church connections entirely and become completely secularized except for fleeting moments of reverie or remorse."[48] Drake and Cayton continued, explaining that the "lower-class" were, in effect, engaged in a "revolt against heaven." "It is a part of the general secularization of life in the urban, industrial society," they said. "In most cases, however, it is not a frank and open atheism. It is not even an attack upon the church *per se,* for Bronzeville's lower class seems to still feel that it ought to be religious. Rather, it takes the form of protest against the alleged cupidity and hypocrisy of church functionaries and devotees."[49]

From another perspective, perhaps an indication that a segment of Chicago's poor had ceased to focus on religion was that city blues singers gave increasingly less attention to criticizing church functionaries and devotees than was customary in country blues and its occasional source, southern jokelore. The declining significance of church functionaries probably signaled the church's loss of moral authority in the city, which resulted in the increase of moral ambiguity. This loss of moral authority was not simply consequential of a new-fashioned religious indifference but of religious unattachment resulting from maladjustment to city life by the victims of the country-to-city culture-shock,[50] a shock that Amiri Baraka said must have been nearly as strange as the transatlantic diaspora of Afro-America's African ancestors.[51]

Some of this maladjustment was due to the "friction of space" in the city and in the black city-within-the-city, the result being the high mobility and social dislocation of the urban individual and family. What southern blacks called a "neighborhood" was, in the North, devoid of the vitality of familiarity. This anonymity in urban "neighborhoods" of the North spilled over into the churches, with their ever-growing memberships. Large memberships not only resulted in waning face-to-face control of church leaders and declining influence of the church faithful, but in diminishing religious guilt on the part of the "somewhat religious," especially blues singers. This subsiding guilt allowed bluesman Doctor Clayton, for instance, to blame the church for blues singers' exclusion from salvation. He sang in his "Angels in Heaven" of 1946, "I know why blues singers don't go to heaven 'cause Gabriel bawls them out." On the other hand, James "Snooky" Pryor confidently sang in his "Judgment Day" of 1969: "Hey Saint Peter, won't you open the door? . . . Yes, I'm comin', feel like my time ain't long." The declining influence of the church faithful not only allowed the "somewhat religious" to feel a sense of justification or exoneration from guilt; it also resulted in the increased possibility that a growing populace would choose, as "blues people" had always chosen, to participate only "representatively" in institutionalized religion. For most of the "classic" blueswomen of the North, who had escaped the oppressive hegemony of the black church in the South, "representatively" was probably the only way they were going to participate in the church; for the freedom of city life had taken them to a new level of self-identity.

Another influence that led to the secularization of black life and the diminishing rural residue of religion in the blues was the rise of a new functionary—the secular journalist. Where the church left off in its polemical influence on the blues, the "new priest" of the city picked up. The medium of this new Race leader—the printer's ink and press and the editorial column—was widely subscribed to in the black communities of the urban North and by white allies of black advancement, such as Clarence Darrow.[52] Among the elite of this new press corps that helped shape the "new Race spirit"—the spirit of the "New Negro"—were the journalists of *The Chicago Defender,* the great uplifter of "the Race." A journalist once said that the *Defender,* always a vanguard in the fight for racial welfare and advancement, was a "defender" not just in name but in fact.[53] Though these new priests resented southern whites trying to give blacks the impression that their race-relatives in the North neither understood nor wanted them,[54] they did find it necessary to give lessons in middle-class behavior to their more "backwards" kindred of the South. "Perhaps it is a matter of impossibility to change in a few months the habits and traits of an individual that have been molded for a quarter of a century or more by a stilted South," a column read. "But such is the task Chicago and many other Northern cities have had thrust upon them during the past few years by reason of the vast number that have migrated from that section."[55]

Abbott, the *Defender* founder and editor, took this yoke of racial uplift directly upon his shoulders and spoke out strongly in a protracted series of editorials that started appearing in the early 1930s and continued up to the time of his death in 1940. In a piece titled "Refinement Sadly Lacking in Modern Youth," Abbott wrote: "At sometime during our intellectual maturity we are expected to have in our repertoire something more than 'St. James Infirmary,' 'Minnie the Moocher,' and 'All God's Chillun Have Shoes.' . . . We must train ourselves to enjoy formal music, symphony concerts and chamber music. Such music tends to purify the senses and edify the imagination. It helps to refine the feelings by appealing to our higher aesthetic selves."[56] Abbott went so far as to suggest that such cultural refinement would bring an end to segregationism.[57] He said, "primitive habits" (presumably this included singing the blues) cause the perpetuation of Jim Crowism.[58] That the blues was viewed by those of Abbott's social class as contributory to Jim Crowism was stated explicitly by Lucius C. Harper, who wrote a column for the *Defender* beginning in the late thirties. In a piece titled "We Prefer the 'Blues' to Our Essential Causes," Harper wrote: "While we have failed in these fundamental instances [gleaning political recognition from whites], we have succeeded in winning favor and almost unanimous popularity in our 'blues' songs, spirituals and 'jitterbug' accomplishments. Why?" Harper answered: "Our blue melodies have been made popular because they are different, humorous and silly. The sillier the better. They excite the primitive emotion in man and arouse his bestiality. He begins to hum, moan and jump usually when they are put into action. They stir up the emotions and fit in handily with bootleg liquor. They break the serious strain of life and inspire the 'on with the dance' philosophy. They are popular because the American people, both white and black, relish nonsense."[59]

Harper's comments were made in 1938, and almost a decade later the same sentiments persisted. In a *Defender* piece titled "If 'Jazz' Isn't Music to the Long Haired Gents, then What about Blues?" Rob Roy commented: "Whenever I read that some long-haired gent has attacked jazz bands as playing something that must not be classed as music, the thought comes that 'Blues' and not 'jazz' is the jam . . . they've been listening to." Supporting the musical quality of jazz over that of the blues, Roy went on to say, "However we do join our long-haired strangers in condemning the current exponents of 'Blues' for asking us to accept, what they sell most easily, as 'music.'" Illustrating the developing preference for blues that was devoid of the old-South cosmology and its attendant expressionism in which the guitar was used only to accompany singing, Roy concluded that an exception to his criticism was T-Bone Walker, "a blues chirper extraordinary."[60] Even the African-American philosopher Alain Locke criticized the city blues despite his aesthetic appreciation of the country blues. Drawing a distinction between "folk blues" and "artificial blues," Locke said in his classic *The Negro and His Music* (1936): "The early blues-singers . . . were far from elegant, but their deadly effective folk speech was clean and racy by contrast with the mawkish sentimentality and concocted lascivity of the contemporary cabaret songs and dances. . . . The older generation sang not for the night clubs and 'hot spots' of Harlem and its Broadway imitations that have spread all over the world of commercialized entertainment, but to the folky people for whom this racy idiom was more a safety valve of ribald laughter than a neurotic stimulant and breaker of Puritan inhibitions."[61]

Langston Hughes, in an essay published six years later in his weekly column "Here to Yonder," criticized the black press for being so "backward" in its coverage of black popular music and musicians. He said, "the Negro newspapers use little material about our sepia greats of the popular music world, except for routine publicity stories. The only regular columnist on a major Negro newspaper writing with enthusiasm occasionally . . . is not a Negro at all." Hughes concluded, "I wish the Race would pay a little more tribute in print to our race leaders in music who don't make speeches, but man, how they can play."[62] So, we see that this push away from southern folkways really existed; in fact, Hughes himself was an unknowing participant in the very "high-hat" attitude he criticized. His column, which commenced in the *Defender* in November of 1942, was clearly a vehicle for race progress. He began the first piece of the weekly with an explanation of the column's title, saying, "Things that happen away off yonder affect us here." He continued, "What happens at the post affects the pillar, and vice versa. Here is yonder, and yonder is here."[63] This meant that, as Abbott said back in 1934, "primitive" folkways (which, we must admit, were part and parcel of country blues), could affect black middle-class progress toward social assimilation.

The old "habits and traits" of southern emigrants, despite the influence of the "new priest" of the city, were not changed within a few months; but, within a few years the process of transmutation was well underway. Thus, at the time St. Clair Drake and Horace Cayton wrote in the early forties, they were able to draw the conclusion that southern "attitudes" existed in Chicago and throughout northern metropolises in "a watered down form."[64] Among the "attitudes" or behaviors "watered down" were African cultural retentions, even though, as Melville Herskovits said, it was wrong to assume that mere contact with city life caused their suppression: "That it discouraged their retention in pure form is undoubtedly true; yet this does not mean that white patterns were taken over without serious revision. Rather, it means that rural and urban Negro cultures took on somewhat different shadings; that the impact of European custom on African aboriginal traditional values and modes of behavior was directed along divergent courses. And hence it is that, while Africanisms are to be found both in cities and in the countryside all over the New World, they differ in intensity and in the specific forms they take."[65] Often the African retentions took on different shadings because the original meaning of certain old words that survived in the rhyme of lyric was forgotten; the meaning was forgotten but there was still a reverence for these mysterious sounds.[66] Decades later, folklorist Richard M. Dorson drew a similar conclusion: "Southern Negro lore had moved north indeed, but only with migrants cradled and nurtured in the yeasty Southern traditions, or with the few still-living children of slaves. Northern-born Negroes, growing up among cities and factories, supercilious toward their Southern brothers, had severed and discarded their folk heritage, and the new migrants grow farther from it as they take on Northern attitudes."[67] One of the political cartoons in the *Defender* correctly portrayed this process of discarding as the result of bombardment from the powerful impetus toward race progress. In the drawing, a missile with the epithet "New Race Spirit" was crashing into the icon of a black mammy representing "Ante-Bellum Traditions"; the pieces of rock that scattered from the explosion read, "fear," "servility," "superstition," and "ignorance."[68]

Among the "superstitions" diffused over the decades by the new priests' propagation of the "new race spirit" was the traditional southern cosmology of the blues. As folklorist Newbell Niles Puckett concluded, the imposition of the progressive race pride on the emigrants from the South resulted in the erasure of the ancient records of folk thought: "Today Negro race pride is forcing many more or less illiterate Negroes to give up, or at least to subdue and refuse to pass on, the old beliefs for fear of ridicule from the more developed members of their race."[69] Puckett devoted an article solely to the subject, "Race-Pride and Folk-Lore," published in the African-American periodical, *Opportunity.* He recognized that "cultured" and college-educated blacks viewed race-pride and folklore (superstition) as "irreconcilable enemies" and that they celebrated the decimation of the "African ghost-heritage" to scanty proportions.[70] He concluded with reference to song, "The quavering whispers of the old 'songster' can no longer be heard above the uncouth blare of modern music—daily, almost hourly, these superb rhythmic masterpieces die down to golden echoes and pass unwritten to the Land of Forgotten Things."[71]

This progressive "race pride" not only impinged upon the blues but upon such southern traditions as singing spirituals, holding house prayer meetings, and preaching street-side. One of the political drawings in the *Defender,* in the long-standing weekly segment titled "People We Can Get Along Without," pursued this criticism. The caption to a gesticulating "jackleg" preacher surrounded by onlookers indicated that among the "people we can get along without" was "the curbstone orator who disgraces the ministry and becomes a nuisance with his idiotic capers."[72] The reason such behaviors and attitudes (also found in black song, jokelore, and slang) were rejected by the progressive element of the city's black society was that these genres preserved backward behavioral responses to the "phantom of the plantation,"[73] a phantom that, especially haunting the mental and social reality of the southern emigrants, perpetuated white segregationism and "James Crow." This is what columnist Lucius Harper was implying in his piece, "We Prefer the 'Blues' to Our Essential Causes." In this piece in which he denounced the blues, Harper also denounced the spirituals as keeping alive the plantation phantom: "The prayerful, moanful themes of the spirituals and slavery songs, sometimes called the sorrow songs of our fathers, have exemplified so much passive submission, such deep religious fervor and fanaticism that American people have found them quite acceptable. . . . By cleaver propaganda the songs of our fathers, rattling chains and stained with human blood have been made quite captivating."[74] Indeed, black Chicagoans of Harper's and Abbott's mindset wanted to forget the years of slavery, of which the spirituals and the blues were a reminder.

While the readership of the *Defender* occasionally came across articles by or about W. E. B. Du Bois, Carter G. Woodson, James Weldon Johnson, Langston Hughes, and George A. Singleton, and, beginning in the 1940s, columns by Hughes, Du Bois, and Mary McLeod Bethune,[75] one of the early appointed "clergy" of the new press corps was columnist Alexander L. Jackson, a graduate of Harvard's class of 1914.[76] All in all, Jackson was a prime mover in the demystification of the South's rural heritage due to his pursuit of racial advancement via the vehicles of education and scientific understanding. The implication was—and the journalism of the *Defender* bore this out from the very beginning—that the more that could be learned by the race educationally, the more that could be understood and explained experientially rather than superstitiously. To this effect, Jackson once commented that, "Our own preachers and ministers must realize that the daily press, which is so powerful an educator in other things, is stirring up the minds and imagination of . . . young people with accounts of what leading members of other churches are thinking and saying."[77] In the late thirties, the journalists still supported this notion, as evidenced in an editorial of 1937 titled "What the Press Does." The writer said, "The newspaper, though not generally regarded as a special medium for intellectual enlargement, nevertheless, has reached a higher plane in bringing to mankind correct world information, than any other institution." The writer concluded, "These things being true, it is all the more fitting that our racial group should read its own periodicals."[78]

Among those whose minds and imaginations had been stirred up by the daily press was one whose letter to the *Defender* editor in March of 1927 was printed in the weekly column "What the People Say." Under the editor's title, "Too Much Religion," the correspondent complained that blacks were afflicted by "a hypertheism superinduced by an inherent tendency to believe in the supernatural."[79] Five years later, in the same column, a Chicagoan commented that, "in Afro-America the Negro leans credulously toward 'conjure' men and spiritualists." He concluded, "The brother is a chump for quackery."[80] In an editorial titled "Joshua Fit the Battle of Jericho," another Chicago writer commented: "The plantation song, later termed the Negro spiritual, is overdone and is on the verge of disaster. It is contended that these songs are the expression of the soul of the Negro, and this is logical. But we must remember that the observation of slaves in that period was limited and because of extreme, oppressive servility ignorance was rampant, crystalizing itself into fear and superstition. The faculty of the slave was not prepared to give significant expression to a soul feeling." The writer went on to say that fifty years later the spirituals, lost in an avalanche of commercial exploitation, would be superseded by a new song that had been filtered through a vocabulary enriched by scientific discovery.[81]

In a feature article of 1934, a Chicago writer named Charles P. Browning elaborated on what one of the above writers to the *Defender* called "hypertheism." He defined this term as enslavement to "traditional mythology" and identified it as one of the great tragedies of modern black life: "Lincoln may have freed the Negro politically in 1863, but the Negro still lives in the shadow of a worse bondage of superstition where the very art of living is taken away from him by supernaturalism and an emotional escape from life."[82] In light of the kind of fear of the devil expressed in the previous chapter by the ex-slave Polly Cancer, Browning called for African Americans to move beyond the point where fear and sorrow were dominant aspects of black religious culture: "No longer must his religion be a defense against fear and a flight from sorrow."[83]

Partly consequential of the constant criticism of old-time religion[84] and the repeated petition for religion to keep up with the findings of science[85] was the increasing demystification of evil, since science tends to replace or attenuate religious cosmology. This commenced with the ascendancy of the scientific spirit in eighteenth-century Christianity, as reflected in the decreased belief in witchcraft and the cessation of witch trials.[86] As put by Paul Carus, "Those who doubt the religious import of science need only consider what science had done for mankind by the radical abolition of witch-prosecution, and they will be convinced that science is not religiously indifferent, but that it is the most powerful factor in the purification of the religions of mankind."[87]

For instance, following the prominent place the *Defender* gave to the approximately two hundred blacks killed in the fire at the Rhythm Night Club in Natchez, Mississippi,[88] letters to the editor in the weeks that followed were concerned not with possible superstitious explanations but with fire safety keeping abreast of technological advancements. As though taunting the religious worldview of southern folks, the staff correspondent wrote a *Defender* piece captioned "Dance Hall Fire Trap was Once a Church." In it he said, "Churchworkers will make much of the charge that Satan visited the place that was once a Sanctified church where congregations of that faith worshipped. Others will say the evils of the sinful cabaret folk who frequented the place while it was a night club were responsible."[89] However, what was said in the *Defender* by correspondents was none of those things; as David Ward Howe put it in his column, "The Observation

Post," "Death rode in Natchez on the wings of inadequate facilities."[90]

Although Carus concluded that the personal devil is dead in science, he also believed that he was still alive in Protestant countries among the uneducated.[91] But there was a change in these old views, he said, as the intellectual life of humankind developed: "The old views are, as a rule, preserved but transformed. There is nowhere an absolutely new start. Either the main idea is preserved and details are changed, or *vice versa,* the main idea is objected to while the details remain the same."[92] The "strong sense" of evil still persisted during the periods of city and urban blues; however, it was increasingly the case that the devil was viewed by "educated" blacks as being not of their own hue, "a big black man," but white—the white courts, the white press, the Dixie white, the white-clad Klan. In a front-page political cartoon in the *Defender,* titled "Take My Seat, Mr. Dixie," a dark, horned devil was turning over his fiery throne to a white man representing "The South." The explanation, which appeared later on the editorial page, said: "His satanic majesty, the devil, has abdicated his throne in favor of the forces of Dixie. Even hell, with all its vaunted evil, with its instruments of torture, with its brimstone and sulphur, with its torturing imps, cannot compete with America's Dixie in barbarity, and the devil grudgingly abdicates his throne." The piece continued, "And Dixie is hell. . . . Slavery was an institution of hell, founded upon the very principles by which that nether world is governed."[93] In another front-page political cartoon, a white man's spirit rose up from a grave that read, "Here Lies Slavery—Died Jan. 1, 1863," above which was the caption, "But It's Evil Spirit Lives."[94] In these political cartoons, the Ku Klux Klan was generally portrayed as in league with the devil, if not as literally "a demon from hell."[95] In a political drawing titled "For Distinguished Service," an award carrying a dangling skull and the recognition "Highest Lynching Score for 1922" was being pinned on the chest of a white Klansman from "Georgia" by the eerie, hairy hand of "His Satanic Majesty."[96] This demystifying of "Kluxism" was the point being made by columnist Jackson when he said that each day led to the end of the Grand Wizard's "Invisible Empire."[97]

In personifying evil in the foregoing ways, viewing it essentially existentially, the journalists of the *Defender* were able to situate it cosmically and thus move toward negotiating with the institutional "powers that be" for the end purpose of its containment and eventual eradication. As anthropologist David Parkin wrote, "Evil may . . . be regarded as ambivalent power, but, through its 'personification,' it becomes more accessible to people's management, even to the point of being temporarily dissolved: to 'know' evil as one might know a person is at least to communicate with it, directly, indirectly through a god, or even as part of a god."[98] To another anthropologist, Alan Macfarlane, evil was not temporarily dissolved, but fully: "Though 'evil' titillates in the films, television, science fiction and children's stories, in ordinary life the concept and reality have largely been banished. Most people move in a one-dimensional world that has expelled Satan, witches, the Evil Eye and fairies. The supernatural dimension is dead, except as 'fantasy.' It appears that 'science' and 'chance' have largely replaced personalized explanation."[99]

As a result of this kind of thought, the "new priests" of the city contributed to the diminishing of the rural residue of religion in city blues as it evolved into its "urban" progeny. Thrown out with the demystification of the evil of white "Jim Crow" was, to a certain degree, the mystery of the "strong sense" of evil and the "theodicy question," both of which had imbued country and city blues with a certain religious cosmology.

CITY AND URBAN BLUES IN CHICAGO

The free verse in Sherwood Anderson's *Mid-American Chants* (1918), akin to the lyric of Chicago's blues, traced the effects of urbanization on the mood and mindset of the citizens who fashioned the "riotous music" of the "Windy" black metropolis. Although Anderson did not write about the black blues singer who migrated to Chicago from the South, the European immigrants he described as having been demented by the city were the very ones who oppressed the black emigrants, driving them to sing the blues with about as much throaty, repressed articulation as they had in Dixie. Thus, a "citified" country blues (city blues), which had already begun to take root in such southern cities as Dallas, Houston, New Orleans, and Memphis, began to take root in Chicago as early as the twenties. By the early sixties, Paul Oliver could say in retrospect that some of the best country blues had been recorded by city-dwellers and that the best location to study Mississippi blues was probably Chicago.[100]

Although the South remained the spiritual home of the blues, Chicago, due to the steady influx of Delta musicians, became the blues capital of the urban North (followed by Memphis during the urban blues phase after World War II). Among the former sharecroppers, tenant farmers, and migrant workers of the southern logging and turpentine camps who came North by highway and railway in search of work in the city's stockyards, steel mills, foundries, and packing plants were blues musicians hoping for recording opportunities with such companies as Paramount, Okeh, Columbia, Vocalion, and, after the depression, Bluebird (RCA Victor) and Decca. From Florida to Chicago came Tampa Red; from Georgia, James Kokomo Arnold and Thomas Dorsey; from Alabama, Charles Davenport; from Tennessee, Sonny Boy Williamson and Jimmy Oden; from Arkansas, Shaky Jake; and from Mississippi to the city Tommy McClennan called "sweet old Chicago," the "land of California" (in his blues "Baby, Don't You Want to Go"), came J. B. Lenoir, Muddy Waters, Tommy McClennan, Big Joe Williams, Big Boy Crudup, Big Bill Broonzy, Jazz Gillum, Little Walker J, Brother John Sellers, Sunnyland Slim, and Jimmy Reed. These were but a few of Chicago's blues musicians who "citified" the country blues, in the process making it religiously transitional in the development of urban blues.

Among the many "classic" blueswomen who lived in Chicago for longer or shorter periods were Sippie Wallace and Victoria Spivey from Texas, Lizzie Miles from Louisiana, Alberta Hunter from Memphis, Lucille Hegamin from Georgia, and Chippie Hill from South Carolina. Their "classic blues" was also religiously transitional. Amiri Baraka essentially drew this conclusion when he said classic blues was the perfect balance between the world of entertainment, racial assimilation, and universality on the one hand, and country blues's world of individuality and segregation on the other.[101] Ralph Ellison said he disagreed with Jones's distinction between country and classic blues because Jones said one was folklore and the other was entertainment. The foregoing point by Jones somewhat discredited the criticism, but Ellison's point supports my view of classic blues as transitional:

> Jones makes a distinction between classic and country blues, the one being entertainment and the other folklore. But the distinction is false. Classic blues were both entertainment *and* a form of folklore. When they were sung professionally in theatres, they were entertainment; when danced to in the form of recordings or used as a means of transmitting the traditional verses and their wisdom, they were folklore. There are levels of time and function involved here, and the blues which might be

used in one place as entertainment (as gospel music is now being used in night clubs and on theatre stages) might be put to a ritual use in another. Bessie Smith might have been a "blues queen" to the society at large, but within the tighter Negro community where the blues were part of a total way of life, and a major expression of an attitude toward life, she was a priestess, a celebrant who affirmed the values of the group and man's ability to deal with chaos.[102]

This very same balance was implied in two editorials of 1933 written by music critic Ralph Matthews about Ethel Waters for *The Pittsburgh Courier* and *The Afro-American* (of Baltimore). In the former, an open letter to Waters, Matthews said, "I can see how you can ignore, after a fashion, what colored folks think about you. Now your dollars are all white dollars and white people have queer appetites where their colored entertainers are concerned. You are trying to please that appetite."[103] Two weeks later he said that, though tainted by her success, she had a right to sing the blues when she remembered "those other days."[104] W. C. Handy, in an essay of 1940 titled "The Heart of the Blues," also alluded to the transitional state of city blues: "I cannot admire the sophisticated, made to order, commercial blues, which mutilate the simple Negro elements by dressing them up. I have the feeling that real blues can be written only by a Negro, who keeps his roots in the life of his race."[105] Daphne Harrison concluded her study of the blues "queens" of the twenties with essentially the same resolve: "Emerging from southern backgrounds rich in religious and folk music traditions, they were able to capture in song the sensibilities of black women—North and South—who struggled daily for physical, psychological, and spiritual balance."[106]

As a religiously transitional music, city blues was not immediately (or ever fully) denuded of its rural religious residue. The city blues singer still insinuated the "country" into the city. City blues had a good three decades to develop before being overshadowed by the urban style of Chicago bluesmen Otis Rush and Jimmy Reed and their Memphis contemporaries Bobby Bland and B. B. King. This was essentially what Richard Wright was saying in 1941 in his lyrical and pictorial history of Afro-America, *12 Million Black Voices*: "On the plantation our songs carried a strain of other-worldly yearning which people called 'spiritual'; but now our blues . . . are our 'spirituals' of the city pavements, our longing for freedom and opportunity, an expression of our bewilderment and despair in a world whose meaning eludes us. The ridiculousness and sublimity of love are captured in our blues, those sad-happy songs that laugh and weep all in one breath, those mockingly tender utterances of a folk imprisoned in steel and stone."[107] The southern religious cosmology of African Americans was maintained in city blues due in part to its constant cross-fertilization with its country precursor. During the approximately three decades (beginning about 1915) that country blues continued to come into the city via the influx of southern emigrants, city blues also returned to the southern folk via the dissemination of blues on radio and recordings. In fact, what some country blues singers brought to the city during the thirties and forties was but their adaptation of styles and verses from the city blues of the twenties and thirties.

As the decades passed, what country blues singers heard in recordings of city blues as it met its destiny with "urbanity" was a music that had distanced itself from its religious roots. As Virginia Piedmont bluesman John Cephas explained, "The younger people growing up . . . didn't want to hear that old hick stuff."[108] Big Bill Broonzy commented similarly in 1953 that "Young people have forgotten how to cry the blues. . . . Back in my day, the people didn't know nothing else to do but cry. They couldn't say about things that hurt 'em. But now they talks and gets lawyers and things. They don't cry no more."[109] Not only did the younger generation forget how to "cry the blues," they also ridiculed the old-fashioned, so-called "countrified" blues singer whose lyrics reflected the old religious cosmology rather than an urbane sophistication. These very factors that caused the blues to distance itself from its religious roots were the same that led soul music to replace the blues as the dominant form of music in the black community of the sixties. As explained by a Detroit disk jockey in the late sixties, "Most people who are rejecting the blues are definitely trying to throw away old clothes."[110]

For blues to have survived in the city for the long run—to have kept pace with the changing tastes of the city citizenry pushing urbanity—it had to merge with musical styles already existing in the metropolises. It had to acquire the sophistication, the aesthetic, of jazz, or, to draw a literary correlation, of Langston Hughes's blues poetry. Hughes, too, had to dilute the religious cosmology of country blues in order to legitimize the folk verse for his target audience, the black middle class.[111] Whatever remaining rural residue of religion was not "watered down" into insignificance was then "dressed up"—language used by Virginia Piedmont bluesman Archie Edwards to describe what happened to country blues when "citified." The "dressed-up blues" was the same blues, explained Edwards, but it sounded different. This could be compared to a country boy who moved to the city and changed from his dungarees into sharp-toed shoes, said Edwards; he was the same country boy but he looked different. "That's the same with the blues. It's the same old song, but the next thing you know its messed up so you don't know it when you hear it."[112] Piedmont blues, the predominant blues style of the Southeast, with its banjo-like acoustic guitar-picking technique, did not adapt well to urban styles. But for the blues that did become "citified" and stylized after jazz, its rural "residue" had to go, just as it had to be excluded from Hughes's blues poetry if it was going to sell well among his middle-class audience.

Hughes, who lived in Chicago during his high-school years (1918–21) and later wrote blues poetry due to the influence of Chicago Renaissance writers Carl Sandburg and Vachel Lindsay,[113] was intimately familiar with city blues. The "riotous music" that Edgar Lee Masters heard down on State Street was, to Hughes's ears, music of folkloric virtue. In his essay titled "I Remember the Blues," Hughes wrote, "in Chicago in my teens, all up and down State Street there were blues, indoors and out, at the Grand and the old Monogram theaters where Ma Rainey sang, in the night clubs, in the dance halls, on phonographs."[114] Later, when Hughes began to write verse using the moods, themes, rhythms, and structures of the blues, he created a poetry of folkloric middle ground that presented his middle-class readership with a professional poet's interpretation of the unpretentious folk.[115] As a result, the imagery in his poetry was not as striking—the folklore not as sincere, accurate, or potent—as that in traditional lyrics of such characters as Robert Johnson and Victoria Spivey. But Hughes's poetry was not only middle ground between the downhome folk and the uptown upward-bound; in our paradigm of the blues continuum, country blues → city blues → urban blues, his poetry was middle ground between city and urban blues: it leaned back toward the purely folkloric (country blues) but could not cross over the boundary of city blues because it was poetry, and poetry (speech), unlike lyric (song), cannot (because it lacks intonation) regress toward the prearticulate cry that was at the root of the hollers; it leaned forward toward the sophisticated urban blues but could not cross over that line because its aesthetic was rooted in the religious cosmology that was essentially denuded from urban blues.

This situating of Hughes's blues poetry within our paradigm of the blues continuum has prepared the way for the crucial question of what city blues looked like about midway through its phase before being largely superseded by urban blues. In terms of its residue of religion, it looked like Hughes's poetry—a product that consciously sought to cash in on the blues craze initiated by the recording industry in 1920 with the immense success of Mamie Smith's "Crazy Blues." "As a creative artist," said Steven Tracy, "Hughes was much like the blues composer or professional musician in seeking to draw on his folk roots not only out of pride and the need for individual artistic freedom but, sometimes, for economic reasons as well. For these reasons he did not reject more commercially oriented blues to express one part of the city side of the blues."[116]

The one thing that this parallel consideration of Hughes's blues poetry does not account for is the way in which the sound of city blues, midway through its phase, affected country blues's residue of southern religious cosmology. The rural residue became buried, in part, beneath a sound that was increasingly modern: more instruments, fuller density, louder volume, and a faster tempo for a more entertaining, dance-like "juke-box." Additionally, while the "voice" of the old "git-fiddle" (the folk guitar) was able to mimic the human voice doing a holler (its instrumental tones and timbres emerging from semi-enclosed inner recesses of natural, resonant wood), the electric guitar of city and urban blues was often made of fiberglass and had not a "mouth" to speak; whatever bit of natural woody resonance remained was denatured by the synthetic sound produced by electrification. Even if consideration were given to the potential meaning within or beyond the surface of sound, the diminishing "residue" was clearly evidenced as the rough edges of the old rural sound smoothed out into a sophisticated "urban" musicality.

Another factor in the diminishing of the southern cosmological residue was that the lone blues guitarist of the country style (the offspring of the lone hollerer) was, in "citified country," joined by piano, bass, drums, and sometimes harp (harmonica) or saxophone—namely, the blues band. This forced blues to become less spontaneous, insofar as band members necessarily had to suppress some of their individual expressiveness for the sake of group homogeneity. While the lone crooning of the rural bluesman better approximated the spontaneity of the old hollers, city blues and its sophisticated urban progeny (like Hughes's blues aesthetic) became stilted by its formality. This point was illustrated by folklorists John and Alan Lomax in their commentary on a 1936 recording of a prisoner in Florida's State Farm, who sang for John Lomax an unaccompanied piece titled "Prisoner Blues":

> If Bessie Smith enthusiasts could hear Ozella Jones or some other clear-voiced Southern Negro girl sing the blues, they might, we feel, soon forget the idol with her brassbound, music-hall throat. The blues, sung by an unspoiled singer in the South, sung without the binding restrictions of conventional accompaniment or orchestral arrangement, grow up like a wild flowering vine in the woods. Their unpredictable, incalculably tender melody bends and then swings and shivers with the lines like a reed moving in the wind. The blues then shows clearly their country origin, their family connection with the "holler."[117]

Contesting Charles Keil's notion that blues performances tended to be more ritualistic than performance oriented, that blues singers tended to be more priestly than artistic, and that blues audiences tended to be more committed than merely appreciative,[118] my contention has been that this became less so as country blues evolved through its "city" adaptation into its sophisticated "urban" phase. Contrariwise, in urban blues (in contrast to country blues), musicians were more artistic than priestly, audiences were more appreciative than committed, and performances were more performance oriented than traditionally ritualistic. As blues became increasingly artistic (its traditional cosmology being reduced and absorbed into a rationalized aesthetic), its increased rationalism resulted in the blues singer *explaining* with the lips (preaching *through* blues) rather than *convincing* by way of articulation with the throat ("preachin' *the* blues"). The throaty, raucous, choked sound of Delta blues conveyed the reality of repression and thus the urgency of the blues being "preached." Without this articulatory urgency, the blues "artist," whose traditional cosmology had been reduced to an aesthetic, was unable to appear very priestly; and without priestliness, the blues "artist" was unable to garner much (if any) commitment—only appreciation. Blues scholar Robert Palmer seemed unable to avoid this conclusion, even though he rejected the idea that blues became something less than it once was. He said, "Blues has lost a lot; it's lost the sense of in-group solidarity that once tied it so closely to its core audience, its crucial context of blackness."[119]

This loss of commitment might explain the abandonment of the "question of evil" in urban blues. In a typical nonthematic (thematically fragmented) country or early city blues, no single theme predominated, so that one or two of the verses were able to make explicit references to aspects of the blues singer's religious cosmology. In urban blues, since a single theme had to be chosen over the many, it was almost always the theme of sexual prowess and unrequited love that won out. Because an entire song progressed toward a single point (the lesson or message), there was increased chance for listener dissatisfaction with a blues song, which likely would have occurred if an entire blues had dealt with such a religiously weighty topic as the "problem of evil." As *Defender* columnist Alexander Jackson stated back in the early twenties, a warning of sorts to blues singers, "It is the fashion to decry religion and the church these days among our younger people who had some education and training."[120]

What made urban blues less priestly, ritualistic, and religious was, in part, capitalism. Capitalism naturally bred artists—artistic entrepreneurs—who *took* (money), rather than fashioning priests—preachers of blues—who *gave* (ministry). This commercializing of black sorrow was perfectly illustrated in a political cartoon in the *Defender* by Jay Jackson, a well-known artist and cartoonist of his day. The cartoon pictured a well-dressed black woman coming out of a "Music Publishing House." The woman was wearing a fur coat and, having just recorded a hit blues, had money overflowing from her pocketbook. The advertisement in the window of the publishing house read, "Divorced Woman Blues. Hear it, Greatest Blues since St. Louis Blues." And who did the newly famed blues singer run into on her way out of the store, begging for money in his tattered clothes; and what did she say? Waving a handful of bills beneath the nose of her ex-husband, the woman said, as the caption read, "Remember when you used to give me the blues? Well I made something out of them."[121]

In terms of capitalism breeding artistic entrepreneurs rather than preachers of blues, blues singer Baby Doo Caston identified the higher social class of urban blues musicians as the distinctive factor distinguishing urban blues from its precursors.[122] Blues scholar Jeff Titon agreed, saying, "Downhome blues steadied the recent migrants; urban blues appealed to those who had made the transition and sought a higher status."[123] Black journalist Del Jones concurred that, now that blues singers such as B. B. King and Joe Williams have ascended to higher class status, the timbre of the blues had changed to the degree that even white audiences can relate to their songs about women.[124] Probably few urban blues singers were "star struck"; they were likely down-to-earth in a "downhome" kind of way. Yet, the result of this breeding of artists of a higher social class was the evolution of audiences that were no longer "committed" but who were "appreciative" for the entertainment their money could afford. The rise of capitalism, which resulted in the production of "art" for sale and profit and the cultivation of patrons to consume the product, went hand-in-hand with the rise of modern rationalism. Blues was increasingly reduced to an ordered system of rules—concretized forms, lyrics, and instrumental combinations—that paralleled the developing rationality found in the social, institutional, and technological life of the period of industrialization. As sociologist Max Weber said, "Rationalization proper commences with the evolution of music into a professional art."[125] Thus, while I agree with Keil that the "affective element" remained "relatively" constant in the development of blues into the sophisticated urban style, and that blues singers developed more rational means toward achieving the affective, I disagree with his contention that the blues tradition evolved in the opposite direction of the Western musical tradition with its emergent rationality, demystification, and diminution of expressiveness.[126] Capitalism bred "art," which, in the effort to develop and capsulize an aesthetic in lyrics, resulted in an emergent rationality, demystification, and diminution of expressiveness. This, in turn, caused the diminution of the residue of religion in city blues as it developed into its "urban" progeny.

Another influence in the commercial reduction of the traditional cosmology of the blues was the trivializing (if not minstrelizing) of the music, first by white-owned vaudeville companies and then by white-owned recording companies. Paramount Records, for instance, advertised Trixie Smith's "Praying Blues" in an almost sacrilegious way, following an excerpt from the blues in which Smith begged the Lord please to hear her plea and send her a man "that wants nobody else but me." The advertisement then read, "It's a riot—a scream—a sensation—that Trixie Smith and Her Downhome Syncopators have made. . . . It's the best prayer we ever heard on record—'Mournful' won't describe it, it's that sad."[127] It is evident in the innumerable advertisements like this one that the promotion of classic blues was plagued by the old "coon song" stereotypes of Tin Pan Alley. For instance, Okeh Race Records advertised Sippie Wallace's "Underworld Blues" with religious indifference: "The newest Okeh

Record of Sippie's is some powerful wicked blues and no mistake. It's probably the sobbin'est, groanin'est, weepin'est, moanin'est blues you ever heard."[128] In handling Victoria Spivey's "Red Lantern Blues," Okeh advertisers also caricatured the southern apparition of the "Jack-o'-lantern" or "Jack-o'-my-lantern," the wandering flames believed to belong to the souls of recently deceased persons.[129] The advertisement read, "Victoria Spivey has been seein' things that will make your blood run cold . . . lanterns movin' from hole to hole . . . curdlin' groans and piercin' screams!"[130] Paramount caricatured hoodoo in their advertisement of Ida Cox's "Mojo Hand Blues": "Yes, sir—Mama's going to Louisiana to get herself a Mojo hand—then, Beware Papa! You'll get a kick and many laughs out of this new Paramount Blues. . . . It's a scream!"[131] Brunswick Race Records similarly advertised a blues by Jim Towel: "Have you ever been hoodooed? If you want to know how it feels to have a hoodoo doctor cast a spell over you, hear Jim Towel tell you about it on the new Brunswick Race Record, 'I've Been Hoodooed.' It's a riot from start to finish."[132]

These advertisements illustrate that white recording executives were significantly responsible for shaping Chicago's city blues. Their concern not for the traditional religious cosmology of many of the artists they recorded, but for money, power, and social relations (which were thought to be able to control good and evil), made blues into an increasingly rationalized "urban" art, one that eventually could be performed by white blues "artists." In this respect, the complaints Mississippian Jimmy Rogers had regarding his recording sessions with Chess in the early fifties are understandable: "Only time it'd be a rerun would be somethin' Chess would want to change, and that would be the end of a good record. When he changed it, he'd take all the soul and everything from it. And that happened quite a few times."[133] Just as the newspaper advertisements of the major record companies reduced the traditional cosmology of the blues to mere vaudeville, so did the record producers, for capitalistic reasons, play a significant part in this denaturement as city blues developed into its sophisticated urban offspring.

Capitalism also helped denude the blues of its mythologies, theologies, and theodicies in that it blurred moral polarities. This blurring of the moral distinction between good and evil, effected by capitalism,[134] also caused African-American culture to shift increasingly from more absolutist judgments of good and evil to more relativist judgments. This is the significance of the front-page *Defender* article of 1950 that carried a large photograph of Billie Holiday and the caption "Billie Holiday Ill Has Right to Sing Blues."[135] Here the jazz-styled blues singer "has the *right* to sing blues," when three decades earlier blues and jazz were severely ridiculed, and blues worse than jazz.

The point is, capitalism blurs moral distinctions. Take for instance the heated debate during the twenties and thirties regarding the morality of jazz. Whites were not the only ones trying to censor musicians of the jazz school who, as one group of white music teachers claimed in a law suit, play their music "in a too seductive manner."[136] Nora Douglas Holt, in her weekly *Defender* column during the twenties, "News of the Music World," sided with negative opinions, describing jazz as "America's enfant terrible, along with the Ku Klux Klan and prohibition."[137] Columnist Alexander Jackson agreed, calling jazz the "new and terrible standard of blues and morals" capable of stunting spiritual growth.[138] Abbott, the *Defender* editor, also had strong feelings about jazz (and no doubt the blues). He commented thus regarding the music and the dance halls, cabarets, and underground taverns that helped scandalize the morals of black youths: "Our sedate young ladies . . . , tearing down every conceivable hope of redemption, abandon themselves into such frenzied, epileptic contortions as 'snake-hip,' 'black-bottom' and the vulgar dance de ventre, known as the 'rhumba,' to the tune of 'Shake That Thing.'"[139] To illustrate how capitalism began to confuse moral distinctions and convictions, Jackson, seemingly sympathetically, reported that a business agent of the Chicago Federation of Musicians said that musicians had a choice between playing jazz or starving.[140] Jackson moved beyond the point of viewing jazz as unconditionally evil—that is, evil without consideration given to motive or intent—but there were, no doubt, those who believed that any attempt to explain such motives or intents behind the perceived evils of jazz was to participate in that evil.

Furthermore, despite what the journalists of the *Defender* thought of the blues and jazz, the "almighty dollar" was all that was requisite for the newspaper to print advertisements of new blues and jazz releases from the major record companies of New York and Chicago, advertisements that portrayed blues singers as great "Race stars." Beginning in the early twenties, the three leading record companies of the period—Okeh, Columbia, and Paramount (which bought Harry Pace's Black Swan Company in the mid-twenties)—were advertising Ethel Waters (Black Swan), Bessie Smith and Clara Smith (Columbia), Trixie Smith, Alberta

Hunter, Ida Cox, and Ma Rainey (Paramount), and Mamie Smith, Sippie Wallace, and Sara Martin (Okeh) as great "Race artists." Their use of the term "Race" was intentional, borrowed from the *Defender*, which coined it to designate the progressive race pride and solidarity of the "New Negro." Compared to the country and city bluesmen, the "queens of the blues" were certainly seen as a "better class" of blues singer. But the African Americans represented by the middle-class standards of the *Defender* did not view the classic blueswomen favorably, because their behavior, language, and attire were generally antithetical to the prevailing model of respectability—the Victorian woman. As one *Defender* reporter wrote, "Stage folks have a wonderful opportunity to help elevate the race—help lift the stamp of inferiority. . . . Vulgarity is a yoke or burden. See it for what it is—a hindrance to our standards of respectability and success."[141] Similarly, a reviewer of Ethel Waters's autobiography, *His Eye Is on the Sparrow* (1951), commented that "Many Negroes resent the book because they believe that it degrades the race, and places it in a very unfavorable light. These people fear that this will give others a distorted picture of Negro life."[142] These critics of the blues "queens" certainly did not view the city bluesmen as any better. When Peetie Wheatstraw died in East St. Louis in a car accident in 1941, the city's black newspaper did not even recognize him. The only way he would have been recognized, said one woman of the community, would have been if he had committed a crime. "No, you won't find any picture of Peetie Wheatstraw, even in the colored newspaper, not unless he got in trouble. They were a different class; lowlife is what they were."[143] If the blues was such a "terrible standard of morals," then the term "Race" should have been reserved for the persons Abbott, Jackson, Holt, Harper, and others on the *Defender* staff perceived to be the "real" Race heroes of upward mobility, of Du Bois's "talented tenth"—the journalists, educators, doctors, lawyers, businessmen, and so on.

To illustrate further how capitalism helped confuse moral distinctions, the same record companies that elevated blues singers to the status of great "Race artists" also traversed upon traditional black Christian belief by advertising sacred and secular music side-by-side. This, of course, had to do with the doctrinal belief adopted from the Christianity that enslaved Africans learned from their captors and not with African traditional religious belief which, comprised of a holistic cosmology, involved no such dichotomizing. From the latter (Afrocentric) perspective, Columbia's side-by-side advertising of Bessie Smith's "Preachin' the Blues" and Rev.

J. C. Burnett's sermon "Daniel in the Lions' Den"[144] illustrated what, for African Americans in touch with their Africanness, was the natural homogeneity of the cosmos (homogeneity personified in the synchronous duplicity of voodoo's god of the crossroads, Legba). But this was not the cosmology that prevailed among blacks of the 1920s who embraced what Haitian voodooists called "the magic of the whites" (Christianity). These were Christians who, in large measure, saw the blues as the progenitor of that allegedly filthy, barbaric, discordant, wild, and shrieky jazz that many thought should be disqualified by the decent element and eliminated from dance halls.[145] Thus, according to the strict doctrinal beliefs of the old black "Bible belt," when Okeh ran an advertisement saying that their race record line included "the bluest blues, the finest spirituals, and the hottest jazz,"[146] black Christians (particularly those whose spirituals were being advertised) should have been up in arms. When Okeh's Christmas advertisements listed, among other pieces, "Go Down, Moses" sung by the Virginia Female Jubilee Singers and "Low-Down Blues" sung by Heywood's Black Bottom Ramblers,[147] the Jubilee Singers (if no one else) should have been enraged, according to the doctrinal beliefs of the black church. Decca Race Records, on the cover of its 1940 catalog, similarly placed a picture of Peetie Wheatstraw, whom their record labels billed as "the Devil's Son-in-Law," adjacent to a picture of the Selah Jubilee Singers.[148] AJAX Records engaged in the same religious impropriety, as was so vividly illustrated in one of its newspaper advertisements. To encourage the purchase of their records over the Christmas holiday, they drew a black Santa Claus whose gift to elated black home-owners was three large records—labeled "Dance Record," "Blues Record," and "Old Time Spirituals"—records almost as large as the grade-school girl and boy helping to roll them into the home.[149] Also advertised alongside the blues on the race records of Okeh, Paramount, and Columbia were recorded sermons that included choral singing, such as those on Vocalion Records by the well-traveled evangelist Rev. A. W. Nix.

Blues scholar Jeff Titon said the record advertisers were likely unaware that their side-by-side listing of religious songs and blues and side-by-side printing of pictures of preachers and blues singers probably hurt the sale of the religious songs.[150] This might have been the case. But one reason the Jubilee Singers or evangelist Nix might not have become enraged about their sacred art being advertised alongside the so-called "devil's music" was because capitalism engendered the demise of moral consensus.

Capitalism caused, among other things, mobilization, which disintegrated community. This, in turn, gave rise to urban anonymity and individualism and thus the demise of moral consensus. In the old South, the country bluesman traveling with his guitar was always identifiable as the stranger in town and therefore as the evil one who challenged the townspeople's moral consensus. But northward migration, urban mobility, and personal anonymity made everyone "the stranger," strangers who were not known to be good or evil within any established consensus. For instance, no consensus was reached regarding the most transient citizens of the northern black metropolises—the classic blueswomen—who were lauded for their success but were also criticized for their non-Victorian lifestyles.[151] In the city, then, everyone was potentially evil, so any earlier consensus regarding what was believed to be morally good or righteous was severely undermined.

Capitalism—the consequence of blues becoming increasingly part and parcel of the commercial industry following the Depression—was also responsible for the decreased expressive flexibility of the blues, expressivity that was probably at its height in the holler. As record companies pursued the commercially successful sounds of their competitors' top sellers, pressuring their contractees to revamp popular conventions derived from earlier hits, lyrics became increasingly trivialized and standardized and the distinctive regional cosmology that came to Chicago with the southern emigrants began to crumble. This is what Howard W. Odum and Guy B. Johnson were saying in their claim that "folk blues," though it would undergo modification, would always reflect early black belief more accurately than "formal blues."[152] Blues scholar William Barlow understood well this price that was paid for the industry's search for song formulas based on earlier hits:

> This tendency was encouraged by the technical demands for the record manufacturers (all songs put on wax during this period had to be three minutes long), as well as by the belief of most record company executives that standardized musical arrangements and lyrics would appeal to a wider audience. These conservative restraints helped to shape a more conventional Chicago blues sound. As a result, some of the unique regional styles and themes that had been brought to Chicago from the rural South began to disappear. The price often paid

for the commercial success of the blues was separation from their folk roots.[153]

Regarding this end result, blues scholar Samuel Charters said that as Blind Lemon Jefferson ran out of songs from downhome Texas he began singing blues that became textually "thin" and musically "dull."[154] This very kind of thing led Texas bluesman Lightnin' Hopkins to complain that Chicago bluesmen only knew how to sing about women.[155] Garon, proceeding even further with his surrealist reading of the blues, said commercialization diluted the blues to the extent that blues singers became "songsters" rather than carrying on their revolt against repression as subversive poets.[156] "Modern blues . . . tends, in its most sophisticated performers, to leave behind the power of the image and the capacity of fantasy, and to concentrate, almost without even a glimmer of imagination, on more mundane activities."[157] Oliver, rather insightfully, saw the reduction of blues lyrics to the common theme of unrequited love and sexual prowess as parallel to the use of amplification and sound stereotypes to mask the "deteriorization" of the music.[158] The emphasis placed on entertainment over social commentary and nonstereotypical sound might have, according to Mike Rowe in his study of Chicago blues, marked the trauma of the Depression or, earlier, the country-to-city diaspora: "Certainly one of the differences between the early singers, who were always ready to comment on current topics, and the postwar inheritors of the tradition was the dwindling range of experiences covered by the latter-day singers. Their subject matter was seriously circumscribed and almost wholly to do with women and love. . . . This may have been another consequence of the overwhelming move from the country to the cities."[159]

One reason the city and urban blues singer placed less emphasis on social commentary than did the country blues singer was that the world of entertainment made modern blues less contemplative. City blues became less contemplative partly because overcrowding and the volume and density of noise in urban areas lessened the human capacity for attention and concentration.[160] Oliver blamed this occurrence on the emergence of electronic instruments,[161] a sense of which is discernible in Langston Hughes's review of Memphis Minnie's club performance on the eve of Chicago's 1943 new year: "The electric guitar is very loud, science having magnified all its softness away. Memphis Minnie sings through a microphone and her voice—hard and strong anyhow for a little woman's—is made harder and stronger by scientific sound. The singing, the electric guitar, and the drums are so hard and so loud, amplified as they are by General Electric on top of the icebox, that sometimes the voice, the words, and the melody get lost under sheer noise, leaving only the rhythm to come through clear."[162] The hardness and loudness of city blues was not only due to the "friction of space" in urban areas and the volume and density of noise but also to the shock effect of city life on first-generation southern emigrants—an effect that lost its force (as reflected in the more relaxed sound of urban blues) only after the first few generations settled into the city.

In addition to the above variables, the city's concrete and noise helped diminish the rural residue of southern religious cosmology because it, respectively, covered up nature and muted its sounds, nature being the key conduit with the spirit world. A city or urban blues singer was unable to go to the crossroads at midnight to learn his or her virtuosity from "the devil," for the city had innumerable crossroads, all of which were busy with the traffic of industrial trucks that did their carrying at night. Along with the noise of these trucks was, according to concerned citizens of Chicago, the honking and grinding of automobiles driven by thoughtless or indifferent "night owls."[163] There were also the taxicab drivers the *Defender* derided for being too lazy to get out of their cabs to ring doorbells: "He sits glued to his seat and honks and honks in the wee hours of early morning, waking up people in the neighborhood."[164] Neither was a crowded (already noisy) streetcar the place to give an old southern "holler." As a writer for the *Defender* said to the emigrants from the South, "Stop [w]hooping from one end of the street car to the other. You are not on a plantation, nor in a minstrel show before an audience."[165]

Even Langston Hughes, in his weekly *Defender* column, criticized this kind of whooping in public. Though he had a sincere appreciation for black folkways, he evidently did not stop to think that the allegedly loud speaking voice of southern blacks might have been of value in the noisy city. He said:

> Miss Zora Neale Hurston once said that the loudness of the Negro voice is probably a carry-over from Africa where people live mostly out-of-doors and use the human voice to call to each other across vast distances, having no telephones. She also said that life in the American South helped to sustain this traditional vocal strength, because people work in big fields,

135

mostly live in cabins and small houses, and often have no telephones either, so they just step out on the back porch and holler four houses down across three vacant lots to a neighbor concerning what is on their minds at the moment.[166]

Hughes went on to say how he thought the naturally loud voice of blacks might have resulted partly from the tradition of fervent praise in the black church, but all in all he saw the city as an inappropriate environment for this southern folkway.[167] Not only were whooping and loud talk inappropriate in the sophisticated city, but so was the loud music that record stores "emptied" into the public streets. Hughes said:

> There is a time and a place for everything. But for those who like dirty records, the place to hear them is hardly over a record shop loud speaker flooding the streets with double meanings, nor is a decent time the daylight hours when children are on their way to and from school.
>
> There ought to be a law against loud speakers emptying sound into the public streets anyhow. Certainly there ought to be restraints on the playing and sale of recorded obscenity, just as there is on the display and sale of dirty pictures or books.
>
> At night clubs and stag parties, songs with double meanings may amuse adults out on a spree. But "Jelly, Jelly" is scarcely suitable for a street corner concert magnified by electronics in broad daylight and repeated interminably at a pitch loud enough to wake up babies.[168]

Hughes concluded his complaint saying, "There is, after all, such a thing as good taste. It is not good taste to flood Negro business streets (or any other streets) with the kinds of dirty lyrics some recording companies permit singers to sing these days."[169] The point is that the subjugation of nature by the urban milieu opened up the way for the suppression of the rural cosmology, so that the total impact of city life (the context) upon the black emigrants from the South profoundly altered the blues (its text and texture).

Urban blues, in the words of T-Bone Walker, was texturally smoother, softer, and more modern, ballad-like, and less downhome than that which preceded it.[170] Like that of Chicagoans Otis Rush and Jimmy Reed, urban blues was not only texturally lighter in feeling, but textually lighter in meaning than its country and city precursors, demystified as it was by the city's concrete and noise. Such weighty, religious concerns as the "problem of evil" were no longer preponderantly pondered; they were subjugated, repressed. Because thinking about evil was about as burdensome and debilitating as the experience of evil itself, its sublimation was liberating to the urbane mentality. Although the reality of the "strong sense" of evil still existed doctrinally for black urban blues singers, urban blues, in relation to its precursor, registered an increasing subjugation of traditional southern cosmology beneath the predominant themes of sex and love.

In sum, in our paradigm of the blues continuum, country blues → city blues → urban blues, there was a diminishing of the rural residue of religion. The ingredient par excellence of the residue—the "strong sense" of evil—was thus reduced to mere misfortune or what was at least scientifically explainable. Thus, while country blues was a product of the mythological world the enslaved made out of the remnants of their African religions and the new cultural and religious influences, city blues was transitional religiously (like Langston Hughes's blues poetry) and urban blues was, in part, city blues denatured of the old cosmology via its subjugation by the black community's progressive element and the resulting sublimation by those who gave in to that social pressure.

NOTES

INTRODUCTION

1. David Evans, "Few Scholars Are Involved in Studying and Preserving the Music We Call the Blues," *The Chronicle of Higher Education,* 9 Nov. 1988, B4.

2. Langston Hughes, "Here to Yonder" (column), *The Chicago Defender,* 13 May 1944, 12.

3. Jeff Todd Titon, *Early Downhome Blues: A Musical and Cultural Analysis* (Urbana: Univ. of Illinois Press, 1977), 269.

4. Paul Oliver, *Blues Fell This Morning: Meaning in the Blues,* 2d ed. (Cambridge: Cambridge Univ. Press, 1990), 95.

5. Giles Oakley, *The Devil's Music: A History of the Blues* (New York: Taplinger, 1977), 50.

6. Oliver, *Blues Fell This Morning,* 118.

7. G. W. F. Hegel, *The Philosophy of History* (New York: Dover, 1956), 96. Cited in Molefi Kete Asante, *Kemet, Afrocentricity and Knowledge* (Trenton, N.J.: Africa World Press, 1990), 34.

8. Richard Wright, *12 Million Black Voices: A Folk History of the Negro in the United States* (New York: Viking, 1941), 128.

9. Richard Wright, foreword to Oliver, *Blues Fell This Morning,* xiv.

10. Ibid., xv.

11. Phil Patton, "Satan, Now On CD," *Esquire,* Oct. 1990, 95–96.

12. Julio Finn, *The Bluesman: The Musical Heritage of Black Men and Women in the Americas* (London: Quartet, 1986), 210.

13. Paul Garon, *Blues and the Poetic Spirit* (1975; New York: Da Capo, 1979), 7, 8.

14. Ibid., 14.

15. Paul Carus, *The History of the Devil and the Idea of Evil: From the Earliest Times to the Present Day* (1899; LaSalle, Ill.: Open Court, 1974), 407–8.

16. Garon, *Blues and the Poetic Spirit,* 149.

17. *The Chicago Defender,* 28 June 1924, 7.

18. *The Chicago Defender,* 23 May 1925, pt. 1, 6.

19. *The Chicago Defender*, 30 Jan. 1926, pt. 1, 7.

20. Titon, *Early Downhome Blues,* 266.

21. Houston A. Baker, Jr., *Modernism and the Harlem Renaissance* (Chicago: Univ. of Chicago Press, 1987), 21.

22. Finn, *The Bluesman,* 192.

23. Charles Keil, *Urban Blues* (Chicago: Univ. of Chicago Press, 1966), 38.

24. Alan Lomax, *The Folk Songs of North America* (Garden City, N.Y.: Dolphin, 1975), 578.

25. David Burrows, *Sound, Speech, and Music* (Amherst: Univ. of Massachusetts Press, 1990), 103–4.

26. Cited in Ray Coleman, *Clapton! An Authorized Biography* (New York: Warner, 1986), 28.

27. Ibid., 8.

28. Nelson George, *The Death of Rhythm & Blues* (New York: Pantheon, 1988), 108.

29. Langston Hughes, "Negro Entertainers Should Look to Our Own Rich Heritage for Material," *The Chicago Defender,* 18 Feb. 1950, 6.

30. "Handy 'Blue' Over Blues," *The Chicago Defender,* 15 Mar. 1952, 23.

31. Langston Hughes, "Negro Entertainers Should Look to Our Own Rich Heritage for Material," 6.

32. W. C. Handy, "The Heart of the Blues," *The Etude,* Mar. 1940, 193.

33. "Snub Handy in Town He Made Great," *The Chicago Defender,* 13 Oct. 1951, 1.

34. Zora Neale Hurston, "Characteristics of Negro Expression," in *Voices from the Harlem Renaissance,* ed. Nathan Irvin Huggins (New York: Oxford Univ. Press, 1976), 235.

35. LeRoi Jones, *Blues People: The Negro Experience in White America and the Music that Developed from It* (New York: Morrow, 1963), 148.

36. Alan Dundes, ed., *Mother Wit from the Laughing Barrel: Readings in the Interpretation of Afro-American Folklore* (Englewood Cliffs, N.J.: Prentice-Hall, 1973), 470.

37. Del Jones, *Culture Bandits* (Philadelphia: Hikeka Press, 1990), 62, 74.

38. Ibid., 62.

39. Asante, *Kemet, Afrocentricity and Knowledge,* 111–12, 120.

40. Jacques Attali, *Noise: The Political Economy of Music,* trans. Brian Massumi (Minneapolis: Univ. of Minnesota Press, 1985), 103–4.

41. Langston Hughes, "Simple Declares Be-Bop Music Comes from Bop! Bop! Bop! Mop!" *The Chicago Defender,* 19 Nov. 1949, 6.

42. Ibid.

43. Oliver, *Blues Fell This Morning,* 283.

44. Wright, foreword to Oliver, *Blues Fell This Morning,* xvi.

45. "Billie Holiday Ill Has Right to Sing Blues," *The Chicago Defender,* 21 Oct. 1950, 1.

46. Dundes, *Mother Wit from the Laughing Barrel,* 470.

47. Jeffrey Burton Russell, *The Devil: Perceptions of Evil from Antiquity to Primitive Christianity* (Ithaca, N.Y.: Cornell Univ. Press, 1977), 18.

48. David Parkin, ed., *The Anthropology of Evil* (Oxford: Basil Blackwell, 1985), 3.

49. Bruce Reed, *Dynamics of Religion: Process and Movement in Christian Churches* (London: Darton, Longman and Todd, 1978), 54, 73, 74, 78–79.

50. Andrew M. Greeley, *Religious Change in America* (Cambridge: Harvard Univ. Press, 1989), 43.

51. Ibid., 66.

52. Barry Lee Pearson, *Virginia Piedmont Blues: The Lives and Art of Two Virginia Bluesmen* (Philadelphia: Univ. of Pennsylvania Press, 1990), 158.

53. Houston A. Baker, Jr., *The Journey Back: Issues in Black Literature and Criticism* (Chicago: Univ. of Chicago Press, 1980), 163.

54. Asante, *Kemet, Afrocentricity and Knowledge,* 27–28.

55. Keil, *Urban Blues,* vii.

56. James H. Cone, *The Spirituals and the Blues: An Interpretation* (New York: Seabury, 1972), 7.

57. Ibid., 115.

58. Pete Chatman (Memphis Slim), oral history interview by Ray Allen, 16 May 1987, Memphis, tape 2, p. 2, Center for Southern Folklore, Memphis.

59. See Houston A. Baker, Jr., *Blues, Ideology, and Afro-American Literature: A Vernacular Theory* (Chicago: Univ. of Chicago Press, 1984).

60. Baker, *The Journey Back,* 164.

61. Booker T. Laury, oral history interview by George McDaniel, 31 Mar. 1983, Memphis, p. 19, Center for Southern Folklore, Memphis.

62. Jones, *Blues People,* 153.

63. Cited in Ollie Stewart, "What Price Jazz," *The Chicago Defender,* 7 Apr. 1934, 12.

64. "What Is Jazz? Convention Held in East to Assemble Stars' Opinions," *The Chicago Defender,* 22 Sept. 1951, 23.

65. Baker's *Blues, Ideology, and Afro-American Literature* and Henry Louis Gates, Jr.,'s *The Signifying Monkey: A Theory of Afro-American Literary Criticism* (New York: Oxford Univ. Press, 1988).

66. Earl Conrad, "Blues School of Literature," *The Chicago Defender,* 22 Dec. 1945, 11.

67. Ibid.

68. Asante, *Kemet, Afrocentricity and Knowledge,* 167.

69. Dundes, *Mother Wit from the Laughing Barrel,* 471.

70. Cited in Paul Oliver, *Conversation with the Blues* (New York: Horizon, 1965), 30.

71. Hughes, "Here to Yonder," 9 Jan. 1943, 14.

72. See Alan Dundes, "Text, Texture and Context," *Southern Folklore Quarterly* 28 (1964): 251–65.

73. Alain LeRoy Locke, *The Negro and His Music* (1936; Salem, N.H.: Ayer, 1988), 12.

CHAPTER 1

1. Zora Neale Hurston, *Mules and Men* (Bloomington: Indiana Univ. Press, 1978), 287.
2. Newman Ivey White, ed., *The Frank C. Brown Collection of North Carolina Folklore* (Durham, N.C.: Duke Univ. Press, 1964), vol. 6: 460.
3. There are recessive forms of the tragic conception of life in the Adamic myth and other parts of the Old and New Testaments—in the Old Testament, God's jealousy of the boldness, inventiveness, and freedom of human beings, which resulted in the expulsion of the primal couple from the garden, and the destruction of Babel; and in the New, the prayer "Lead us not into temptation." Paul Ricoeur, *The Symbolism of Evil*, trans. Emerson Buchanan (Boston: Beacon, 1969), 156, 240, 254, 325.
4. See the advertisement in *The Chicago Defender*, 23 July 1927, pt. 1, 6.
5. Howard W. Odum and Guy B. Johnson, *Negro Workaday Songs* (Chapel Hill: Univ. of North Carolina Press, 1926), 142–43.
6. Daphne Duval Harrison, *Black Pearls: Blues Queens of the 1920s* (Brunswick, N.J.: Rutgers Univ. Press, 1988), 116–17.
7. Ricoeur, *The Symbolism of Evil*, 213–14.
8. Ibid., 173.
9. Ibid., 227.
10. Hurston, *Mules and Men*, 254.
11. Peter Guralnick, *Searching for Robert Johnson* (New York: Dutton, 1989), 45.
12. Samuel B. Charters, *The Country Blues* (New York: Rinehart, 1959), 66. See also E. S. Virgo, "A Note on the Death Date of Blind Lemon Jefferson," *Black Music Research Bulletin* 10, no. 2 (Fall 1988): 14–15.
13. Cited in Paul Garon, *The Devil's Son-in-Law: The Story of Peetie Wheatstraw and His Songs* (London: Studio Vista, 1971), 99.
14. "Natchez Fire Brings Songs by Lewis Set," *The Chicago Defender*, 29 June 1940, 21.
15. Ricoeur, *The Symbolism of Evil*, 173.
16. John W. Roberts, *From Trickster to Badman: The Black Folk Hero in Slavery and Freedom* (Philadelphia: Univ. of Pennsylvania Press, 1989), 1, 13.
17. Ibid., 176.
18. Ibid.
19. Ibid., 179.
20. "Bad Nigger Makes Good Minstrel," *Life*, 19 Apr. 1937.
21. Roberts, *From Trickster to Badman*, 173–74.
22. Ibid., 200.
23. Ibid., 186, 189.
24. Ibid., 200.
25. Ibid.
26. Ibid., 201, 211.
27. Ibid., 203.
28. Ibid., 213.

29. Mimi Clar Melnick, "'I Can Peep Through Muddy Water and Spy Dry Land': Boasts in the Blues," in *Mother Wit from the Laughing Barrel*, ed. Dundes, 268.
30. Ibid., 276.
31. William Barlow, *"Looking Up at Down": The Emergence of Blues Culture* (Philadelphia: Temple Univ. Press, 1989), 327.
32. Garon, *The Devil's Son-in-Law*, 38, 63–64.
33. Cited in Garon, *The Devil's Son-in-Law*, 64.
34. Newbell Niles Puckett, *Folk Beliefs of the Southern Negro* (Chapel Hill: Univ. of North Carolina Press, 1926), 79, 554.
35. Bruce Bastin, *Red River Blues: The Blues Tradition in the Southeast* (Urbana: Univ. of Illinois Press, 1986), 281.
36. David Evans, *Big Road Blues: Tradition and Creativity in the Folk Blues* (New York: Da Capo, 1982), 114–15.
37. *The Chicago Defender,* 30 Jan. 1926, pt. 1, 7.
38. Newbell S. Booth, Jr., "God and the Gods in West Africa," in *African Religions: A Symposium*, ed. Newbell S. Booth, Jr. (New York: NOK, 1977), 170.
39. Cited in Julius Lester, "Preachin' the Blues," *Sing Out!* 15, no. 3: 46. Cited in Paul Oliver, *Screening the Blues: Aspects of the Blues Tradition* (New York: Da Capo, 1968), 49.
40. *The Chicago Defender,* 22 Aug. 1931, 3.
41. Robert D. Pelton, *The Trickster in West Africa: A Study of Mythic Irony and Sacred Delight* (Berkeley: Univ. of California Press, 1980), 256.
42. Ibid., 261.
43. Ibid., 245–46.
44. George P. Rawick, ed., *The American Slave: A Composite Autobiography* (Westport, Conn.: Greenwood, 1977), suppl. ser. 1, vol. 6, pt. 1, 271.
45. Puckett, *Folk Beliefs of the Southern Negro,* 526.
46. Jessie Gaston Mulira, "The Case of Voodoo in New Orleans," in *Africanisms in American Culture*, ed. Joseph E. Holloway (Bloomington: Indiana Univ. Press, 1990), 56, 62–63.
47. Rawick, ed., *The American Slave,* suppl. ser. 1, vol. 8, 1207.
48. Titon, *Early Downhome Blues,* 33.
49. *The Chicago Defender,* 9 Apr. 1932, 3.
50. Zora Neal Hurston, *Tell My Horse* (Berkeley, Calif.: Turtle Island, 1981), 257; *Mules and Men,* 205, 234.
51. Finn, *The Bluesman,* 188.
52. Hurston, *Mules and Men,* 193.
53. Michel S. Laguerre, *Voodoo and Politics in Haiti* (New York: St. Martin's, 1989), 36.
54. Ibid., 56–57, 70.
55. Hurston, *Mules and Men,* 254.
56. Richard M. Dorson, *American Negro Folktales* (Greenwich, Conn.: Fawcett, 1967), 212–13, 237.
57. White, ed., *The Frank C. Brown Collection* 7: 41.
58. Ibid., 41–42.

59. Mike Waldman, "Superstitions? No? Then You Can Not Be an Actor or Singer," *The Chicago Defender*, 26 Nov. 1949, 26.

60. Puckett, *Folk Beliefs of the Southern Negro*, 113–34, 135; and White, ed., *The Frank C. Brown Collection* 7: 148–49.

61. Cited in William Ferris, *Blues From the Delta* (Garden City, N.Y: Anchor/ Doubleday, 1979), 86.

62. Cited in Stefan Grossman, *Delta Blues Guitar* (New York: Oak, 1969), 115.

63. Donald Taylor, "Theological Thoughts about Evil," in *The Anthropology of Evil*, ed. Parkin, 28.

64. See Clifton H. Johnson, ed., *God Struck Me Dead: Religious Conversion Experiences and Autobiographies of Ex-slaves* (Philadelphia: Pilgrim, 1969), 17, 59, 91, 100, 121, 143, 146, 149.

65. Ibid., 14.

66. *The Chicago Defender*, 21 June 1930, 5.

67. Puckett, *Folk Beliefs of the Southern Negro*, 110, 498.

68. Ibid., 248, 252, 551.

69. Melville J. Herskovits, *The Myth of the Negro Past* (1941; rpt. Gloucester, Mass.: Peter Smith, 1970), 251.

70. John Ashton, *The Devil in Britain and America* (London: Ward and Downey, 1896), 311.

71. Carus, *The History of the Devil and the Idea of Evil*, 282.

72. Jean Delumeau, *Sin and Fear: The Emergence of a Western Guilt Culture 13th– 18th Centuries*, trans. Eric Nicholson (New York: St. Martin's, 1990), 554–55, 556.

73. Ashton, *The Devil in Britain and America*, 2.

74. Ibid., 109, 159.

75. Ibid., 148.

76. Ibid., 108.

77. Ibid., 111.

78. Ibid., 265.

79. Ibid., 257–58.

80. Ibid., 271.

81. Ibid., 290.

82. *The Chicago Defender*, 22 Oct. 1927, pt. 1, 3.

83. Ashton, *The Devil in Britain and America*, 3–4, 22–23.

84. Puckett, *Folk Beliefs of the Southern Negro*, 550.

85. Carus, *The History of the Devil and the Idea of Evil*, 284.

86. Rawick, ed., *The American Slave*, suppl. ser. 1, vol. 7, pt. 2, 344–45. Dialect omitted.

87. Delumeau, *Sin and Fear*, 3, 4, 189, 482, 490.

88. Ibid., 502.

89. Charles P. Browning, "Religion a 'Way of Escape'," *The Chicago Defender*, 14 July 1934, 10.

90. Puckett, *Folk Beliefs of the Southern Negro*, 550.

91. Harold Courlander, *A Treasury of Afro-American Folklore* (New York: Crown, 1976), 456.

92. Virginia Frazer Boyle, *Devil Tales* (Freeport, N.Y.: Books for Libraries, 1972), 161.

93. Courlander, *A Treasury of Afro-American Folklore*, 454–55.

94. Puckett, *Folk Beliefs of the Southern Negro*, 188, 551; White, ed., *The Frank C. Brown Collection* 7: 136; Boyle, *Devil Tales*, 107.

95. Grossman, *Delta Blues Guitar*, 115.

96. Dorson, *American Negro Folktales*, 137.

97. Puckett, *Folk Beliefs of the Southern Negro*, 551, 557; see also Boyle, *Devil Tales*, 113, 124, 164.

98. Boyle, *Devil Tales*, 185.

99. Ibid., 83.

100. Ibid., 113.

101. White, ed., *The Frank C. Brown Collection* 7: 276.

102. Carus, *The History of the Devil and the Idea of Evil*, 438.

103. James R. Aswell, et al., eds., *God Bless the Devil!: Liar's Bench Tales* (Chapel Hill: Univ. of North Carolina Press, 1940), x.

104. Ibid., xi.

105. Ibid., 194–98, the tale "Luster an de Devil."

106. Even in early modern Britain where the devil was a far greater terror than in early African-American culture, he was still put into comic situations and joked about. Often depicted as being intellectually deficient, he was actually capable of being outwitted by shrewd human beings (Ashton, *The Devil in Britain and America*, 16–17).

107. See Robert M. W. Dixon and John Godrich, *Recording the Blues* (New York: Stein and Day, 1970), 69.

108. Boyle, *Devil Tales*, 181.

109. Ashton, *The Devil in Britain and America*, 168, 258.

110. Carus, *The History of the Devil and the Idea of Evil*, 114–15.

111. Langston Hughes and Arna Bontemps, *The Book of Negro Folklore* (New York: Dodd, Mead, 1958), xiii–iv.

112. White, ed., *The Frank C. Brown Collection* 7: 151, 154.

113. Puckett, *Folk Beliefs of the Southern Negro*, 150–51.

114. Hurston, *Mules and Men*, 229.

115. Ashton, *The Devil in Britain and America*, 272.

116. Puckett, *Folk Beliefs of the Southern Negro*, 554.

117. Ibid.

118. Cited in David Evans, *Tommy Johnson* (London: Studio Vista, 1971), 22–23.

119. Bruce Bastin, "The Devil's Goin' to Get You," *North Carolina Folklore Journal* 21, no. 4 (Nov. 1973): 190.

120. Oliver, *Conversation with the Blues*, 29. Dialect omitted.

121. See Boyle, *Devil Tales*, 72.

122. Rawick, ed., *The American Slave*, suppl. ser. 1, vol. 10, pt. 5, 2010.

123. Evans, *Tommy Johnson*, 30.

124. Johnson, ed., *God Struck Me Dead*, xvii.

125. Ibid., 19, 21.

126. See Roberts, *From Trickster to Badman*, 201–2.

127. John F. Szwed, "Afro-American Musical Adaption," in *Afro-American Anthropology: Contemporary Perspectives,* ed. Norman E. Whitten and John F. Szwed (New York: Free Press, 1970), 221.
128. See Johnson, ed., *God Struck Me Dead,* 99.
129. Ibid., 58.
130. Carter G. Woodson, "And the Negro Loses His Soul," *The Chicago Defender* 25 June 1932, 14.
131. Cited in Giles Oakely, *The Devil's Music: A History of the Blues* (New York; Taplinger, 1977), 50–51.
132. Zora Neale Hurston, *Dust Tracks on a Road: An Autobiography,* 2d ed. (Urbana: Univ. of Illinois Press, 1984), 270, 272.
133. Hurston, *Mules and Men,* 254.
134. Cited in Puckett, *Folk Beliefs of the Southern Negro,* 252.
135. Dorson, *American Negro Folktales,* 255.
136. William Francis Allen, Charles Pickard Ware, and Lucy McKim Garrison, eds. *Slave Songs of the United States* (New York: Peter Smith, 1929), 108.
137. See Martin Southwold, "The Popular Culture of Evil in Urban South India," in *The Anthropology of Evil,* ed. Parkin, 132, 136.
138. Herskovits, *The Myth of the Negro Past,* 251.
139. Ibid., 253, 254.
140. Ibid., 252–53.

CHAPTER 2

1. Rod Gruver, "The Blues as a Secular Religion," *Blues World,* no. 29 (Apr. 1970): 3, 5.
2. Ibid., no. 29: 5; no. 32: 9.
3. Ludwig Feuerbach, *The Essence of Christianity,* ed. E. Graham Waring and F. W. Strothmann (New York: Continuum, 1989), vii, viii, ix, 11, 39, 47.
4. Gruver, "The Blues as a Secular Religion," no. 32: 7.
5. Ibid., no. 31: 6.
6. Ibid., no. 32: 7.
7. Larry Neal, "The Ethos of the Blues," *Black Scholar* 3, no. 10 (Summer 1972): 45.
8. Ibid., 44.
9. Ibid., 47.
10. Cone, *The Spirituals and the Blues,* 5.
11. Ibid., 110.
12. Ibid., 128, 132.
13. Ibid., 112.
14. Oliver, *Blues Fell This Morning,* 227.
15. Ibid., 278.
16. Ibid., 255.
17. Cone, *The Spirituals and the Blues,* 114, 119.
18. Evans, *Big Road Blues,* 54, 58.
19. Albert Murray, *Stomping the Blues* (New York: Vintage, 1982), 42.

20. Oliver, *Blues Fell This Morning,* 255.
21. Cited in Oakley, *The Devil's Music,* 60.
22. Ferris, *Blues from the Delta,* 28.
23. See Odum and Johnson, *Negro Workaday Songs,* 144.
24. Evans, *Big Road Blues,* 30.
25. Garon, *Blues and the Poetic Spirit,* 134.
26. See Ashton, *The Devil in Britain and America,* 154.
27. Cited in Ferris, *Blues from the Delta,* 79.
28. Cited in Houston A. Baker, Jr., *Afro-American Poetics: Revisions of Harlem and the Black Aesthetic* (Madison: Univ. of Wisconsin Press, 1988), 158. See Larry Neal, "Aesthetics and Culture," *The Drum* 9 (1978): 11–12.
29. "You all may not know what a juke house is. That's way back out in the country, them old raggedy houses. You didn't have but one night to have a good time so we stay up all Saturday night and try to get some rest on Sunday." James "Son" Thomas, interview by William Ferris, New Haven, Feb. 27–28, 1974, roll 1, p. 2. William Ferris Collection, Archives and Special Collections Dept., Univ. of Mississippi, University, Miss.
30. Murray, *Stomping the Blues,* 38.
31. Van Zula Hunt (b. 1902), oral history interview by George McDaniel, 5 Jan. 1983, Memphis, tape 3, p. 13, Center for Southern Folklore, Memphis, Tenn.
32. Cited in Derrick Stewart-Baxter, "The Story of Memphis Slim," *Sing Out!* 11, no. 3 (Summer 1961): 4.
33. Finn, *The Bluesman,* 207.
34. Leonard Goines, "The Blues as Black Therapy," *Black World,* Nov. 1973, 31.
35. Keil, *Urban Blues,* 143–44, 145.
36. Ibid., 164.
37. Ibid., 143.
38. Cited in Oakely, *The Devil's Music,* 216.
39. Robert Palmer, *Deep Blues* (New York: Viking, 1981), 81.
40. "Ethel Waters Recalls Being Stranded in 1931," *The Chicago Defender,* 1 Dec. 1939. 15.
41. Gene Ray, "Bronze Blues Queen Greeted at Cleveland by Huge Audience," *The Chicago Defender,* 14 Nov. 1936, 20.
42. "Billie Holiday Goes on Tour," *The Chicago Defender,* 15 Sept. 1945, 16.
43. Alan Lomax, "'Sinful' Songs of the Southern Negro," *Southwest Review* 19, no. 2 (Jan. 1934): 109.
44. Oliver, *Conversation with the Blues,* 145.
45. Keil, *Urban Blues,* 145.
46. Oliver, *Screening the Blues,* 49, 66.
47. Ibid., 67.
48. Ibid., 47.
49. Chris Albertson, *Bessie* (New York: Stein and Day, 1972), 130.
50. Cone, *The Spirituals and the Blues,* 127.
51. Oliver, *Conversation with the Blues,* 167. Dialect omitted.
52. Wright, *12 Million Black Voices,* 128; Cone, *The Spirituals and the Blues,* 108–42.

53. Oliver, *Blues Fell This Morning*, 279.

54. Oliver, *Conversation with the Blues*, 18, 108–9, 167, 160, 168.

55. Ibid., 16.

56. Handy, "The Heart of the Blues," 193.

57. Cited in Oliver, *Conversation with the Blues*, 168.

58. Cited in Oakley, *The Devil's Music*,116.

59. Evans, *Big Road Blues*, 44.

60. Cited in Oliver, *Conversation with the Blues*, 168.

61. Pearson, *Virginia Piedmont Blues*, 74.

62. Ibid., 145.

63. Ibid., 201.

64. Cited in Oakely, *The Devil's Music*, 115.

65. Garon, *Blues and the Poetic Spirit*, 7, 8, 107, 134.

66. Oliver, *Blues Fell This Morning*, 117, 279.

67. Ibid., 279.

68. "Tragic Scenes in Fire which Took More than 200 Lives in Natchez, Miss.," *The Chicago Defender*, 4 May 1940, 6.

69. "Local Groups of Both Races Give to Fund," *The Chicago Defender*, 4 May 1940, 5.

70. Oliver, *Blues Fell This Morning*, 231. Emphasis added.

71. Ronald Inden, "Hindu Evil as Unconquered Lower Self," in *The Anthropology of Evil*, ed. Parkin, 150.

72. John A. Burrison, ed., *Storytellers: Folktales and Legends from the South* (Athens: Univ. of Georgia Press, 1989), 176. Dialect omitted.

73. Oliver, *Screening the Blues*, 56, 75–76.

74. James "Son" Thomas, interview by William Ferris, Leland, Miss., 1968, tape 5, p. 18; tape 30, p. 21. William Ferris Collection, Archives and Special Collections Dept., Univ. of Mississippi, University, Miss.

75. Pearson, *Virginia Piedmont Blues*, 150.

76. Ibid., 152.

77. Oliver, *Screening the Blues*, 23.

78. Ibid.

79. Gruver, "The Blues as a Secular Religion," no. 32: 7–8.

80. Garon, *Blues and the Poetic Spirit*, 66.

81. Michel Foucault, *The History of Sexuality* 1, trans. Robert Hurley (New York: Vintage, 1989), 6.

82. Lomax, *The Folk Songs of North America*, 577.

83. Frantz Fanon, *Toward the African Revolution* (New York: Grove, 1967), 37. Cited in Ortiz M. Walton, *Music: Black, White and Blue* (New York: Morrow, 1972), 33.

84. Cited in James H. Cone, *God of the Oppressed* (New York: Seabury, 1975), 185.

85. See Harrison, *Black Pearls*, 138.

86. Ricoeur, *The Symbolism of Evil*, 101, 104.

87. Ibid., 146.

88. Ibid., 104.

89. Ibid., 69.

90. Cited in Oliver, *Conversation with the Blues,* 165.
91. Thomas, interview, 1968, tape 30, p. 17.
92. "Singing for the Devil," *Time,* 15 Sept. 1947.
93. Lester, "Preachin' the Blues," 46. This comment was made by Son House as he introduced his song "Preachin' the Blues" (first recorded in 1930) before a concert audience in Wabash, Indiana, in 1964.
94. Flora Molton, unpublished interview by Eleanor Ellis, p. 7, *Living Blues* files, Center for the Study of Southern Culture, University of Mississippi, University, Miss.
95. Thomas, interview, 1974, roll 15, p. 5.
96. Ibid., roll 18, p. 2.
97. Oliver, *Screening the Blues,* 69–70.
98. Friedrich Nietzsche, *Beyond Good and Evil: Prelude to a Philosophy of the Future,* trans. Walter Kaufmann (1886; New York: Vintage, 1989), 1.
99. Chatman, oral history interview, 16 May 1987, tape 2, pp. 7–8.
100. Thomas, interview, 1968, tape 5, p. 17.
101. Odum and Johnson, *Negro Workaday Songs,* 20–21.
102. Cited in Oliver, *Conversation with the Blues,* 169–70.
103. "The Rev. Rubin Lacy," interview by David Evans, *Blues Unlimited,* no. 42 (Mar.–Apr. 1967): 5.
104. "New Dinah Washington: She Sings Sundays Now," *The Chicago Defender,* 4 Mar. 1950, 20.
105. Hunt, oral history interview, tape 3, pp. 6, 11–12.
106. "The Rev. Rubin Lacy," interview by David Evans, *Blues Unlimited,* no. 44 (June–July, 1967): 7.
107. "The Rev. Rubin Lacy," interview by David Evans, *Blues Unlimited,* no. 43 (May 1967): 13–14.
108. Oliver, *Conversation with the Blues,* 168.
109. Ibid., 160, 168.
110. Pearson, *Virginia Piedmont Blues,* 150.
111. Hunt, oral history interview, tape 3, pp. 6, 11–12.
112. Oliver, *Conversation with the Blues,* 167.
113. Pearson, *Virginia Piedmont Blues,* 38.
114. Oliver, *Conversation with the Blues,* 25.
115. "Bostic's Prof. Does Not Like 'Barfly Baby' Blues," *The Chicago Defender,* 24 July 1948, 8.
116. Molton, unpublished interview, 8.
117. "Living Blues Interview: Lowell Fulson," *Living Blues* 2, no. 5 (Summer 1971): 22.
118. "Reverend Robert Wilkins," interview by Pete Welding, *Blues Unlimited,* no. 55 (July 1968): 11.
119. "Blues Singer Believes New Day Coming," [Arkansas] *State Press,* 15 Dec. 1944.
120. Clyde E. B. Bernhardt, oral history interview by Sandy Lieb (Newark, N.J., 31 Dec. 1974), pp. 34, 40, *Living Blues* Archival Collection, Mississippi Blues Archive, University of Mississippi, University, Miss.

121. Bill Phillips, "Piedmont Country Blues," *Southern Exposure,* Summer 1974, 60.
122. "Georgia Tom Dorsey" (interview by Jim and Amy O'Neal, 27 Nov. 1974; 17 Jan. and 24 Jan. 1975, Chicago), *Living Blues,* no. 20 (Mar.–Apr. 1975): 17, 18, 29, 30, 33, 34.
123. "Charges Singers with 'Jazzing' Gospel Music," *The Chicago Defender,* 11 Aug. 1951, 2.
124. Cited in Keil, *Urban Blues,* 147.
125. Cited in Garon, *Blues and the Poetic Spirit,* 9.
126. St. Clair Drake and Horace R. Cayton, *Black Metropolis: A Study of Negro Life in a Northern City* (New York: Harcourt, Brace, 1945), 616.
127. Keil, *Urban Blues,* 147.
128. Titon, *Early Downhome Blues,* 37.
129. Gatemouth Moore, oral history interview by George McDaniel, 25 Jan. 1983, Memphis, tape 4, p. 81, Center for Southern Folklore, Memphis, Tenn.
130. David Evans, "Charley Patton; the Conscience of the Delta," in *The Voice of the Delta: Charley Patton and the Mississippi Blues Traditions, Influences and Comparisons,* ed. Robert Sacre (De Liege, Belgium: Presses Universitaires, 1987, 136, 137, 139, 142, 171.
131. "Reverend Robert Wilkins," 11.
132. Evans, *Tommy Johnson,* 30–31.
133. Mike Rowe, *Chicago Blues: The City and the Music* (New York: Da Capo, 1975), 194.
134. Keil, *Urban Blues,* 145.
135. Bastin, *Red River Blues,* 138–39.
136. Molton, unpublished interview, 8.
137. The twist to this story is that James (1902–1969) was rediscovered and returned to performing blues in 1964. Often it was the wife who talked her husband out of playing the blues. Sometimes when the wife died the husband went back to playing the blues.
138. Joan Fenton, "Rev. Gary Davis 1896–1972," *Sing Out!* 21, no. 5 (1972): 4.
139. Carey James Tate, "Famed Lizzie Miles' Death Ends Era of Blues Singing," *The Louisiana Weekly,* 30 Mar. 1963.
140. Gatemouth Moore, oral history interview, 25 Jan. 1983, tape 2, pp. 40–41.
141. "The Rev. Rubin Lacy," *Blues Unlimited,* no. 42: 5–6.
142. "Reverend Jack Harp," interview by Jeff Godrich, *Blues Unlimited,* no. 26 (Oct. 1965): 4, 5. See also Rev. Walter Davis's story in Oliver, *Conversation with the Blues,* 167.
143. Oliver, *Conversation with the Blues,* 160.
144. Thomas, interview, 1968, tape 5, p. 18; tape 30, p. 21.
145. Thomas, interview, 1974, roll 15, p. 5.
146. "The Rev. Rubin Lacy," *Blues Unlimited,* no. 43: 13.

CHAPTER 3

1. Stanley Hauerwas, *Naming the Silences: God, Medicine, and the Problem of Suffering* (Grand Rapids, Mich.: Eerdmans, 1990), 62.

2. Cone, *The Spirituals and the Blues,* 125–26.

3. Lawrence W. Levine, *Black Culture and Black Consciousness: Afro-American Folk Thought from Slavery to Freedom* (New York: Oxford Univ. Press, 1977), 234.

4. Garon, *Blues and the Poetic Spirit,* 135–36.

5. Ibid.

6. Cited in Baker, *Afro-American Poetics,* 157–58.

7. Albert Camus, *The Rebel: An Essay on Man in Revolt,* trans. Anthony Bower (New York: Knopf, 1969), 101.

8. Kenneth Surin, *Theology and the Problem of Evil* (Oxford: Basil Blackwell, 1986), 100.

9. Camus, *The Rebel,* 24, 101.

10. Oliver, *Screening the Blues,* 33.

11. Ibid., 35.

12. Asante, *Kemet, Afrocentricity and Knowledge,* 181.

13. See C. G. Jung, "On the Psychology of the Trickster Figure," the postscript to Paul Radin, *The Trickster: A Study in American Indian Mythology* (London: Routledge and Kegan Paul, 1956), 195–211.

14. John A. Sanford, "The Problem of Evil in Christianity and Analytical Psychology," in *Carl Jung and Christian Spirituality,* ed. Robert L. Moore (New York: Paulist Press, 1988), 129–30.

15. Ibid., 129.

16. Puckett, *Folk Beliefs of the Southern Negro,* 546.

17. Newbell Niles Puckett, "Race-Pride and Folk-Lore," *Opportunity* 4, no. 39 (Mar. 1926): 83.

18. Zora Neale Hurston, *The Sanctified Church* (Berkeley, Calif.: Turtle Island, 1983), 103.

19. Jones, *Blues People,* 92.

20. Sanford, "The Problem of Evil," 113.

21. Cone, *The Spirituals and the Blues,* 131.

22. Murray, *Stomping the Blues,* 27.

23. Don McClean, "Josh White; a Farewell," *Sing Out!* 19, no. 4 (Winter 1969–70): 12.

24. Sanford, "The Problem of Evil," 125.

25. Ibid.

26. Surin, *Theology and the Problem of Evil,* 48.

27. Camus, *The Rebel,* 20. Emphasis added.

28. Oliver, *Blues Fell This Morning,* 275.

29. Cited in Oliver, *Conversation with the Blues,* 25.

30. Ibid., 102.

31. Ibid., 25.

32. Baker, *Afro-American Poetics,* 157.

33. Baker, *Blues, Ideology, and Afro-American Literature,* 30.

34. William Barton, ed., *Old Plantation Hymns: A Collection of Hitherto Unpublished Melodies of the Slave and the Freedman, with Historical and Descriptive Notes* (1895; New York: AMS Press, 1972), 252.

35. Rawick, ed., *The American Slave,* suppl. ser. 1, vol. 6, 81.
36. Murray, *Stomping the Blues,* 24.
37. Palmer, *Deep Blues,* 68.
38. See John 9:1–4 and Luke 13:2–6.
39. Ricoeur, *The Symbolism of Evil,* 31–32, 43–44.
40. Ibid., 31, 78, 261.
41. Oliver, *The Meaning of the Blues,* 322. Dialect omitted.
42. Ibid., 70.
43. Puckett, "Race-Pride and Folk-Lore," 83. Dialect omitted.
44. Baker, *Modernism and the Harlem Renaissance,* 17.
45. Ibid., 20, 22, 27, 33, 49, 75.
46. Ibid., 31.
47. See Odum and Johnson, *Negro Workaday Songs,* 210.
48. Cited in Steven C. Tracy, *Langston Hughes and the Blues* (Urbana: Univ. of Illinois Press, 1988), 115. Originally cited in Carl Van Vechten, "The Black Blues," *Vanity Fair* 26, no. 1 (1926): 86.
49. Oliver, *Screening the Blues,* 70–71.
50. Baker, *Blues, Ideology, and Afro-American Literature,* 194.
51. Burrison, ed., *Storytellers,* 160.
52. Camus, *The Rebel,* 25.
53. Oliver, *Screening the Blues,* 48.
54. "Negro Woman Held in Slavery for 29 Years; Society Couple Jailed," *The Chicago Defender,* 8 Mar. 1947, 2. Also see "'Slave Woman' Due Back Wages," *The Chicago Defender,* 29 Mar. 1947, 6.
55. Cited in Cone, *The Spirituals and the Blues,* 136. Emphasis added.
56. Ernest Becker, *The Structure of Evil: An Essay on the Unification of the Science of Man* (New York: Free Press, 1976), 18. Also see Surin, *Theology and the Problem of Evil,* 42.
57. William R. Jones, *Is God a White Racist?: A Preamble to Black Theology* (Garden City, N.Y.: Anchor/Doubleday, 1973), 59.
58. Ibid., 195.
59. Cited in Garon, *Blues and the Poetic Spirit,* 136.
60. Rawick, ed., *The American Slave,* suppl. ser. 1, vol. 7, 41. Dialect omitted.
61. Ibid., 96. Dialect omitted.
62. Johnson, ed., *God Struck Me Dead.* 161.
63. Ibid., 107.
64. Ibid., 161.
65. Cited in Oliver, *Conversation with the Blues,* 169.
66. Justin O'Brien, "The Dark Road of Floyd Jones," *Living Blues* 58 (Winter 1983–84): 5.
67. Cited in Levine, *Black Culture and Black Consciousness,* 267.
68. Oliver, *Conversation with the Blues,* 70.
69. Garon, *Blues and the Poetic Spirit,* 133.
70. Ibid., 130, 133.
71. Surin, *Theology and the Problem of Evil,* 11.

72. Paul D. L. Avis, "The Atonement," in *Keeping the Faith: Essays to Mark the Centenary of Lux Mundi,* ed. Geoffrey Wainwright (Philadelphia: Fortress; Allison Park, Penn.: Pickwick, 1988), 124.

73. Major J. Jones, *The Color of God: The Concept of God in Afro-American Thought* (Macon, Ga: Mercer Univ. Press, 1987), viii.

74. James H. Cone, *A Black Theology of Liberation* (New York: Lippincott, 1970), 111. Emphasis added.

75. Camus, *The Rebel,* 15.

76. "The Rev. Rubin Lacy," *Blues Unlimited,* no. 43: 13.

77. Ralph Ellison, *Invisible Man* (New York: Vintage, 1972), 51.

78. Baker, *Blues, Ideology, and Afro-American Literature,* 187–88.

79. Hunt, oral history interview, 5 Jan. 1983, p. 14.

80. Ibid., 15.

CONCLUSION

1. Cited in Tracy, *Langston Hughes and the Blues,* 32.

2. William L. Offord, "Other Causes of Migration from Dixie," *The Chicago Defender,* 26 July 1924, pt. 2, 1.

3. Langston Hughes, "U.S. Likes Nazis and Franco Better than Its Own Negroes," *The Chicago Defender.* 6 Nov. 1948, 6.

4. Offord, "Other Causes of Migration from Dixie."

5. *The Chicago Defender,* 14 Feb. 1925, pt. 1, 12.

6. "Convict Leasing," *The Chicago Defender,* 24 Nov. 1923, pt. 2, 1.

7. See the use of the phrases "negro heaven" and "kitchen heaven" in the narrative of Mississippi ex-slave Jack Jones in *The American Slave: A Composite Autobiography,* ed. Rawick, suppl. ser. 1, vol. 8, 1212.

8. Alan Lomax, "I Got the Blues," in *Mother Wit from the Laughing Barrel,* ed. Dundes, 484.

9. Alexander L. Jackson, "The Onlooker" (column), *The Chicago Defender,* 5 May 1923, 24.

10. *The Chicago Defender,* 17 Feb. 1923, 12.

11. "Exodus Continues from South by Thousands," *The Chicago Defender,* 2 June 1923, pt. 2, 13.

12. *The Chicago Defender* 17 Nov. 1923, pt. 2, 1.

13. "Letters of Negro Migrants of 1916–1918," *Journal of Negro History* 4 (July 1919): 304.

14. Cited in Lomax, "I Got the Blues," 485.

15. Cited in Langston Hughes, "U.S. Likes Nazis and Franco Better than Its Own Negroes," 6.

16. "Additional Letters of Negro Migrants of 1916–1918," *Journal of Negro History* 4 (Oct. 1919): 452.

17. See "'Back to Southland' Train Fails to Move," *The Chicago Defender,* 15 Dec. 1923, 1; and "'Plantation Special' Blows Up Again; Promoters Sorry," *The Chicago Defender,* 12 Jan. 1924, 2.

18. *The Chicago Defender,* 13 Oct. 1923, 10.

19. Ibid., 3.

20. *The Chicago Defender,* 16 Feb. 1924, pt. 2, 12.

21. Arna Bontemps and Jack Conroy, *They Seek a City* (Garden City, N.Y.: Doubleday, Doran, 1945), 133.

22. Sears, Roebuck catalogs advertised guitars as early as 1893 and by 1897 devoted a full page to their advertisement. See more in Bastin, *Red River Blues,* 17.

23. *The Chicago Defender,* 9 Feb. 1924, 1.

24. *The Chicago Defender,* 25 Dec. 1926, pt. 2, 8.

25. "Letters of Negro Migrants of 1916–1918," 293.

26. "Additional Letters of Negro Migrants of 1916–1918," 452.

27. Robert S. Abbott, "A Recapitulation of 25 Years Work," *The Chicago Defender,* 3 May 1930, pt. 1, 21.

28. W. O. Saunders, "Why Jim Crow Is Flying North," *The Chicago Defender,* 22 Dec. 1923, pt. 2, 1.

29. Ibid.

30. See an advertisement of Darrow and his complete writings in *Crisis,* Apr. 1929, 113. See also, "John Brown, Darrow and Us," in the column "What the People Say," *The Chicago Defender,* 7 May 1932, 14; "Clarence Darrow, Friend of Race, Dies," *The Chicago Defender,* 19 Mar. 1938, 2; and Darrow's own article, published posthumously, "John Brown," *Chicago Defender Magazine,* 18 Dec. 1948, 2. The annotation to the latter piece said the article was written by Darrow expressly for the readers of the *Defender.*

31. Clement Wood, "The Problem of James Crow: 'Jim' Grown Up," *The Chicago Defender,* 6 Jan. 1923, pt. 2, 1.

32. Keil, *Urban Blues,* 59.

33. Ibid., 76.

34. Cited in Samuel Charters, *The Legacy of the Blues: Art and Lives of Twelve Great Bluesmen* (New York: Da Capo, 1977), 133–34.

35. *The Chicago Defender,* 27 Oct. 1923, 14.

36. Wright, *12 Million Black Voices,* 88.

37. Richard Wright, introduction to Drake and Cayton, *Black Metropolis,* xxxi.

38. Edgar Lee Masters, *The Tale of Chicago* (New York: Putnam's Sons, 1933), 288.

39. Ibid., 287.

40. Ibid., 255, 281.

41. Drake and Cayton, *Black Metropolis,* 418.

42. Wright, *12 Million Black Voices,* 130.

43. Kenny Williams, *A Storyteller and a City: Sherwood Anderson's Chicago* (DeKalb: Northern Illinois Univ. Press, 1988), 21.

44. Masters, *Tale of Chicago,* 287.

45. Ibid., 338.

46. Drake and Cayton, *Black Metropolis,* 388.

47. Ibid., 385, 387, 669.

48. Ibid., 653.
49. Ibid., 650.
50. Niles Carpenter, *The Sociology of City Life* (New York: Longmans, Green, 1932), 272–73.
51. Jones, *Blues People*, 105.
52. "Clarence Darrow, Friend of Race, Dies," *The Chicago Defender*, 19 Mar. 1938, 2.
53. *The Chicago Defender*, 9 Feb. 1924, 1.
54. *The Chicago Defender*, 3 Nov. 1923, 9.
55. *The Chicago Defender*, 10 Nov. 1923, 12.
56. Robert S. Abbott, "Refinement Sadly Lacking in Modern Youth," *The Chicago Defender*, 10 Mar. 1934, 11.
57. Robert S. Abbott, "No Racial Group Can Make Gains Where Culture is Lacking," *The Chicago Defender*, 3 Mar. 1934, 16.
58. Robert S. Abbott, "Depression No Reason for Lack of Culture," *The Chicago Defender*, 28 Apr. 1934, 12.
59. Lucius C. Harper, "We Prefer the 'Blues' to Our Essential Causes," *The Chicago Defender*, 1 Oct. 1938, 16.
60. Rob Roy, "If 'Jazz' Isn't Music to the Long Haired Gents, then What about Blues?" *The Chicago Defender*, 1 Feb. 1947, 19.
61. Locke, *The Negro and His Music*, 87–88.
62. Hughes, "Here to Yonder," 13 May 1944, 12.
63. Ibid., 21 Nov. 1942, 14.
64. Drake and Cayton, *Black Metropolis*, 267.
65. Herskovits, *The Myth of Negro Past*, 125.
66. Puckett, *Folk Beliefs of the Southern Negro*, 16.
67. Dorson, *American Negro Folktales*, 38.
68. *The Chicago Defender*, 25 Apr. 1925, pt. 2, 10.
69. Puckett, *Folk Beliefs of the Southern Negro*, 581.
70. Puckett, "Race-Pride and Folk-Lore," 82–83.
71. Ibid., 84.
72. *The Chicago Defender*, 10 Dec. 1921, 16.
73. Na'im Akbar, *Chains and Images of Psychological Slavery* (Jersey City, N.J.: New Mind Productions, 1984), 4, 7, 11.
74. Harper, "We Prefer the 'Blues' to Our Essential Causes," 16.
75. Hughes's column in *The Chicago Defender* began on 21 Nov. 1942 (it drops the column title on 16 Oct. 1948), Du Bois's on 20 Jan. 1945 and concluded on 22 May 1948, and Bethune's began on 16 Oct. 1948.
76. Jackson was, in addition to being on the staff of the *Defender*, secretary of the Chicago YMCA and educational secretary of the National Urban League. "A. L. Jackson is Offered Position in Labor Bureau," *The Chicago Defender*, 16 Feb. 1924, 2.
77. Jackson, "The Onlooker," 5 Jan. 1924, 12.
78. "What the Press Does," *The Chicago Defender*, 15 May 1937, 17.
79. *The Chicago Defender*, 12 Mar. 1927, pt. 2, 2.

80. *The Chicago Defender*, 15 Oct. 1932, 14.

81. Barney E. Page, "Joshua Fit the Battle of Jericho," *The Chicago Defender*, 16 Apr. 1932, 14.

82. Browning, "Religion a 'Way of Escape,'" 10.

83. Ibid.

84. See "Spiritualism," *The Chicago Defender*, 20 May 1922, 12.

85. See Killy Miller, Jr., "Religion Must Change Method for New Issues," *The Chicago Defender*, 10 Nov. 1923, pt. 2, 1.

86. Carus, *The History of the Devil and the Idea of Evil*, 305.

87. Ibid., 406.

88. See *The Chicago Defender*, 4 May 1940, 4–8.

89. "Dance Hall Fire Trap Was Once a Church," *The Chicago Defender*, 4 May 1940, 5.

90. David Ward Howe, "The Observation Post" (column), *The Chicago Defender*, 4 May 1940, 14.

91. Carus, *The History of the Devil and the Idea of Evil*, 401.

92. Ibid., 444–45.

93. "It Beats the Devil," *The Chicago Defender*, 23 July 1927, pt. 1, 1; pt. 2, 2.

94. *The Chicago Defender*, 12 Feb. 1927, pt. 1, 1.

95. *The Chicago Defender*, 23 Apr. 1921, 16.

96. *The Chicago Defender*, 20 Jan. 1923, 12.

97. *The Chicago Defender*, 24 Sept. 1921, 16.

98. Parkin, ed., *The Anthropology of Evil*, 18.

99. Alan Macfarlane, "The Root of Evil," in *The Anthropology of Evil*, ed. Parkin, 60.

100. Oliver, *Conversation with the Blues*, 11, 13.

101. Jones, *Blues People*, 86–87.

102. Ralph Ellison, "Blues People," in *Shadow and Act* (New York: Random, 1964), 249–50.

103. *The Pittsburgh Courier*, 2 Dec. 1933.

104. *The Afro-American*, 16 Dec. 1933.

105. Handy, "The Heart of the Blues," 193.

106. Harrison, *Black Pearls*, 221.

107. Wright, *12 Million Black Voices*, 128.

108. Cited in Pearson, *Virginia Piedmont Blues*, 177.

109. Cited in *Time*, 1 Sept. 1953.

110. Michael Haralambos, "Soul Music and Blues: Their Meaning and Relevance in Northern United States Black Ghettos," in *Afro-American Anthropology: Contemporary Perspectives*, ed. Whitten and Szwed, 371.

111. Tracy, *Langston Hughes and the Blues*, 45–46.

112. Cited in Pearson, *Virginia Piedmont Blues*, 81.

113. Tracy, *Langston Hughes and the Blues*, 142.

114. Langston Hughes, "I Remember the Blues," in *Missouri Reader*, ed. Frank Luther Mott (Columbia: Univ. of Missouri Press, 1964), 153. Cited in Tracy, *Langston Hughes and the Blues*, 108.

115. Tracy, *Langston Hughes and the Blues,* 47.

116. Ibid., 123, 143.

117. John A. Lomax and Alan Lomax, *Our Singing Country* (New York: Macmillan, 1941), 364–65. Cited in Bastin, *Red River Blues,* 60.

118. Keil, *Urban Blues,* 164.

119. Palmer, *Deep Blues,* 275.

120. *The Chicago Defender,* 17 Sept. 1921, 16.

121. Jay Jackson, "So What?" (weekly), *The Chicago Defender,* 25 Apr. 1942, 15.

122. Cited in Jeff Todd Titon, *Downhome Blues Lyrics: An Anthology from the Post–World War II Era,* 2d ed. (Urbana: Univ. of Illinois Press, 1990), 9.

123. Ibid., 10.

124. Jones, *Culture Bandits,* 50–51.

125. Max Weber, *The Rational and Social Foundations of Music,* trans. Don Martindale, Johannes Riedel, Gertrude Neuwirth (Carbondale: Southern Illinois Univ. Press, 1958), 41.

126. Keil, *Urban Blues,* 74–75.

127. *The Chicago Defender,* 25 Oct. 1924, 7.

128. *The Chicago Defender,* 28 June 1924, 7.

129. Puckett, *Folk Beliefs of the Southern Negro,* 133–34.

130. *The Chicago Defender,* 28 Apr. 1928, pt. 1, 2.

131. *The Chicago Defender,* 12 Nov. 1927, pt. 1, 7.

132. *The Chicago Defender,* 27 Apr. 1929, 6.

133. Jim O'Neal and Bill Greensmith, "Living Blues Interview: Jimmy Rogers," *Living Blues* 14 (Fall 1973): 15.

134. Macfarlane, "The Root of Evil," 71–72.

135. "Billie Holiday Ill Has Right to Sing Blues," *The Chicago Defender,* 21 Oct. 1950, 1.

136. "New York Judge Says Jazz Music Cannot Be Indecent," *The Chicago Defender,* 2 Apr. 1932, 5.

137. *The Chicago Defender,* 1 Oct. 1921, 5.

138. Jackson, "The Onlooker" 14 Jan. 1922., pt. 2, 4.

139. Abbott, "Refinement Sadly Lacking in Modern Youth," 11.

140. Jackson, "The Onlooker," 14 Jan. 1922, pt. 2, 4.

141. Cited in Harrison, *Black Pearls,* 30.

142. Luix Virgil Overbea, "Ethel Waters Book Unique," *The Chicago Defender,* 28 Apr. 1951, 21.

143. Garon, *The Devil's Son-in-Law,* 19.

144. *The Chicago Defender,* 18 June 1927, pt. 1, 6.

145. Dave Payton, "What Jazz Has Done," *The Chicago Defender,* 16 July 1927, pt. 1, 6.

146. *The Chicago Defender,* 20 Dec. 1924, pt. 1, 6.

147. Ibid.

148. See Dixon and Godrich, *Recording the Blues,* 87.

149. Ibid., 8.

150. Titon, *Early Downhome Blues,* 255.

151. Harrison, *Black Pearls*, 31.
152. Odum and Johnson, *Negro Workaday Songs*, 34.
153. Barlow, *"Looking Up at Down,"* 293.
154. Charters, *The Country Blues*, 64.
155. Rowe, *Chicago Blues*, 97.
156. Garon, *Blues and the Poetic Spirit*, 40–41.
157. Ibid., 49.
158. Oliver, *Blues Fell This Morning*, 17.
159. Rowe, *Chicago Blues*, 97.
160. Carpenter, *The Sociology of City Life*, 208–9.
161. Oliver, *Blues Fell This Morning*, 281.
162. Hughes, "Here to Yonder," 9 Jan. 1943, 14.
163. *The Chicago Defender*, 28 Mar. 1925, pt. 2, 8.
164. "Folks We Can Get Along Without," *The Chicago Defender*, 27 Aug. 1932, 2.
165. "Neighborhood Improvements," *The Chicago Defender*, 2 Apr. 1921, 16.
166. Hughes, "Here to Yonder," 15 Jan. 1944, 10.
167. Ibid.
168. Langston Hughes, "Loud Speakers and Dirty Records would be No Loss to Civilization," *The Chicago Defender*, 16 Feb. 1952, 10.
169. Ibid.
170. Oakley, *The Devil's Music*, 232.

SELECT BIBLIOGRAPHY

Allen, William Francis, Charles Pickard Ware, and Lucy McKim Garrison, eds. *Slave Songs of the United States.* New York: Peter Smith, 1929.

Asante, Molefi Kete. *Kemet, Afrocentricity and Knowledge.* Trenton, N.J.: Africa World Press, 1990.

Ashton, John. *The Devil in Britain and America.* London: Ward and Downey, 1896.

Aswell, James R., et al., eds. *God Bless the Devil!: Liar's Bench Tales.* Chapel Hill: Univ. of North Carolina Press, 1940.

Attali, Jacques, *Noise: The Political Economy of Music.* Trans. Brian Massumi. Minneapolis: Univ. of Minnesota Press, 1985.

Baker, Houston A., Jr. *Afro-American Poetics: Revisions of Harlem and the Black Aesthetic.* Madison: Univ. of Wisconsin Press, 1988.

————. *Blues, Ideology, and Afro-American Literature: A Vernacular Theory.* Chicago: Univ. of Chicago Press, 1984.

————. *The Journey Back: Issues in Black Literature and Criticism.* Chicago: Univ. of Chicago Press, 1980.

————. *Modernism and the Harlem Renaissance.* Chicago: Univ. of Chicago Press, 1987.

Barlow, William. *"Looking Up at Down": The Emergence of Blues Culture.* Philadelphia: Temple Univ. Press, 1989.

Barton, William E., ed. *Old Plantation Hymns: A Collection of Hitherto Unpublished Melodies of the Slave and the Freedman, with Historical and Descriptive Notes.* 1895. New York: AMS Press, 1972.

―――. "The Devil's Goin' to Get You," *North Carolina Folklore Journal* 21, No. 4 (Nov. 1973): 189–94.

Bastin, Bruce. *Red River Blues: The Blues Tradition in the Southeast.* Urbana: Univ. of Illinois Press, 1986.

Becker, Ernest. *The Structure of Evil: An Essay on the Unification of the Science of Man.* New York: Free Press, 1976.

Bontemps, Arna, and Jack Conroy. *They Seek a City.* Garden City, N.Y.: Doubleday, Doran, 1945.

Booth, Newell S., Jr., ed. *African Religions: A Symposium.* New York: NOK, 1977.

Boyle, Virginia Frazer. *Devil Tales.* 1900. Rpt. Freeport, N.Y.: Books for Libraries, 1972.

Burrison, John A., ed. *Storytellers: Folktales and Legends from the South.* Athens: Univ. of Georgia Press, 1989.

Burrows, David. *Sound, Speech, and Music.* Amherst: Univ. of Massachusetts Press, 1990.

Camus, Albert. *The Rebel: An Essay on Man in Revolt.* Trans. Anthony Bower. New York: Knopf, 1969.

Carpenter, Niles. *The Sociology of City Life.* New York: Longmans, Green, 1932.

Carus, Paul. *The History of the Devil and the Idea of Evil: From the Earliest Times to the Present Day.* 1899. Rpt. LaSalle, Ill.: Open Court, 1974.

Charters, Samuel B. *The Country Blues.* New York: Rinehart, 1959.

―――. *The Legacy of the Blues: Art and Lives of Twelve Great Bluesmen.* New York: Da Capo, 1977.

Cone, James H. *A Black Theology of Liberation.* New York: Lippincott, 1970.

―――. *God of the Oppressed.* New York: Seabury, 1975.

———. *The Spirituals and the Blues: An Interpretation.* New York: Seabury, 1972.

Courlander, Harold. *A Treasury of Afro-American Folklore.* New York: Crown, 1976.

Delumeau, Jean. *Sin and Fear: The Emergence of a Western Guilt Culture 13th–18th Centuries.* Trans. Eric Nicholson. New York: St. Martin's, 1990.

Dixon, Robert M. W., and John Godrich. *Recording the Blues.* New York: Stein and Day, 1970.

Dorson, Richard M. *American Negro Folktales.* Greenwich, Conn.: Fawcett, 1967.

Drake, St. Clair, and Horace R. Cayton. *Black Metropolis: A Study of Negro Life in a Northern City.* New York: Harcourt, Brace, 1945.

Dundes, Alan, ed. *Mother Wit from the Laughing Barrel: Readings in the Interpretation of Afro-American Folklore.* Englewood Cliffs, N.J.: Prentice-Hall, 1973.

———. "Text, Texture and Context." *Southern Folklore Quarterly* 28 (1964): 251–65.

Eliade, Mircea. *Myth and Reality.* Trans. Willard R. Trask. New York: Harper and Row, 1963.

———. *The Sacred and the Profane: The Nature of Religion.* New York: Harcourt, Brace, 1959.

Ellison, Ralph. *The Invisible Man.* New York: Vintage, 1972.

———. *Shadow and Act.* New York: Random, 1964.

Evans, David. *Big Road Blues: Tradition and Creativity in the Folk Blues.* New York: Da Capo, 1982.

———. *Tommy Johnson.* London: Studio Vista, 1971.

Ferris, William. *Blues from the Delta.* Garden City, N.Y.: Anchor/ Doubleday, 1979.

Feuerbach, Ludwig. *The Essence of Christianity.* Ed. E. Graham Waring and F. W. Strothmann. New York: Continuum, 1989.

Finn, Julio. *The Bluesman: The Musical Heritage of Black Men and Women in the Americas.* London: Quartet, 1986.

Foucault, Michel. *The History of Sexuality* 1. Trans. Robert Hurley. New York: Vintage, 1989.

Garon, Paul. *Blues and the Poetic Spirit.* 1975. Rpt. New York: Da Capo, 1979.

———. The Devil's Son-in-La*w: The Story of Peetie Wheatstraw and His Songs.* London: Studio Vista, 1971.

Gates, Henry Louis, Jr. *The Signifying Monkey: A Theory of Afro-American Literary Criticism.* New York: Oxford Univ. Press, 1988.

Goines, Leonard. "The Blues as Black Therapy." *Black World,* Nov. 1973, 28–40.

Greeley, Andrew M. *Religious Change in America.* Cambridge: Harvard Univ. Press, 1989.

Gruver, Rod. "The Blues as a Secular Religion." *Blues World,* no. 29 (Apr. 1970): 3–6; no. 30 (May 1970): 4–7; no. 31 (June 1970): 5–7; no. 32 (July 1970): 7–9.

Guralnick, Peter. *Searching for Robert Johnson.* New York: Dutton, 1989.

Harrison, Daphne Duval. *Black Pearls: Blues Queens of the 1920s.* Brunswick, N.J.: Rutgers Univ. Press, 1988.

Hauerwas, Stanley. *Naming the Silences: God, Medicine, and the Problem of Suffering.* Grand Rapids, Mich.: Eerdmans, 1990.

Herskovits, Melville J. *The Myth of the Negro Past.* 1941. Rpt. Gloucester, Mass.: Peter Smith, 1970.

Holloway, Joseph E., ed. *Africanisms in American Culture.* Bloomington: Indiana Univ. Press, 1990.

Huggins, Nathan Irvin, ed. *Voices from the Harlem Renaissance.* New York: Oxford Univ. Press, 1976.

Hughes, Langston, and Arna Bontemps, eds. *The Book of Negro Folklore.* New York: Dodd, Mead, 1958.

Hurston, Zora Neale. *Dust Tracks on a Road: An Autobiography,* 2d ed. Urbana: Univ. of Illinois Press, 1984.

———. *Mules and Men.* Bloomington: Indiana Univ. Press, 1978.

———. *The Sanctified Church.* Berkeley, Calif.: Turtle Island, 1983.

———. *Tell My Horse.* Berkeley, Calif.: Turtle Island, 1981.

Johnson, Clifton H., ed. *God Struck Me Dead: Religious Conversion Experiences and Autobiographies of Ex-slaves*. Philadelphia: Pilgrim, 1969.

Jones, Del. *Culture Bandits*. Philadelphia: Hikeka Press, 1990.

Jones, LeRoi (Amiri Baraka). *Blues People: The Negro Experience in White America and the Music that Developed from It*. New York: Morrow, 1963.

Jones, Major J. *The Color of God: The Concept of God in Afro-American Thought*. Macon, Ga.: Mercer Univ. Press, 1987.

Jones, William R. *Is God a White Racist?: A Preamble to Black Theology*. Garden City, N.Y.: Anchor/Doubleday, 1973.

Keil, Charles. *Urban Blues*. Chicago: Univ. of Chicago Press, 1966.

Laguerre, Michel S. *Voodoo and Politics in Haiti*. New York: St. Martin's, 1989.

Levine, Lawrence W. *Black Culture and Black Consciousness: Afro-American Folk Thought from Slavery to Freedom*. New York: Oxford Univ. Press, 1977.

Locke, Alain LeRoy. *The Negro and His Music* and *Negro Art: Past and Present*. 1936. Rpt. Salem, N.H.: Ayer, 1988.

Lomax, Alan. *The Folk Songs of North America*. Garden City, N.Y.: Dolphin, 1975.

———. "'Sinful' Songs of the Southern Negro," *Southwest Review* 19, No. 2 (Jan. 1934): 105–31.

Lomax, John A., and Alan Lomax. *Our Singing Country*. New York: Macmillan, 1941.

Masters, Edgar Lee. *The Tale of Chicago*. New York: Putnam's Sons, 1933.

Moore, Robert L., ed. *Carl Jung and Christian Spirituality*. New York: Paulist Press, 1988.

Murray, Albert. *Stomping the Blues*. New York: Vintage, 1982.

Neal, Larry. "The Ethos of the Blues." *Black Scholar* 3, No. 10 (Summer 1972): 42–48.

Nietzsche, Friedrich. *Beyond Good and Evil: Prelude to a Philosophy of the Future*. Trans. Walter Kaufmann. 1886. New York: Vintage, 1989.

Noddings, Nel. *Women and Evil.* Berkeley: Univ. of California Press, 1989.

Oakley, Giles. *The Devil's Music: A History of the Blues.* New York: Taplinger, 1977.

Odum, Howard, W. *The Way of the South: Toward the Regional Balance of America.* New York: Macmillan, 1947.

————, and Guy B. Johnson. *Negro Workaday Songs.* Chapel Hill: Univ. of North Carolina Press, 1926.

Oliver, Paul. *Blues Fell This Morning: Meaning in the Blues,* 2d ed. Cambridge: Cambridge Univ. Press, 1990.

————. *Conversation with the Blues.* New York: Horizon, 1965.

————. *Screening the Blues: Aspects of the Blues Tradition.* New York: Da Capo, 1968.

Palmer, Robert. *Deep Blues.* New York: Viking, 1981.

Parkin, David, ed. *The Anthropology of Evil.* Oxford: Basil Blackwell, 1985.

Pearson, Barry Lee. *Virginia Piedmont Blues: The Lives and Art of Two Virginia Bluesmen.* Philadelphia: Univ. of Pennsylvania Press, 1990.

Pelton, Robert D. *The Trickster in West Africa: A Study of Mythic Irony and Sacred Delight.* Berkeley: Univ. of California Press, 1980.

Puckett, Newbell Niles. *Folk Beliefs of the Southern Negro.* Chapel Hill: Univ. of North Carolina Press, 1926.

————. "Race-Pride and Folk-Lore." *Opportunity* 4, No. 39 (Mar. 1926): 82–84.

Radin, Paul. *The Trickster: A Study in American Indian Mythology.* London: Routledge and Kegan Paul, 1956.

Rawick, George P., ed. *The American Slave: A Composite Autobiography.* Westport, Conn.: Greenwood, 1977.

Ricoeur, Paul. *The Symbolism of Evil.* Trans. Emerson Buchanan. Boston: Beacon, 1969.

Roberts, John W. *From Trickster to Badman: The Black Folk Hero in Slavery and Freedom.* Philadelphia: Univ. of Pennsylvania Press, 1989.

Rowe, Mike. *Chicago Blues: The City and the Music.* New York: Da Capo, 1975.

Russell, Jeffrey Burton. *The Devil: Perceptions of Evil from Antiquity to Primitive Christianity*. Ithaca, N.Y.: Cornell Univ. Press, 1977.

Sacre, Robert, ed. *The Voice of the Delta: Charley Patton and the Mississippi Blues Traditions, Influences and Comparisons*. De Liege, Belgium: Presses Universitaires, 1987.

Sandburg, Carl. *The American Songbag*. New York: Harcourt, Brace, 1927.

Spear, Allan H. *Black Chicago: The Making of a Negro Ghetto 1890–1920*. Chicago: Univ. of Chicago Press, 1967.

Spencer, Jon Michael. *Protest and Praise: Sacred Music of Black Religion*. Minneapolis: Fortress, 1990.

———, ed. *Sacred Music of the Secular City: From Blues to Rap*. Durham, N.C.: Duke Univ. Press. Special issue of *Black Sacred Music: A Journal of Theomusicology* 6, no. 1 (Spring 1992).

———. *Theological Music: Introduction to Theomusicology*. Westport, Conn.: Greenwood, 1991.

Surin, Kenneth. *Theology and the Problem of Evil*. Oxford: Basil Blackwell, 1986.

Taft, Michael. *Blues Lyric Poetry: An Anthology*. New York: Garland, 1983.

Titon, Jeff Todd, ed. *Downhome Blues Lyrics: An Anthology from the Post–World War II Era*. 2d ed. Urbana: Univ. of Illinois Press, 1990.

———. *Early Downhome Blues: A Musical and Cultural Analysis*. Urbana: Univ. of Illinois Press, 1977.

Tracy, Steven C. *Langston Hughes and the Blues*. Urbana: Univ. of Illinois Press, 1988.

Walton, Ortiz M. *Music: Black, White and Blue*. New York: Morrow, 1972.

Weber, Max. *The Rational and Social Foundations of Music*. Trans. Don Martindale, Johannes Riedel, Gertrude Neuwirth. Carbondale: Southern Illinois Univ. Press, 1958.

White, Newman Ivey, ed. *The Frank C. Brown Collection of North Carolina Folklore*. Durham, N.C.: Duke Univ. Press, 1964.

Whitten, Norman E., Jr., and John F. Szwed, eds. *Afro-American Anthropology: Contemporary Perspectives*. New York: Free Press, 1970.

Williams, Kenny. *A Storyteller and a City: Sherwood Anderson's Chicago.* DeKalb: Northern Illinois Univ. Press, 1988.

Wright, Richard. *12 Million Black Voices: A Folk History of the Negro in the United States.* New York: Viking, 1941.

INDEX

"A Green Gal Can't Catch On," 45
Abbott, Robert S., 106, 107, 113, 116, 130, 131
"Adam and Eve" (Anderson), 2
"Adam and Eve" (Bradley), 2
"Adam and Eve Had the Blues," 2
Adam and Eve Root, 15
Afro-American, The, 122
AJAX Records, 132
Alexander, Texas, 86, 87, 88, 93
"All God's Chillun Have Shoes," 113
American Record Company, 26
An Eye for an Eye, 107
Anderson, Sherwood, 110, 120
Anderson, Talking Billy, 2
"Angels in Heaven," 54, 112
Armstrong, Louis, xvii
Arnold, Kokomo, 2, 3, 121
Asante, Molefi, xviii, xxiv, xxvii
Ashton, John, 21, 33
Aswell, James, 26
Attali, Jacques, xviii
Avis, Paul, 95

"Baby," 93
"Baby, Don't You Want to Go," 121
"Back to the Woods Again," 87
bad nigger, 6–7
"Bad Notion Blues," 39
"Bad Woman Blues," 25
badman, 4, 6–13
Baker, Houston, xvi, xxiv, xxv, xxvi, 75, 83, 84, 97
Baldwin, James, 63–64, 90
Baraka, Amiri, xii, xviii, xxv, xxvii, 72, 111, 131
Barbecue Bob, 46
"Barfly Baby," 61
Barlow, William, 8, 133–34
Barnes, Walter, 5, 6
Barton, William E., 32, 76
Batts, Will, 88
bebop, xviii–xix
Bennett, Will, 8
Bernhardt, Clyde, 62
Bethune, Mary McLeod, 117, 155n75

Beyond Good and Evil, 57

Bible, 32, 88, 107; source of blues mythology, 1–4, 72; source of blues theodicy, 74, 75–76, 77

"Big Fat Mama Blues," 16

Bilbo, Theodore, xx, xxi

"Black and Evil Blues," 22, 82

"Black Cat Crossed Your Path," 26

"Black Man Blues," 58

Black Metropolis, 109

black preacher: compared to blues singer, 40–41; polemics with blues singer, 49–53, 97

Black Sacred Music: A Journal of Theomusicology, x

Black Swan company, 130

Blackwell, Francis Scrapper, 75

Bland, Bobby, xxix, 122

Blind Percy, 19

"Blue Spirit Blues," 20

Bluebird Records, 9, 121

blues: churches influence on, 34; compared to spirituals, 43–46; defined, xx–xxi, 61; eulogies in, 48–49; its misunderstanding, xii; poetic representation of, 124–25; relationship to gospel, 40, 61–62; relationship to hymns, 44; relationship to prayer, 46–49, 56–58, 61, 87, 88, 93, 97, 98; relationship to preaching, 40–43; ritual of, 39, 40–43; truth in, xxv, 32, 37, 59, 67, 96

Blues and the Poetic Spirit, xiv

blues god, 36, 71–74, 75, 86, 87, 88, 89, 94, 96, 97, 98

Blues, Ideology, and Afro-American Literature, xxvi

blues singer: compared to black preacher, 40–41; polemics with black preachers, 49–53, 73, 93–96

Bogan, Lucille, 80, 82, 90, 91

Bontemps, Arna, 27, 105

Boogie Woogie Red, 75

Bostic, Earl, 61

"Bourgeoisie Blues," 53

"Bo-Weavil Blues," 7

Bowling Green State University, ix, x

Boyd, Eddie, 90, 91

Boyle, Virginia Frazer, 33

Bracey, Mississippi, 44

Bradley, Tommie, 2, 3, 89

Brewer, Blind James, 43, 44, 61

"Bright Lights, Big City," 79

"Bring Me Flowers While I'm Living," 5

"Broke Down Engine Blues," 88

Bronzeville Five, 6, 48

Broonzy, Big Bill, 42, 43, 78, 108, 121, 123

"Brother James," 49

Brown, Hi Henry, 44, 49

Brown, John, 107, 154n30

Brown, Sterling, xxiv, 99

Browning, Charles P., 23–24, 118

Brunswick Race Records, 129

Burnett, J. C., 132

"Burnin' Hell," 85

Burns, Eddie, 25

"Bye-Bye Blues," 78

"C and A Blues," 93

Camus, Albert, 71, 74, 85, 95

Cancer, Polly, 23, 118

"Can't Be Trusted Blues," 12

Carr, Leroy, 19, 75, 82, 90, 91

Carter, Bo, 50

Carus, Paul, xiv, 21, 23, 27, 118, 119

Caston, Baby Doo, 127

"Catfish Blues," 93

Cayton, Horace, 64, 109, 110, 111, 115

Cephas, John, xxii–xxiii, 46, 51, 61, 123

Charters, Samuel, 5, 134

Chatman, Sam, 84
Chess Records, 129
Chicago Defender, The, xx, 6, 24, 100, 101, 102–3, 104, 105, 106, 108, 109, 112–15, 116, 117, 118, 119, 127, 129, 130, 131, 135
Chicago Federation of Musicians, 130
Chicago Renaissance, 107, 124
"Chock House Blues," 59
"Christmas Mornin' Blues," 71
Chronicle of Higher Education, The, xi
"Church Bell Blues," 49
Church of God in Christ, 65
city blues: defined, xxviii–xxix, 121
city life: affect on rural customs, 111–20; in Chicago, 109–20
Clapton, Eric, xvii
classic blues: defined, xxix, 121–22
Clayton, Doctor, 54, 112
"Coal River Blues," 19
Collier's Weekly, 106
Collins, Sam, 12, 13
Color of God, The, 95
Columbia Records, 11, 121, 130, 131, 132
Cone, James H., xii, xxiii, xxiv, 36, 43, 46, 69, 73, 95
conjuration, 15, 72
conjurers, 6, 7, 31, 32, 33
Conrad, Earl, xxvi
Conroy, Jack, 105
conversion, religious, 64–67
convict lease system, 89, 101–2
Cotten, Elizabeth, 62–63
Council, Floyd "Dipper Boy," 9
Count Basie Orchestra, 45
Country Blues, 5
country blues: defined, xxviii, xxx
Cousin Joe, 91
Conversation with the Blues, 44
Cox, Ida, xxix, 15, 16, 129, 131
"Crazy Blues," 125

Crisis, 102
crossroads, 27–30, 135
Crudup, Big Boy, 121
"Crying Mother Blues," 44
"Crying Won't Help You," 80
Culture Bandits, xviii
"Cypress Grove," xxx
"Cypress Grove Blues," 78

"Daniel in the Lions' Den," 132
Darby, Teddy Roosevelt "Blind," 44
"Dark Road," 92
Darrell, John, 22
Darrow, Clarence, 107, 154n30
Davenport, Charlie, 91, 93, 121
Davis, Blind Gary, 10, 66
Davis, Walter, 57, 89, 108
"Death Sting Me Blues," 86
Decca Race Records, 9, 121, 132
"Deep Down in the Ground," 25
"Denomination Blues," 50
devil, 18–26, 30–34, 145n106; as a scapegoat, 76; as black, 22–23, 24; as white, 91, 119; descriptions of, 24–25; influence of, 25; instruments of, 26–30; selling one's soul to, 27–29, 33–34
"Devil Dance Blues," xv
Devil in Britain and America, The, 21, 33
"Devil in the Lion's Den," 12
"Devil Sent the Rain," 25
Devil Tales, 33
"Devil's Got the Blues," 19, 86, 92
Devil's Music, The, xiii
"Dirty Deal Blues," 78, 81
"Done Sold My Soul, Sold It to the Devil," 33
Dorsey, Thomas A., 45, 61, 63, 121
Dorson, Richard, 23, 115
"Down Hearted Blues," 78
Doyle, Little Buddie, 98

Drake, St. Clair, 64, 109, 110, 111, 115
"Drunken Hearted Man," 55, 87
Du Bois, W. E. B., 109, 116, 117, 131, 155n75
Duke Divinity School, ix, x
Dunbar, Paul Laurence, xxiv
Dundes, Alan, xviii, xxvii

Easton, Amos, 57, 87, 88
Edwards, Archie, 46, 61, 124
Ellison, Ralph, xxvi, xxvii, 9, 51, 96–98, 121
"Empty House Blues," 5
ethnomusicology, xxi, xxiii
Evans, David, xi, xii, 10, 37, 38, 46, 54
Evans, Joe, 18
"Everybody Wants to Know," 53, 90
evil, xxi–xxii, 52, 53; and good integrated, 71–74; black as not, 82–84; in the Adamic myth, 2–4; in the tragic-hero myth, 3–6; repression of, 73–74; strong sense of, 19, 20, 23, 26, 32, 119, 120, 137; weak sense of, 19
"Evil Blues" (Jackson), 22, 54
"Evil Blues" (Washboard Sam), 81
"Evil Devil Woman Blues," 80
evil eye, 24, 120
"Evil-Hearted Woman," 19
"Evil Woman Blues," 19
"Eyesight to the Blind," 57

Fair Employment Practice Commission, xx, xxi
Fanon, Frantz, 52
Ferris, William, 38
Feuerbach, Ludwig, 35
Finn, Julio, xii, xiii, xvi, 16, 39
"First and Last Blues," 75
Folk Beliefs of the Southern Negro, 20

"Fool's Blues," 58, 59, 83–84
Foucault, Michel, 52
Fuller, Blind Boy, 49, 80
Fulson, Lowell, 62

Garon, Paul, xiv, xv, 38, 46, 52, 54, 69–71, 73, 85–86, 94, 134
George, Nelson, xvii
Georgia Pine Boy, 88
Gibson, Clifford, 79
Gillum, Bill Jazz, 46, 121
Gilmore, Gene, 48
"Go Down, Moses," 132
God, xxii, 27, 95; reference to in blues, 37–39, 54, 58
"God Bless the Child," 42
Goines, Leonard, 39–40
"Going Down Slow," xxiii, 77
"Gonna Hit the Highway," 57
Good Luck Dust, 16
"Good Woman Blues," 82
Goofer Dust, 16
"Goofey Dust Blues," 16
Gordon, Jimmie, 9
gospel music, 40, 52, 60, 61, 62, 63, 64, 66, 67
"Got to Reap What You Sow," 46
Great Awakening, 23
Great Black Migration, 15, 18, 26, 100–9; leadership of, 105–6
Greeley, Andrew, xxii
Gruver, Rod, 35–36, 51–52
guilt, xvi, 23, 53–54, 56, 91, 112
Guitar Slim. See Jones, Eddie
Guralnick, Peter, 5

"Ham Hound Crave," 66
Handy, W. C., xvii, 45, 122
"Hard Scufflin' Blues," 98
"Hard Time Blues," 75
"Hard Time Killin' Floor Blues," 86

Harp, Jack, 66
Harper, Lucius C., 113, 116, 131
Harrison, Daphne Duval, xii, 122
"He Calls That Religion," 50
Healer, The, ix
Hegamin, Lucille, 121
Hegel, G. W. F., xii, xiv
hell, 42; description of, 20, 32
"Hell and What It Is," 26
"Hell Hound on My Trail," 9
Henderson, Bertha, 81
"Henry's Worried Blues," 88
Herskovits, Melville, 20–21, 32, 115
Heywood's Black Bottom Ramblers, 132
"Highway No. 61 Blues," 88
Hill, Chippie, 55, 121
Hill, King Solomon, 25
Himes, Chester, xxvi
His Eye Is on the Sparrow, 131
History of the Devil and the Idea of Evil, The, xiv, 23
Holiday, Billie, xvii, xx, 41, 42, 102, 130
Holiness church, 27, 50, 62, 65, 70
hollers, xxviii, 124, 125, 126, 133, 135, 136
Holt, Nora Douglas, 130, 131
"Hoodoo, Hoodoo," 15–16
Hooker, John Lee, ix, xxvi, 44, 58, 61, 74, 85
Hopkins, Lightnin', xxiii, 47, 56, 93, 134
House, Son, xxviii, 11, 41, 42, 43, 55, 56, 62, 65, 84–85, 93
"How Long Daddy, How Long," xxix
"How You Want Your Rollin' Done," 56
Howe, David Ward, 118
Howell, Peg Leg, 76
Howlin' Wolf, 24

"Howling Wind Blues," 108
"Howling Wolf Blues," 58, 83
Hughes, Langston, xi, xvii, xviii–xix, xx, xxiv, xxviii–xxix, 83, 101, 114, 116, 117, 123–25, 134, 135–36, 137, 155n75
Hunt, Van, 39, 60, 61, 98
Hunter, Alberta, xxix, 46, 79, 121, 131
"Hurry Blues," 73
Hurston, Zora Neale, xvii–xviii, 4, 16, 17, 32, 72, 74, 135

"I Ain't Superstitious," 24
"I Packed My Suitcase, Started to the Train," 6
"I Thought I'd Do It," 80
If He Hollers Let Him Go, xxvi–xxvii
"If I Had Possession Over Judgment Day," 79
"I'll Go with Her Blues," xxiii, 47
"I'll Overcome Some Day," 44
"I'm a Guitar King," 67
"I'm On My Way Blues," 78
Invisible Man, 9, 51, 96–98
Is God a White Racist?, 82, 91
"It's Tight Like That," 62
"I've Been Hoodooed," 129
"I've Been Treated Wrong," 45, 89

Jack-o-lantern, 17, 129
Jackson, Alexander L., 103, 117, 119, 127, 130, 131, 155n76
Jackson, Jay, xx, 127
Jackson, Lil' Son, 22, 54–55
Jackson, Papa Charlie, 25
James, Jesse, 79, 86
James, Skip, xxx, 18, 19, 20, 24, 65–66, 78, 86, 150n137
Jefferson, Blind Lemon, xxviii, 5, 6, 11, 47, 49, 59, 60, 134
"Jelly, Jelly," 136

Jesus Christ, xxii, 18, 24, 31, 32, 43, 57, 58, 84, 95, 96
"John the Revelator," 62
Johnson, Charles S., 31
Johnson, Guy B., 2, 58, 133
Johnson, James "Stump," 98
Johnson, James Weldon, xxiv, 116
Johnson, LaDell, 29, 31, 65
Johnson, Lonnie, xxviii, 8, 19, 68, 86, 92
Johnson, Louise, 87
Johnson, Robert, xiii, xvi, xx, xxviii, 4, 5, 6, 9–10, 11, 16, 31, 55–56, 79, 87, 92, 124
Johnson, Tommy, xxiii, 29, 31, 65, 78
Jones, Del, xviii, 127
Jones, Eddie, 79
Jones, Floyd, 92
Jones, Jordon, 26
Jones, LeRoi. See Baraka, Amiri
Jones, Little Hat, 64, 73, 98
Jones, Maggie, 47, 78, 93
Jones, Major, 95
Jones, Moody, 65
Jones, Ozella, 126
Jones, William R., 82, 91
Jordan, Luke, 49
"Judgment Day," 112
juke house: defined, 147n29
Jung, C. G., 13, 70, 71–72, 73
"Justice Blues," 88

Keil, Charles, xvi, xxiv, xxvii, 40, 64, 108, 126, 128
Kelly, Jack, 88
"Key to the Highway," 78
King, B. B., xxix, 122, 127
Ku Klux Klan, xxi, 91, 92, 119, 130

Lacy, Rubin, 59, 60–61, 66, 67, 96, 98
Langston University, 61

"Laplegged Drunk Again," 83
Laskie, Louie, 56, 87, 88
Laury, Booker T., xxv
"Lawdy Lawdy Blues," xxix
"Lead Hearted Blues," 81
Leadbelly, 7, 52–53
Legba, 11, 13, 28–30, 72, 74, 132; identified with the devil, 12, 17, 28, 32–33
Lenoir, J. B., xxviii, 30, 53, 65, 90, 91, 121
Leslie, Lew, 41
Levine, Lawrence, 69
Lewis, Furry, 56
liar's bench tales, 26
Life magazine, 7
"Lifeboat Blues," 57
Lindsay, Vachel, 124
"Little Hat Blues," 64
Littlefield, Little Willie, 16
Locke, Alain, xxx, 114
Lomax, Alan, xvi, 52, 102, 126
Lomax, John, 126
Lomax, Lonnie, 83
"Lonesome Day Blues," 79, 86
"Lonesome Home Blues," xxiii
"Lonesome Man Blues," 88
"Long Train Blues," 57
"Long Way From Home," 87
"Louisiana Blues," 15
"Love Me Like You Used To," 79
"Low-Down Blues," 132
"Low-Down Mississippi Bottom Man," 24
Lucas, James, 91
Lucas, Jane, 41
lynching, 102

McClennan, Tommy, xxvii, 67, 121
McCoy, Joe, xxiii, 18, 49, 80
McCoy, Robert Lee, 9

McDaniel, Hattie, 80
Macfarlane, Alan, 120
McGhee, Brownie, 49, 62
McLean, Don, 73
McTell, Blind Willie, xxviii, 65, 81, 88
"Mama's Baby Child," xxiii
Mamiya, Lawrence, x
Manning, Leola, 39
Martin, Roberta, 60
Martin, Sara, 45, 86, 131
Masters, Edgar Lee, 109, 110, 124
Matthews, Ralph, 122
"Me and the Devil Blues," 4, 10, 55, 92
Melnick, Mimi, 8
Memphis Minnie, xxviii–xxix, 62,
  134–35
Memphis Slim, xxiv, 39, 57
Mid-America Chants, 120
Miles, Lizzie, 17, 66, 121
"Minnie the Moocher," 113
Miss Rhapsody, 62
"Mississippi Fire Blues," 6, 48
Mississippi Sheiks, 50
"Mistreatin' Blues," 79
"Mistreatin' Mama," 56
"Moan, Mourners," 20, 41, 43
"Mojo Hand Blues," 129
Molton, Flora, 55, 62, 65
Montgomery, Eurreal, 44
Moore, Alice, 22, 82
Moore, Gatemouth, 64, 66
Morton, Jelly Roll, 104
Moss, Buddy, 48
"Motherless Child Blues," 46
"Motherless Children Have a Hard
  Time," 46
"Mr. Devil Blues," 18, 92
Muddy Waters, xxviii, 15–16, 41, 121
Murray, Albert, xii, 37, 39, 73, 77
"My Babe My Babe," 18
"My Black Mama," 84–85

"My Wash Woman's Gone," xxiii
Myth of the Negro Past, The, 20
myths: Adamic, 1–4, 6, 9, 13, 17, 18,
  30, 56, 57, 72, 74, 87, 88, 142n3;
  prodigal son, 5, 6, 13, 31, 63–67,
  96; tragic-hero, 1–2, 3–6, 8–9, 11,
  13, 17, 18, 142n3

NAACP, 102
"Natchez Mississippi Blues," 6, 48
National Convention of Gospel
  Choirs and Choruses, 63
Native Son, xxvii
Neal, Larry, 36, 39, 71, 75
"Nearer My God to Thee," 44, 73
Negro and His Music, The, 114
Negro Workaday Songs, 2
Nelson, Angela, x
Nelson, Red, 44
"Never Drive a Beggar from Your
  Door," 78
"New Huntsville Jail," 18
"New Orleans Goofer Dust Blues," 16
New Orleans Luck Powder, 15
New Orleans States, 104
"New Two Sixteen Blues," 98
Newbern, Hambone Willie, 38
Ngugi wa Thiong'o, xviii
Nickerson, Charlie, 73
Nietzsche, Friedrich, 57, 94
Nix, A. W., 132
"No Woman No Nickel," 57, 87
"Nobody Knows," 45
"Nobody Knows My Trouble," 44
"Nobody Knows the Trouble I've
  Seen," 44, 45
"North Bound Blues," 93

Oakley, Giles, xii, xiii
O'Brien, Justin, 92

Oden, Jimmy, xxiii, 2, 77, 121
Odum, Howard, 2, 58, 133
Office of Price Administration, xx, xxi
Offord, William, 100–1
Okeh Race Records, xv, 121, 128–29, 130, 131, 132
Old Plantation Hymns, 32, 76
Oliver, Paul, xvi, 38, 54, 55, 63, 71, 72, 74, 120, 134; misunderstanding of blues, xii–xiii, xv, xix–xx, xxvii, 37, 41, 43–44, 46, 47, 48, 50–51, 74, 81, 82, 83, 85–86, 87, 94
"On Revival Day," 43
"On the Road Again," 92
Opportunity, 116
original sin, 56, 76
Oriole Records, 26

Pace, Harry, 130
Palmer, Robert, 41, 77, 126
Paramount Records, xv, 5, 10, 11, 13, 121, 128, 129, 130, 131, 132
Parker, Little Jr., 63
Parkin, David, 119–20
"Patience Like Job," 2
Patton, Charlie, xxviii, 25, 37, 38–39, 47, 64, 65, 80, 81
"Pea Vine Blues," 80, 81
"Peetie Wheatstraw Stomp," 12
Pelton, Robert, 11, 12, 13
"Pennsylvania Woman Blues," 19
Pentecostal church, 27, 50, 70
Petway, Robert, 93
Phillips, Washington, 50
Philosophy of History, xii
"Pig Iron Sally," 82
Pittsburgh Courier, The, 122
Platt, James, 47
"Pleading Blues," 44
Pleasant Joe. *See* Cousin Joe
"Poor Boy Blues," 38

"Poor Man Blues," 53
"Praying Blues," 45, 88, 128
"Preacher Blues," 49
"Preachers Blues," 49
"Preachin' the Blues" (House), 11, 41, 56, 93
"Preachin' the Blues" (Smith), 41, 43, 131
"Preaching the Blues" (Broonzy), 42, 43
"Preaching the Blues" (Johnson), xx
"Prisoner Blues," 126
Pryor, James "Snooky," 112
Puckett, Newbell Niles, 20, 21, 22, 28, 72, 82, 83, 115–16
"Pussy Cat Blues," 41

racism, 52–53, 82–84, 89–93; in the North, 107–9; in the South, 100–5
"Rag, Mama, Rag," 80
Railroad Bill, xv, 4, 8
Rainey, Ma, xv, xxix, 7, 10, 62, 89, 124, 131
Rankin, John, xx, xxi
Ray, Harmon, 9
"Reap What You Sow" (Jones), 79
"Reap What You Sow" (Rush), 80
"Red Hot Blues," 39
"Red Lantern Blues," 17, 129
Reed, Bruce, xxii
Rhapsody in Black, 42
Ricoeur, Paul, 4, 54, 91
"Risin' High Water Blues," 47
Roberts, John, 7
"Rocky Road Blues," 3
Rogers, Jimmy, 129
"Round and Round," 73
Rowe, Mike, 134
Roy, Rob, 113–14
Rush, Otis, xxix, 80, 122, 137
Rushing, Jimmy, xxix, 45
Russell, Jeffrey Burton, xxi–xxii

"Sam, You're Just a Rat," 8
Sanctified church 51, 65. *See also* Holiness church and Pentecostal church
Sandburg, Carl, 124
Sanford, John, 71, 73
Saunders, W. O., 107
"Sawmill Blues," 91
"Screamin' and Hollerin' Blues," 38–39
Seaching for Robert Johnson, 5
Selah Jubilee Singers, 132
Sellers, John, 92, 121
Sermon on the Mount, 58, 59
sexuality, xiii, 36, 52, 72, 73, 87, 88, 89
Shade, Will, 6
"Shake That Thing," 130
Shaky Jake, 67, 121
"She Belongs to the Devil," 25
"Shelby County Workhouse Blues," 38
"Shootin' Star Blues," 17
Short, J. D. "Jelly Jaw," 37
shouting, 41
Signifying Monkey, xxvi
sin, 91; consciousness of, 53–56, 57, 81; justification for, 57–63, 77–78, 112
Singleton, George A., 116
Sissle, Noble, xxvi
"Sittin' on a Log," 93
"Slave to the Blues," xv, 10, 89
slavery, new forms of black, 89–90, 93, 100–5, 109, 119
Smith, Bessie, xxix, 11, 13, 20, 41, 42, 43, 53, 57, 62, 86, 87, 122, 126, 130, 131
Smith, Clara, 33, 130
Smith, Funny Papa, 58, 59, 83–84
Smith, Mamie, 125, 131
Smith, Six Cylinder, 19

Smith, Trixie, 45, 79–80, 88, 128, 130
Snow, Susan, 31
"Someday I'll Be in the Clay," 18
"Sometimes I Feel Like a Motherless Child," 44, 45, 46
sorcerers, 33
soul music, 123
"Southern Can Mama," 81
Spand, Charlie, 16, 87
Spann, Otis, 44–45
spirituals, 32, 36, 38, 61, 62, 64, 67, 69, 79, 83, 116, 117–18, 132
Spirituals and the Blues, The, xxiii, 36, 43
Spivey, Victoria, xxix, 9, 17, 71, 121, 124, 129
Spruell, Freddie, 24
"St. James Infirmary," 113
"St. Louis Blues," xvii, 127
"St. Louis Cyclone Blues," 68
St. Louis Jimmy, 74
"St. Peter Blues," 85
Stackolee, xv, 4, 8, 9
"Starvation Blues," 108
State Press (Little Rock, Arkansas), 62
Stokes, Frank, 79, 85, 86
"Stop Your Rambling," 79
"Strange Fruit," 42, 102
Sunnyland Slim, 2, 42, 108, 121
superstition, 17, 24, 26, 99, 115, 116, 117–18; black cat, 24, 26, 27–28; black cat bone, 17, 27–28; falling star, 17; shooting star, 17
Surin, Kenneth, x, 71, 94–95
"Sweet Atlanta Blues," 73
"Sweet Home Blues," 19
Swing Harlem Swing, 42
Sykes, Roosevelt, 38

"Take Me for a Buggy Ride," 87
Tale of Chicago, 109
"Talking to Myself," 88

Tampa Red, 80, 121
"Teasin' Brown Blues," 87
Tennessee Valley Authority, xx, xxi
Terry, Sonny, 62
"Texas Worried Blues," 86
"That's No Way to Get Along," 65
"The Blues Is All Wrong," 39
"The Cats Got the Measles," 25
"The Cockeyed World," 92
"The Death of Blind Boy Fuller," 49
"The Devil Is a Busy Man," 42
"The Down Home Blues," xxix
"The First Shall Be Last and the Last Shall Be First," 75
"The Flood Blues," 68
"The Good Lawd's Children," 94
"The Natchez Fire," 48
"The Panama Limited," 46
"The Prodigal Son," 65
"The Right Kind of Life," 56
"The Twelves," 2
theodicy: contrasted with threat, 79–80; defined, xxvi, 68–69, 91; secular, 91; types of in blues, 74–81, 86–87
theomusicology, xxi, xxvii
They Seek a City, 105
"[Thirty-four] 34 Blues," 47
Thomas, Henry, 86, 87
Thomas, Hociel, 2–3
Thomas, James Son, 18, 19, 20, 38, 51, 55, 57, 67
Thomas, Willie, 44, 61
"Thunderstorm Blues," 47
"Tight Time Blues," 75, 90
Tindley, Charles Albert, 44
"Titanic Blues," 44
Titon, Jeff, xii, xv–vi, 15, 64, 127, 132
Toomer, Jean, xxiv
Torey, George, 88
Towel, Jim, 129

Townsend, Henry, 31–32, 37, 58–59, 88
Tracy, Steven, 125
"Travelin' This Lonesome Road," 89
Trice, Luther, 29–30, 33
Trice, Willie, 29–30
trickster, 6–13, 28, 32, 33, 74; as source of theory, xxvi, xxvii, 71–74
Trickster to Badman, 7
"Twelve Gates to the City," 62
[Twelve] 12 Million Black Voices, 43, 122

"Underworld Blues," 128–29
"Unkind Blues," 56
urban blues: defined, xxix–xxx, 137

Vaughn, Sarah, xvii
Vincson, Walter, 50, 88
Virgial, Otto, 39
Virginia Female Jubilee Singers, 132
Vocalion Records, 121, 132
voodoo-hoodoo, 9, 13, 14–18, 28, 30–31, 33, 129, 132

Walker, Little J, 121
Walker, Margaret, xxiv
Walker, T-Bone, xxix, 114, 137
Wallace, Minnie, 92
Wallace, Sippie, xv, 2–3, 53, 68, 121, 128–29, 131
Washboard Sam, 25, 45, 57, 78, 81, 89
Washington, Booker T., 109
Washington, Dinah, 59–60
"Wasn't It Sad about Lemon," 5, 49
Waters, Ethel, xxix, 41–42, 122, 130, 131
Weaver, Sylvester, 12, 13
Weber, Max, 128
Weldon, Will, 39
Welsh, Nolan, 85

INDEX

INDEX

"Western Union Man," 57
Wheatstraw Peetie, xxviii, 5, 6, 9, 10, 11, 12, 13, 19, 75, 93, 94, 131, 132
White, Bukka, xxviii, 46
White, Josh, 62, 73
"Whoopee Blues," 25
Wiggins, James, 19
Wilber, Bill, 18
"Wild Cow Blues," 80, 81
Wilkins, Robert, xxiii, 47–48, 57, 61, 62, 65, 78, 81
Wilkins, Roy, 100
Williams, Joe, 18, 49, 80, 81, 92, 121, 127
Williams, Kenny, 110
Williams, Robert Pete, 45–46
Williamson, John Lee, 15–16

Williamson, Sonny Boy, 25, 38, 52, 56, 57, 80, 121
Williamson, Sonny Boy No. 2 (Rice Miller), 57
Winston, George "Devil," xv, 4, 31
witches, 28, 33, 118, 120
Woodson, Carter G., 31, 116
"Workhouse Blues," 86
Wright, Richard, xii–xiii, xx, xxvi, xxvii, 43, 109, 110, 122–23

"Yellow Girl Blues," 86
"You Got to Die Some Day!," 80
"You Shall," 85, 86
"Your Funeral and My Trial," 80
"You're Going to Reap Just What You Sow," 79